T0338214

KYOTO AREA STUDIES ON ASIA

CENTER FOR SOUTHEAST ASIAN STUDIES, KYOTO UNIVERSITY

VOLUME 11

After the Crisis

KYOTO AREA STUDIES ON ASIA

CENTER FOR SOUTHEAST ASIAN STUDIES, KYOTO UNIVERSITY

KYOTO AREA STUDIES ON ASIA

CENTER FOR SOUTHEAST ASIAN STUDIES, KYOTO UNIVERSITY

VOLUME 11

After the Crisis

Hegemony, Technocracy and Governance in Southeast Asia

Edited by

SHIRAISHI Takashi

and

Patricio N. ABINALES

Kyoto University Press

First published in 2005 jointly by:

Kyoto University Press
Kyodai Kaikan
15-9 Yoshida Kawara-cho
Sakyo-ku, Kyoto 606-8305, Japan
Telephone: +81-75-761-6182
Fax: +81-75-761-6190
Email: sales@kyoto-up.gr.jp
Web: http://www.kyoto-up.gr.jp

Trans Pacific Press
PO Box 120, Rosanna, Melbourne
Victoria 3084, Australia
Telephone: +61 3 9459 3021
Fax: +61 3 9457 5923
Email: info@transpacificpress.com
Web: http://www.transpacificpress.com

Copyright © Kyoto University Press and Trans Pacific Press 2005

Set by digital environs, Melbourne

Printed in Melbourne by BPA Print Group

Distributors

Australia
Bushbooks
PO Box 1958, Gosford, NSW 2250
Telephone: (02) 4323-3274
Fax: (02) 4323-3223
Email: bushbook@ozemail.com.au

USA and Canada
International Specialized Book
Services (ISBS)
920 NE 58th Avenue, Suite 300
Portland, Oregon 97213-3786
USA
Telephone: (800) 944-6190
Fax: (503) 280-8832
Email: orders@isbs.com
Web: http://www.isbs.com

UK and Europe
Asian Studies Book Services
Franseweg 55B, 3921 DE Elst, Utrecht
The Netherlands
Telephone: +31 318 470 030
Fax: +31 318 470 073
Email: info@asianstudiesbooks.com
Web: http://www.asianstudiesbooks.com

Japan
Kyoto University Press
Kyodai Kaikan
15-9 Yoshida Kawara-cho
Sakyo-ku, Kyoto 606-8305
Telephone: (075) 761-6182
Fax: (075) 761-6190
Email: sales@kyoto-up.gr.jp
Web: http://www.kyoto-up.gr.jp

Japan, Asia and the Pacific
Kinokuniya Company Ltd.
Head office:
38-1 Sakuragaoka 5-chome
Setagaya-ku, Tokyo 156-8691
Japan
Phone: +81 (0)3 3439 0161
Fax: +81 (0)3 3439 0839
Email: bkimp@kinokuniya.co.jp
Web: www.kinokuniya.co.jp
Asia-Pacific office:
Kinokuniya Book Stores of Singapore Pte., Ltd.
391B Orchard Road #13-06/07/08
Ngee Ann City Tower B
Singapore 238874
Tel: +65 6276 5558
Fax: +65 6276 5570
Email: SSO@kinokuniya.co.jp

ISSN 1445–9663 (Kyoto Area Studies on Asia)
ISBN 1–920–901–06X

Contents

Tables

Figures

List of Contributors

Takashi Shirashi, professor, Center for Southeast Asian Studies, Kyoto University.

Akira Suehiro, professor, Institute of Social Science, University of Tokyo.

Ukrist Pathmanand, assistant professor, Institute of Asian Studies, Chulalongkorn University.

Takashi Torii, associate professor, Department of Commerce, Meiji University.

Teresa S. Encarnacion-Tadem, associate professor of political science and director of Third World Studies Center, University of the Philippines, Diliman.

Vedi R. Hadiz, associate professor, Department of Sociology, National University of Singapore.

Patricio N. Abinales, associate professor, Center for Southeast Asian Studies, Kyoto University.

Khoo Boo Teik, associate professor and deputy dean, School of Social Sciences, Universiti Sains Malaysia, Penang, Malaysia.

Kasian Tejapira, assistant pofessor, Faculty of Political Science, Thammasat University.

Pasuk Phongpaichit, professor, Faculty of Economics, Chulalongkorn University.

Acknowledgements

This book has its origins in the Shizuoka Asia-Pacific Forum on Governing in Asia and the Prospects for a 'New Asia' which was organized by Shizuoka Research Institute in 2000. Funding for further research and the 2002 workshop on Hegemony, Technocracy and Networks was provided by the Japan Society for the Promotion of Science (JSPS) under the aegis of the JSPS-National Research Council of Thailand Core University Program. We thank the JSPS for its Grant-in-Aid for Publication of Scientific Results. We also thank the CSEAS faculty and staff for their help in ensuring the success of the Core workshop, and Donna J. Amoroso for editing the manuscript.

1
Introduction: States, Markets and Societies after the Asian Crisis[1]

Takashi Shiraishi

This book is about Southeast Asia—above all Thailand, Indonesia, Malaysia and the Philippines—after the Asian financial crisis.[2] The crisis began in 1997 when short-term portfolio investors, jittery about Thai ability to maintain the pegged exchange rate between the Thai baht and the US dollar, pulled their capital out from Thailand. The government used up its foreign exchange reserves in a vain attempt to defend the baht and then turned to the International Monetary Fund (IMF) for emergency assistance. In line with IMF conditionality, Thai officials floated the currency and raised domestic interest rates. Since many firms could not service their loans, non-performing loans mounted, causing insolvency of the domestic banking system. Financial institutions could not repay loans denominated in foreign currencies. The stock market collapsed. Jobs were lost. What began as a currency crisis deepened into a financial, economic and social one. The contagion quickly reached Indonesia, the Philippines, South Korea and Malaysia, which had comparable experiences (though different in degree of severity) of drastic currency depreciation, increased bankruptcies, financial system failures and stock market collapse. The crisis had huge political consequences, most visible in the new constitutional system in Thailand which paved the way for the emergence of Thaksin Shinawatra, the collapse of Soeharto's New Order regime in Indonesia, the near collapse of Mahathir Mohamad's National Front in Malaysia, and continuing political and social crises in the Philippines under Fidel Ramos, Joseph Estrada and Gloria Macapagal Arroyo.

While there exists a substantial body of literature on the Asian financial crisis, it has been concerned mainly with diagnosing the crisis, explaining its causes, and prescribing remedies (for example, Zhang 1998; Jackson 1999; Noble and Ravenhill 2000; Tan 2000). Studies that link economic and political analyses often dwell on issues of power relationships, capital movement and institutional structures and regulation in order to stress the dynamic interaction between states and markets on national, regional and global levels (Pempel 1999; Robison et al 2000). While these studies allude to the enormous social costs and consequences of the crisis, they do not adequately address the longterm political, economic and social implications of these costs and consequences. Although some observers note, for example, attempts on the part of Asian countries to seek greater national autonomy in policy making, they generally dismiss "nationalist" responses as either manifestations of elite manipulation of nationalist rhetoric to protect and preserve vested interests or instances of populism and mass politics which cannot be sustained in the long run because of economic irrationality (see Higgott 2000, 261–82).

This book foregrounds analyses of the Asian crisis that take up the complex interactions and tensions among Southeast Asian states, markets and societies within the context of a regional order under American hegemony, with emphasis on individuals and collectivities whose thoughts and actions actively intervene in the shaping of relations between and among the three realms. In particular, this book is concerned with two kinds of *claims* made on the state: one is by the market, here understood as the global market dominated by American capitalism and its ideological armature of neo-classical economics; the other is by different sectors of society within particular national states.[3] These claims are embodied by technocracy (representing the claims of the market) and popular and elite nationalisms (representing the claims of society). Institutionally, technocracy advocates "economic rationality" (defined in terms of neo-classical economics) within the state, while popular and elite nationalisms press the state to respond to particular and general social needs and demands—all the more so when the state is no longer "authoritarian" but "democratic."

This introduction argues that the claims made on the Southeast Asian state by market and society can only be understood by examining the history of the regional order and the way this order was shaped during the post-World War II period by US strategic and economic interests. US hegemony in the region was based on the creation of an East Asian security system controlled by the United States in alliance with Japan and other East Asian developmental states; the promotion of a politics of development and productivity in Southeast Asia through a triangular trade system between the US, Japan and Southeast Asia; and the nurturing of a technocracy manned by US-trained economists. What follows discusses the formation of the regional order, the shift in US policy from condoning to dismantling authoritarian developmentalist regimes in light of challenges posed by Asian global competitiveness, and US deployment of a multilateral neoliberal economism mediated by the IMF as a way of imposing "structural reforms" on now-"democratizing" states. This introduction also examines the social and political impact and consequences of the Asian crisis in Thailand, Indonesia, Malaysia and the Philippines, with particular emphasis on the social responses which took the form of elite and popular nationalist "backlash" against globalization and Americanization.

———

The wars, revolutions and counterrevolutions of the 1940s and 1950s changed the political topography of this region dramatically. To better appreciate the nature of this change, it is useful to consider the political map of East Asia as we know it today. Continental Asia is dominated by the People's Republic of China. North and South Korea share the Korean Peninsula uneasily, while China and Taiwan continue to glare at one another across the Taiwan Strait. To the east lies Japan and to the south Southeast Asia—a vast area encompassing Vietnam, the Philippines, Indonesia and all the countries in between. This map is a product of the political changes of the 1940s: the dismantling of the Japanese empire, the emergence of the United States as a superpower, the founding of the People's Republic of China and the decolonization of the countries of Southeast Asia. What sort of regional order emerged as this map took shape?

The United States played the decisive role in the formation of an East Asian order after World War II, which is not to say that everything went according to Washington's plan. However, as the upheavals of the 1940s began to subside, it was Washington that provided the blueprint. And it was the United States that had the will, the power and the wealth to set about building an order based on that blueprint.

At the end of the 1940s, when the People's Republic of China was in its infancy and the American occupation of Japan was nearing an end, Washington faced two major problems in East Asia. The first was how to respond to the "threat" of communism—that is, how to contain the Soviet Union and China. The second was how to revive the Japanese economy and create an independent nation capable of supporting Washington's geopolitical strategy while ensuring that Japan would never again threaten the United States. What the US was looking for in East Asia was a workshop and a logistical base, and the only suitable candidate was Japan.

Washington's answer to these problems from a security angle was a policy of double containment. The first component of this was what Secretary of State Dean Acheson referred to as the "great crescent," a bulwark designed to contain communism, extending from Japan through

Southeast Asia and India to the oil-rich Persian Gulf. The underlying structure of this bulwark was a hub-and-spokes framework of bilateral treaties and base agreements between the United States and the countries of the region, including Japan, South Korea, Taiwan, Thailand and the Philippines.

The other object of double containment was Japan itself. By the end of the 1940s, the US was preparing to end the occupation of Japan and Washington was wary that an independent and economically resurgent Japan would once again rise up and constitute a threat. State Department director of policy planning George Kennan believed that a mechanism was needed whereby Japan's artery could be cut off at any time. His solution was to integrate the Japanese military into an East Asian security system under American leadership, while at the same time controlling Japan's energy supply. The incorporation of Japan's military power into an East Asian security system of US making became the basic premise of the Japan–US alliance, and this alliance in turn became the linchpin of Washington's East Asian strategy.

On the economic front, the solution devised by Washington was to create a triangular trade system built around Japan, Southeast Asia and the US. The thinking behind this was very straightforward: To rebuild its economy, Japan needed markets from which it could import raw materials and to which it could export manufactured goods. Before the war, China had supplied such markets, but this economic relationship collapsed with the dissolution of the Japanese empire and the advent of the People's Republic of China. Furthermore, for Japan to depend on China for raw materials and an export market did not mesh with American policy. The solution was to replace China with Southeast Asia, which would promote development in that region while helping Japan rebuild its economy. To facilitate the arrangement, the US would provide currency for the creation of a triangular trade system. Through this scheme, Southeast Asia took on new importance for Japan. Postwar relations between Japan and Southeast Asia, in other words, have their beginnings in the triangular trade system envisioned by the United States.

Following World War II, the countries of Southeast Asia achieved independence from the latter half of the 1940s through the 1950s. Some, like Indonesia and Vietnam, did so through revolution, while others, such as Malaysia (then Malaya) and the Philippines, were "granted" independence by their colonizers. Nationalist sentiment ran high in all of these countries, however, and their governments were initially less than enthusiastic about the US plan for a Japan – US – Southeast Asia triangular trade system;

Japan's calls for economic cooperation in fact meant accepting Japanese exports and granting Japan access to the region's raw materials. But when a country becomes independent, it must pursue nation building on some model. Countries like Vietnam and Burma chose the model offered by Communist China. Thailand, Malaysia, Indonesia, the Philippines and Singapore, which were incorporated into the US-led order, opted for an authoritarian system. This was the "nation building from above" of "developmental states." The point here is the close relationship between nation building from above and the regional system under which these countries were incorporated. What tied them together was the ideology of development.

The significance of this can be understood by examining the historical origins of developmentalism. One of the key characteristics of this phenomenon is the fusion of nation building from above with the ideology of economic growth. In his excellent essay on developmentalism, Akira Suehiro (1999) pinpoints the typical origin of this model in the following way.

Around the beginning of the 1950s, Max Millikan, an expert on the Soviet economy who had served as assistant director of the Central Intelligence Agency, and Walter Rostow, later famous for his "take-off theory," were at the center of a research team set up at the Massachusetts Institute of Technology's Center for International Studies to explore the question of underdeveloped regions and US foreign aid policy. In 1957, the team published its findings in a book entitled *Proposal: Key to Effective Foreign Policy*. The book argued that for underdeveloped countries to stand up to communism and avoid violent revolution from below, what was required was the kind of internal social change made possible by economic development. The thesis placed particular importance on development plans undertaken at the initiative of the developing countries' leaders. According to Suehiro, the book was distinguished by the fact that it downplayed the promotion of such American values as individual freedom and economic liberalism and instead emphasized a national development effort embracing all classes, government leadership in economic policy and development from above. Suehiro notes that this concept contained almost all the elements of the developmentalism that emerged in the late 1950s.

Why then did authoritarian developmentalism prevail in noncommunist East Asia? The reason is simple. During the 1950s and 1960s, Southeast Asia had no means to resist the "threat" posed by communist and domestic revolutionary forces except through social change. But what could serve as the agent for such change in the absence of industrial capitalism? Under the circumstances, governments attempted to nurture capitalism through development from above, often by violently suppressing resistance from below. To support these government efforts, the US launched what has been termed the developmentalist project.

One element of this project was a program of Americanization in which the US invested in education and training to foster "experts" who "spoke the same language" and thought the same way as Americans. This was an extremely wide-ranging undertaking, but here I will limit myself to one example—the training of Indonesian economists.

The effort began in the early 1950s with the establishment of the Faculty of Economics at the University of Indonesia (UI) through a grant from the Ford Foundation. Economists were sent to Indonesia from US universities to teach in the capacity of visiting professors. The UI economics curriculum, which had formerly been taught in Dutch by Dutch professors using Dutch textbooks, was replaced by an American curriculum, taught in English by US professors using American textbooks. Graduates from this faculty received Ford Foundation fellowships to do graduate studies in the US. As a result, by the early 1960s, the Economics Faculty of the University of Indonesia had become an enclave of American economists and American-educated Indonesian economists.

Subsequently, under the Soeharto regime, a national economic de- velopment apparatus emerged with the establishment of the National Development Planning Agency, government-affiliated development banks and the Government Board of Investment. Many technocrats entered government service. US-educated Indonesian economists were appointed to high-ranking posts in the government and managed the Indonesian economy in cooperation with the IMF and World Bank; the government signed consulting contracts with the Harvard Center for International Development and investment banks like Lehman Brothers. This is not to say that such relationships completely controlled the Indonesian economy. But it is undeniable that in Soeharto's Indonesia, Americans and technocrats who "spoke their language" had a stronghold inside the Indonesian government and that they brought with them the Trojan horse of Americanism.

In short, American intellectual hegemony was built into the economic policy-making structure of its Asian allies through technocracy. Technocrats belong to an international network of people who share the language of economics. This network is nestled in universities (especially economics departments), international multilateral lending agencies and government ministries and agencies. In this perspective, technocratic development in Southeast Asia (and elsewhere) can be understood as an extension and entrenchment of an American-centered technocratic network in Southeast Asia. Indeed, the development and the expansion of US-centered technocratic networks in Southeast Asia not only cemented the incorporation (in different degrees) of Southeast Asian countries into the US orbit. More importantly, in the wake of the 1997 crisis, technocrats would form part of a broad ideological consensus of policy-makers drawn from the ranks of academia, government and business, as well as of elites and middle classes, which clamored for free-market and political reforms. Academics, business managers, bankers and politicians who had received their advanced academic training during the 1970s and 1980s—a time when neo-classical economics overshadowed Keynesian economics in academic departments in the United States and Southeast Asia—proved influential during this time (see Bello in Robison et al., 2000).

In this volume, Akira Suehiro examines the transformation of Thai economic policy making through the history of the Thai technocracy, which was rooted in the creation of four core economic agencies in the 1960s. The National Economic and Social Development Board (NESDB), the Fiscal Policy Office (FPO) in the Ministry of Finance, the Bureau of Budget (BOB) in the Prime Minister's Office and the Bank of Thailand (BOT) all featured Dr. Puey Ungpakon as the central figure. Sarit Thanarat and other leaders delegated authority to technocrats in non-rent producing areas such as macro-economic management. This system of economic policy making began to undergo changes in the 1970s, when the democratically elected government began to challenge the autonomy of economic technocrats, but the full collapse of BOT autonomy occurred in the 1990s with the disintegration of the system after the crisis. If, previously, economic rationality was equated with the presence of a technocracy insulated from the patronage that thrived in sectoral politics, by the time Thaksin came to power in 2001, party politics began to dominate economic policy and planning without help from economic technocrats in government agencies. The current policy-making structure is built around the economic policy team of the Thai Rak Thai Party, and the Prime Minister's Office has replaced the MOF and the NESDB as the headquarters for formulating and monitoring all important government policies.

Ukrist Pathmanand, in his chapter, argues that the Thai developmental state was fashioned as part of Thai anti-communism, which in turn depended on US support. During the crisis, the Thai government turned to the IMF for assistance, but the United States seized the opportunity to pressure Thailand into liberalizing its economic system, in Deputy Secretary of Treasury Lawrence Summers' words, a matter of "exporting institutions and ideas" to Thailand. Thai leaders responded favorably to the US, complied with IMF conditionality and adjusted their regional policy; instead of placing its economy in the forefront, penetrating Indochina and strengthening ties with China and Japan, Thailand accepted US supremacy and "flexible engagement."

Teresa Encarnacion Tadem's analysis of technocracy in the Philippines also points to the creation of a broad neoliberal consensus. Technocrats were once viewed as an important pillar of the Marcos regime, along with the military and cronies. But after the 1986 People Power revolution, owing to the regime's dependence on US military and economic assistance (via the IMF and World Bank), technocrats disappeared into a much larger group of people in government, who constituted the "faceless" catalyst of US hegemony with strong support from the local and international business community and academics. Tadem notes that the ideology of technocracy exhibits a marked distaste for politics, which is seen as irrational and thus anathema to the development of scientific expertise, and an obsesssion with the creation of a strong state. Under Fidel Ramos, technocrats came from the private sector; bankers, academics and politicians (including Gloria Macapagal Arroyo) are now the lead advocates and agents of globalization.

Takashi Torii's chapter on Malaysia's "age of development" focuses on the formation and implementation of Mahathir's industrialization policies. He argues that the Prime Minister's Office controlled both development planning and implementation and the evaluation of development projects, while actively promoting the private sector. Not only did Mahathir's policies create professional Malays and put them in charge of Malaysian economic development. They also instituted a forum, the Industrial Coordination Council, which effectively linked the Malay and non-Malay private sectors to the government.

The Suehiro, Ukrist, Tadem and Torii chapters show how technocrats have traditionally depended on state intervention in the economy to promote development, even as they viewed politics as "irrational" and sought to "rationalize" the political economy. The crisis became a point of convergence at which the US, IMF and national technocratic world views intersected and formed a critical mass that weighed politically on the state.

The Indonesian case is again instructive. When the crisis started in Bangkok in July 1997, the Indonesian economy was still doing well. Its economy was growing by 7.5 percent annually; exports were increasing by 10.4 percent; its budget deficit was below 2 percent of GDP; it had $21 billion foreign reserves; inflation was under control; and the rupiah looked stable. Confident of sound economic fundamentals, technocrats seized the opportunity of "mini-crisis" to persuade Soeharto to introduce structural reforms with the help of the IMF and to address structural problems such as expanding bad loans in the banking sector, the dependence of business groups on short-term dollar-denominated funds from foreign sources and the control of Soeharto's children, lieutenants and crony business tycoons over the commanding heights of the economy.

When there were signs in September 1997 that the crisis was spreading to Indonesia, the government thus announced a comprehensive economic policy package that technocrats called their own IMF conditionality; it called for financial and fiscal tightening, structural reforms (including the suspension of government development projects) and banking sector reform. Technocrats also persuaded Soeharto to ask for IMF assistance to shore up international confidence and in October 1997 concluded an agreement with the IMF, which required, among other things, the closure of sixteen private banks (including one owned by Soeharto's son) and additional structural reform measures.

But the reforms required by the IMF threatened not only to hurt the business interests of Soeharto's children, cronies and lieutenants, but also to undermine Soeharto's patronage networks, which served as the informal funding mechanism of state agencies including the military. When the government closed troubled banks and suspended government development projects immediately after signing the IMF agreement, Soeharto learned that he had been duped. He allowed his son to take over another bank and revived suspended development projects controlled by his family's and cronies's businesses. He no longer trusted his technocrats, above all the finance minister and the central banker. The closure of banks caused bank runs, leading to the systemic crisis of the banking sector. Thus the agreement the technocrats had engineered with the IMF backfired, as Soeharto's lack of commitment to structural reforms was exposed and the rupiah slid downward.

Then, in December 1997, Soeharto fell seriously ill and did not attend the ASEAN summit meeting. This instantly transformed the situation from an economic crisis to a political and social crisis. The rupiah plummeted 70 percent, reaching 10,000 rupiah to the US dollar in January 1998. Unable to repay dollar-denominated loans, many business groups, including those established and owned by Soeharto's relatives and cronies, went bankrupt. The informal funding mechanism of the state, a mainstay of Soeharto's staying power, was also destroyed. Prices of goods, including rice, cooking oil and sugar, rose steeply. The social crisis manifested itself in increasing unemployment, widespread anti-Chinese riots, lootings, disturbances and rising criminality. A new IMF program was worked out in January 1998 with Soeharto alone—technocrats were no longer consulted—and replaced by yet another program in April 1998. But it did not help restore political, economic and social stability. The crisis destroyed Soeharto's politics of stability and economic development and led to the fall of his regime in May 1998 in the wake of massive riots in Jakarta and elsewhere.

In his chapter, Vedi Hadiz looks at post-Soeharto Indonesia and argues that the current system is not in transition. Examining how the prevailing configuration of power and interests informs the shaping of the political and economic regimes (above all under Abdurrahman Wahid), Vedi states that social, political and economic change is "now being presided over largely by predatory interests incubated under the New Order"; these predators have learned to secure their preeminence by exploiting new and shifting alliances in a fluid, democratic space that is "powered by money politics, bossism, thuggery, and violence." With Soeharto in retirement, no one has achieved the commanding heights of the oligarchy. Oligarchic interests now operate within a more diffuse and decentralized political framework. With reformist forces not yet in a position to challenge the oligarchy, a coalition politics is now in place.

Hadiz sees the future of Indonesia in the Philippines. His insight is borne out by Patricio Abinales' study of coalition politics in the Philippines after the fall of Marcos, which reveals how coalition politics accommodates different political actors, including traditional politicians, local bosses and caciques, as well as social movements, NGOs and POs (people's organizations). Shifting coalitions are created in support of presidential candidates, and the winning coalition apportions government agencies, which become autonomous spheres in which to operate. The diverse and often divergent agendas of the various factions of the coalition cause it to pursue contradictory policies and programs. Further, maintaining the coalition requires that resources be allocated and channeled for this purpose, delimiting the political choices the president can make and undermining long-term financial sustainability. The state—although dotted with pockets of efficiency—comes to an impasse; its resources, reach and functions are delimited by coalition politics, even while it is forced to contend with ever-present and deepening social and political crises.

Southeast Asian states followed their own trajectories of economic development, in which state corporations were often used to nurture native capitalists and in which Chinese businesses thrived in alliance with native political elites. But with the Cold War over and in the face of Asian global competitiveness, the United States now equated the anti-communist developmental state it had hitherto supported with "crony capitalism" and seized the opportunity offered by the crisis to "democratize" the region's developmentalist regimes. It relied on the IMF to impose reforms in the name of transparency, accountability and good governance and to force open the national economies of East Asia to US goods and services and multinational investment and ownership.

IMF policies during the Asian monetary crisis were seen to favor foreign banks and investors, provoking both elite and popular nationalist outcries. Elites sought to use the rhetoric of nationalism to shield their businesses and vested interests, while people who bore the brunt of the social crisis engendered by structural adjustment turned to nationalism to articulate their demand for social justice.

Khoo Boo Teik's chapter on the Mahathirist project deals with the ideology and historical unfolding of a state-led nationalist-capitalist venture of late industrialization. Founded on a good relationship between the state, foreign capital (in the form of foreign direct investment) and domestic conglomerates, this project sought to create a corps of "new Malay" capitalists and professionals. During the crisis, pro-market reform was viewed as a threat to Mahathirism, and Anwar Ibrahim's fall signified the scuttling of free-market structural reform. In order to rescue the conglomerates it had nurtured, the state had to negotiate a new stance vis-à-vis the international money market, opting for recapitalization of the financial sector, reflation to stimulate the economy and the rescue of imperiled conglomerates behind an economic shield of capital controls and a currency peg. The alliance of the state and domestic conglomerates was preserved. But Mahathirism as the code for capitalist rationalization ended with conglomerate-dominated national capital remaining weak. As the United Malay National Organization was built into an economic empire and individual Malay capitalists emerged under Mahathir, coalitions created for power, access to resources and opportunities for accumulation exacerbated intra-ethnic rivalry and competition within the UMNO. Malay capitalists now clamor for shelter from the challenges of globalization, while politicizing business and commercializing politics. But the Anwar affair undermined the appeal of Malay economic nationalism, which is now associated with the rescue of Malay cronies. Mahathirism has thus become the ideology of crony nationalism while being forced to grapple with challenges from Islam and populism that are underpinned by the popular demand for social justice.

Kasian Tejapira's chapter argues that the main problem of the current Thai economy is the contradiction between the globalized banking sector and the still-Thai non-financial corporate sector. The globalizing/neo-liberalizing economic reform strategy of the Chuan Leekpai-Tarrin Nimmanhaeminda government (1997–2001) upheld this contradiction, which caused the resurgence of populist-nationalist sentiment and movements and the decline of its domestic political feasibility. Financially cornered debtors struck back politically by supporting Thaksin Shinawatra, while the middle class remained divided over globalization. This kind of impasse allowed politics to stage a comeback in the form of mass protest movements challenging the Washington/Thai technocratic consensus and sowing the seeds of strategic alternatives to the globalist/neo-liberal vision. These economic populist-nationalist forces—representing the crony-capitalist and radical populist reform agendas—moved from the political margins to center stage and propelled Thaksin to power. His government represents an unstable amalgam of these competing concepts of the Thai nation, with their potentially conflicting demands, interests and concerns.

In her chapter, Pasuk Phongpaichit examines the phenomenon of social movements in Thailand, which has witnessed an outburst of demonstrations, protest marches and new organizations in the past decade. She argues that participants organize themselves and others into movements to demand their rights or to fight to protect the environment and their livelihood on a long-term basis. Society-based initiatives come to the fore when the state becomes subject to the market and when democratic processes are contaminated by money politics and ineffective in rectifying inequalities. The sphere of public intervention henceforth shifts from democratization to people politics, which expresses the people's desire and demand for more direct participation in decision making on matters affecting their livelihood and way of life. Social movements operate both at the local level to critique the power structure of society and market forces and at the global level to challenge the forces of global capitalism and multinational corporations. They draw their base of support from the ranks of the underprivileged, the marginalized, workers and poor farmers. In Thailand, the combination of democratization, economic growth and globalization has produced contradictory results. These processes encroach on people's lives and livelihood, but at the same time open up political opportunities and give legitimacy to social movements.

Finally, the crisis in 1997–1998 marked a major watershed in the history of East Asia, not just nationally but regionally. The ASEAN plus 3 (China, Japan and Korea) framework, inaugurated with the first summit meeting of December 1997, has since become institutionalized with the annual summit and ministerial meetings. The crisis also marked the beginning of Japan's new regional engagement, as evidenced by its call in 1997 for the establishment of an Asian Monetary Fund (AMF), the Miyazawa Initiative in 1998 to stimulate economies hit by the crisis, the Chiang Mai Initiative in 2000 to create a zone of currency stability and, in 2001, the conclusion of the Japan–Singapore Economic Partnership Agreement and Prime Minister Junichiro Koizumi's proposal in Singapore for a Japan–ASEAN economic partnership as the first step in building an East Asian community. Any regional initiative that emerges from this crisis will necessarily be shaped by the national imperatives of each of the countries in East and Southeast Asia. Although Americanization and globalization still have enormous impact both nationally and regionally, in the long run both elite and popular nationalisms and their collaborative-conflictive relationship with global capitalism are forces that will influence the fashioning of national and regional systems.

Notes

1 I thank Dr. Caroline Sy Han for her careful reading of and commenting on this introduction.
2 The chapters of this book are revised versions of papers first presented at the Core University Program Workshop on "Networks, Hegemony and Technocracy," held at Kyoto University, March 25-26, 2002.
3 This argument does not discount the regional implications of the crisis as seen in calls for, and initiatives toward, economic coordination, the development of institutional mechanisms to create a zone of currency stability (the Chiang Mai Initiative), and liberalization of trade and investment. But it is still the case that these initiatives are made and coordinated on the level of nation-states.

References

Bello, Walden. 2000. The Philippines: The making of a neo-classical tragedy. In *Politics and Markets in the Wake of the Asian Crisis*, ed. Richard

Robison, Mark Beeson, Kanishka Jayasuriya, and Hyuk-Rae Kim, 238–57. London: Routledge.

Higgott, Richard. 2000. The international relations of the Asian economic crisis: A study in the politics of resentment. In *Politics and Markets in the Wake of the Asian Crisis*, ed. Richard Robison, Mark Beeson, Kanishka Jayasuriya, and Hyuk-Rae Kim, 261–82. London: Routledge.

Jackson, Karl, ed. 1999. *Asian Contagion: The Causes and Consequences of a Financial Crisis*. Oxford: Westview Press.

Maier, Charles S. 1978. The politics of productivity: Foundations of American international economic policy after World War II. In *Between Power and Plenty: Foreign Economic Policies of Advanced Industrial States*, ed. Peter J. Katzenstein. Madison: University of Wisconsin Press.

Noble, Gregory W., and John Ravenhill. 2000. *The Asian Financial Crisis and the Architecture of Global Finance*. Cambridge: Cambridge University Press.

Pempel, T.J., ed. 1999. *The Politics of the Asian Economic Crisis*. Ithaca: Cornell University Press.

Robison, Richard, Mark Beeson, Kanishka Jayasuriya, and Hyuk-Rae Kim, eds. 2000. *Politics and Markets in the Wake of the Asian Crisis*. London: Routledge.

Suehiro, Akira. 1999. Kaihatsu-shugi to wa nani ka? In *Tokyo Daigaku Shakai Kagaku Kenkyusho*, ed. 20-seiki Sisutem. Tokyo: Tokyo Daigaku Shuppankai.

Tan, Gerald. 2000. *The Asian Currency Crisis*. Singapore: Times Academic Press.

Zhang, Peter, ed. 1998. *IMF and the Asian Financial Crisis*. Singapore: World Scientific.

2
Who Manages and Who Damages the Thai Economy? The Technocracy, the Four Core Agencies System and Dr. Puey's Networks

Akira Suehiro

Before the currency crisis of 1997, many scholars attempted to explain the reasons for Thailand's outstanding record of macroeconomic stability, including its stable growth under the military regime of the 1960s and 1970s, its successful structural adjustment to external shock under the quasi-democracy of the early 1980s and its unprecedented "economic boom" under the corrupt political regime of the 1990s. Some stressed the importance of policy making in stabilizing the macroeconomy and traditional conservatism in fiscal and monetary policies for the economic fundamentals (Warr and Bhanupong eds. 1996, 228–36). Others turned their attention to the "institutional capacity" required for economic development rather than to the policies themselves. For instance, Muscat, who had comprehensively surveyed Thai development policy for three decades, emphasized the deepening process of "institutional capacities required, the development of a modern state and…the education and training of Thai elites and professionals to lead and staff these institutions" (Muscat 1994, 7).

Maxfield argued that institutional capacity is one reason for the strong autonomous position of Thailand's central bank in formulating and determining economic policies. After conducting an international comparative study on the role of the central bank in developing countries, she concluded:

> The Bank of Thailand charter makes no mention of central bank autonomy. The executive branch has unconditional discretion to dismiss the governor, and the bank has no legal role in the budget process or legal authority over the formulation of monetary policy. Government borrowing from the central bank is relatively unrestricted. In reality, however, in terms of its ability to influence economic policy broadly, the Bank of Thailand is one of the strongest central banks in the world (Maxfield 1994, 560).

Likewise, Doner and Unger insisted that the financial liberalization reforms the Bank of Thailand (BOT) initiated at the end of the 1980s increased BOT independence from political influence and autonomy in economic policy (Doner and Unger 1993, 121–122). Where they found good economic performance before the crisis, they positively evaluated the institutional capacities of key government agencies, including the BOT.

After the crisis, however, scholars began to attack both institutional failure and the incapability of the BOT to deal with the fallout. For instance, Ammar Siamwalla, a leading Thai economist, severely criticized the BOT for erroneous projections about the changing world economy, incorrect foreign currency policies and personal conflict within its top management (Ammar 1997, 63–75). The official committee set up to investigate BOT responsibility in the currency crisis (the Nukun Committee or So. Po. Ro.) revealed poor management by responsible persons of Thailand's monetary position vis-à-vis the attack of international hedge funds. They also concluded that personal conflict between top BOT leaders had contributed to Thailand's critical condition in 1997 (So. Po. Ro. 1998). After the publication of this committee's report in May 1998, the public no longer believed in the BOT's capability and autonomy.

How can we reconcile these two quite different views of the BOT's role before and after the crisis? How can we evaluate the institutional elements which contributed to the economic "miracle" of the 1990s, but which also caused the economic "meltdown" after 1997? To answer these questions, we must reconsider the role of the major economic agencies engaged in formulating and implementing economic policies in Thailand. As Warr and his associates have already argued, there are *four core economic agencies* in Thailand: the National Economic and Social Development Board (NESDB), which is the government's main economic planning agency; the Fiscal Policy Office (FPO) of the Ministry of Finance; the Bureau of the Budget (BOB) of the Prime Minister's Office; and the BOT (Warr and Bhanupong 1996, 69–70) (See Figure 2-1).

These four agencies have played a significant role in the national budget process since the 1960s. Before submitting the final budget plan to the cabinet, the four agencies usually come together to discuss the plan for about a month between mid-December and mid-January (the budget year in Thailand starts on October 1 and ends on September 30). The NESDB principally screens the investment plans of each department, while the BOB investigates revenue aspects. The FPO proposes an annual expenditure plan according to its policy, and the BOT presents its estimate of the maximum possible government spending consistent with monetary

Figure 2-1. Policymaking Structure and The Four Core Agencies

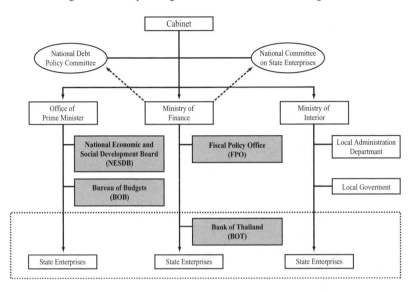

Source: Revised by the author from Warr and Bhanupong 1996, 70.

stability.[1] Coordination among the four agencies has been crucial to both economic stability and economic growth. It is therefore important for us to study inter-agency relationships when we examine the institutional capacities of economic policy making in Thailand.

This paper aims to clarify the role of the technocracy in the management of Thailand's macroeconomy with reference to: 1) the *major actors or players*, including finance ministers, four core agencies and international finance organizations such as the International Monetary Fund (IMF) and World Bank; 2) the *major determinants of economic policymaking*, including the power structure (military rulers, political party leaders and technocrats), the relationship between finance ministers and BOT governors and the extent of cooperation or conflict between the four core agencies; and 3) the *major policy targets* affecting relationships between political leaders and economic technocrats, between finance ministers and BOT governors and between the four core agencies.

Possible conflicts in policy targets among the major actors can be found in the three major fields of macroeconomic management (economic stability vs. economic growth), fiscal policy (strict budget balancing vs. spending policy for economic expansion or economic recovery from recession) and monetary policy (strict control of the money supply vs.

financial liberalization to support economic expansion). These issues are closely connected to conflict or collaboration between political leaders and economic technocrats and between finance ministers and BOT governors, regardless of differences in Thailand's power structure over time.

On the basis of these criteria, I divide the development and decline of the technocracy in Thailand into four periods and explore the characteristics of each period. The first covers the establishment of BOT autonomy and the creation of the four core agencies system in the 1960s. The second period, from the mid-1970s to the mid-1980s, was distinguished by changes in the four core agencies system and conflict between a finance minister and a BOT governor. The third period started with the collapse of BOT autonomy during the 1990s economic boom, and the fourth period saw the complete disintegration of the four core agencies system after the currency crisis.

This paper also focuses on the occupational careers of finance ministers and top leaders of the four core agencies—governors of the BOT, secretaries-general of the NESDB and directors of the FPO and the BOB—and examines their personal relationship with the key person of Dr. Puey Ungpakon (1917–1999). It was Dr. Puey who initiated the financial reforms of the 1960s and who created the four core agencies system when he was BOT governor between 1959 and 1971. In the conclusion, I suggest that although Thailand seemed to have developed institutional capacities for implementing economic policies, the autonomy of the technocracy in general and the BOT in particular depended principally on the personality and leadership of key persons such as finance ministers and BOT governors.

The Careers of Finance Ministers and Top Leaders of the Four Core Agencies

Careers of Finance Ministers

To begin the discussion of the role played by economic agencies in policy making, let us examine the age, educational attainment and occupational career of Thailand's finance ministers. Table 2-1 summarizes the career characteristics of finance ministers between 1958 and 1998, an era that can be divided into six periods according to the characteristics of the government regime: military government (1958–73); political party-based government (1974–76); quasi-democratic government (1977–88); political party-based government (1988–91); military government (1991–92); and political party-based government (1992–present). Table 2-1 makes very

Table 2-1. Distribution of Finance Ministers[a] by Career[b] (1958–1998)

	Military Government 1958–73	Party-based Politics 1974–76	Quasi-democratized 1977–88	Party-based Politics 1988–91	Military + Tentative 1991–92	Party-based Politics 1992–98
Predominant Classification by Regime	Bureaucrat	Mixed	Bureaucrat	Politician	Bureaucrat	Politician
Bureaucrat/Finance	5	1	1	-	2	-
Bureaucrat/Economic	2	3	5	-	1	2
Bureaucrat/Interior	-	-	1	-	-	-
Bureaucrat/Politician	-	3	-	-	-	-
Businessman/Politician	-	1	-	2	-	6
Scholar/Politician	-	-	-	1	-	1
Other	-	-	-	-	-	-
Total	7	8	7	3	3	9

Notes:
a. Counted once for each appointment in a different government or a reshuffled cabinet.
b. In case of persons with multiple occupations, identifies the career immediately preceding appointment. For instance, Amnuai Wirawan is identified as a financial bureaucrat (Ministry of Finance) for the purpose of his 1980 appointment as finance minister. In 1996, however, he is identified as a businessman/politician because he was the chairman of the executive committee of the Bangkok Bank as well as a member of the New Aspiration Party when he was appointed finance minister.

Sources: Compiled by the author from data in Appendices 1a and 1b.

clear that all finance ministers under military regimes were financial or economic bureaucrats (technocrats), while political party-based governments mostly appointed party leaders of varying backgrounds. This suggests that a military regime does not necessarily see military leaders directly involved in national economic affairs. It is in fact democratic governments that tend to involve themselves in economic policies by appointing leading figures of political parties as finance ministers.

Table 2-3 shows that finance ministers in Thailand have been well qualified in their educational attainment. Eighteen out of 20 obtained a bachelor's or higher degree, and 15 of these 18 studied abroad, especially in the United States. The two exceptions were General Marshal Kriangsak Chamanan, who attended a military academy in the United States, and Banharn Silpa-archa, who attended a commercial college in Bangkok.

Careers of the Top Leaders of the Four Core Agencies

Table 2-2 summarizes the occupational careers of the top leaders of the economic quartet. The table indicates that the majority—34 of 38—were recruited from economic bureaucrats (technocrats) in general and financial bureaucrats in particular. By carefully examining Table 2-2 and the Appendices, we can see some variation among the agencies. The secretaries-general of the NESDB and the governors of the BOT were recruited from the ranks of both financial bureaucrats and non-financial bureaucrats, while directors of the FPO were found exclusively among financial bureaucrats or the staff of the Ministry of Finance.

An equally important feature was the emergence of internally promoted persons (*luk mo*). Up to the 1980s, all top leaders of the NESDB, BOT and BOB were appointed from outside, with the Ministry of Finance serving as the largest human resource pool. By the 1990s, however, persons within each agency were promoted to the top position. The earliest case was Bodi Chunnanon, who was appointed BOB director in 1983. In the NESDB, Phisit Pakkasem was promoted from deputy secretary-general to secretary-general in 1989, and after his retirement in 1995, three more secretaries-general (Sumet, Wirat and Charnchai) were promoted from positions as deputy secretary or director.

The government also selected BOT governors from within the agency in the 1990s. Wichit Suphinit (1990–96), who received the first BOT scholarship in 1961, was the pioneer, followed by Roengchai Marakanon (1996–97) and Chaiwat Wibunsawat (1997–98). After the currency crisis, however, the government reverted to the traditional practice, dismissing Chaiwat and appointing Chatumonkhon Sonakun, the permanent secretary

Table 2-2. Distribution of Top Leaders of the Four Core Agencies by Career

	TOTAL FOR FOUR CORE AGENCIES[a]	NESDB 1959–97	BANK OF THAILAND 1942–98	BUREAU OF BUDGET 1959–90	FISCAL POLICY OFFICE 1962–90
Bureaucrat/Finance	23	4	7	4	8
Bureaucrat/Economic	11	3	5	2	1
Bank of Thailand	4	-	4	-	-
Bureaucrat/Interior	1	-	-	1	-
Total	39	7	16	7	9

Notes:
Top leader positions: NESDB—Secretary-General; Bank of Thailand—Governor; Bureau of the Budget—Director; Fiscal Policy Office—Director.
a. Data on directors of the Bureau of the Budget and the Fiscal Policy Office cover the period up to 1990.

Sources: Compiled by the author from data in Appendices 1b-d and 2b-d.

of the Ministry of Finance, as new BOT governor in 1998. The Thaksin government continued in this fashion when it dismissed Chatumongkhon and invited Pridiyathorn Thewakun (Devakul) (former senior vice-president of the Thai Farmers Bank) to take the top post of the BOT from the President of the Export-Import Bank of Thailand in May 2001.

Table 2-3 shows that the top leaders of the four core agencies have had higher educational attainment than Thailand's finance ministers. Twenty-five out of 39 obtained a master's or doctoral degree from European (9) or American (16) universities, the latter attended by the majority of those graduating after the 1960s. Rangsan, who studied the political economy of economic policies, attempted to classify Thai economic technocrats into the *first generation group* (Puey Ungpakon, Chalong Pungtrakun, Phisut Nimmanhemin, Sommai Huntrakun, etc.) and the *second generation group* (Amnuai Wirawan, Sanoh Unakun,

Table 2-3. Final Academic Attainment of Finance Ministers and Top Leaders[a] of the Four Core Agencies

ACADEMIC ATTAINMENT	FINANCE MINISTERS 1958–98	NESDB 1959–97	BANK OF THAILAND 1942–98	BUREAU OF BUDGET[b] 1959–90	FISCAL POLICY OFFICE[b] 1962–90
Senior High School/College	1	-	-	1	1
Bachelor's Degree (Thailand)[c]	3	-	-	1	-
Bachelor's Degree (Europe)	1	-	7	-	-
Bachelor's Degree (US)	-	-	-	1	-
MA or PhD (Europe)	2	2	4	1	2
MA, MBA, PhD (US)	10	4	5	3	4
MA (Japan)	2	-	-	-	-
Military Academy (US)	1	-	-	1	-
Data not available	-	1	-	-	1
Total	20	7	16	7	9

Notes:

Top leader positions: NESDB—Secretary-General; Bank of Thailand—Governor; Bureau of the Budget—Director; Fiscal Policy Office—Director.

a. In case of persons appointed to multiple positions, counted once for each appointment.

b. Data on directors of the Bureau of the Budget and the Fiscal Policy Office cover the period up to 1990.

c. Three out of four persons who graduated from universities in Thailand studied in the Faculty of Commerce and Accounting of Thammasat University.

d. Persons whose final educational attainment is below the bachelor's degree include Banharn (Finance Minister), Siri (director of the BOB) and Banthit (director of the PFO).

Sources: Compiled by the author from data in Appendices 1a-d.

Charnchai Leethawon, Phanat Simasathian, etc.) (Rangsan 1989, 40, 49fn). According to his classification, the first generation group were graduates of European universities, while the second generation were mostly educated in the United States.

Interlocking Relationships and Dr. Puey's Personal Networks

The Appendices show another important characteristic of top leaders—the fact that a single person frequently occupied two or three top posts in the four core agencies. Dr. Puey exemplified this trend; he served as governor of the BOT (1959–71), first director of the BOB (1959–61), first director of the FPO (1961–67) and NESDB committee member. After working in the Comptroller Department (Krom Banchi Klang) of the Ministry of Finance, Sanoh was appointed twice as secretary-general of NESDB (1973–1975 and 1980–1988) and served as BOT governor from 1975 to 1979. The practice of rotating posts seemed to cement the organizational unity of the four core agencies and enhance cooperation among them.

The personal connection of top leaders with Dr. Puey himself was even more crucial to the creation and continuity of the four core agencies system. Therefore, let us move to the issue of how Dr. Puey created the system of macroeconomic management and enhanced the autonomy of the BOT against the involvement of military leaders.

Dr. Puey's Financial Reforms and the Four Core Agencies System

Dr. Puey's Resistance against the Military Leaders

Puey Ungpakon (Puey Khiam sae Ung; 黄培謙) was born to a Chinese merchant family in 1917.[2] After graduating from the famous Bangkok high school, the Assumption School, he went to the London School of Economics (LSE), where he obtained a PhD in economics with honors in 1949. Returning to Thailand, he was appointed to the professional post of Economist (*setthakan*) attached to the Ministry of Finance. Immediately after entering the Ministry, he was dispatched as a trainee to the World Bank headquarters in Washington, D.C. (1950–1951), where he mastered policy making in international financial organizations (Wanrak ed. 1996, 36–38). Two years later (1953) he was appointed deputy governor of the BOT at the age of only 32 years.

During his term as deputy governor, two interesting episodes demonstrated Dr. Puey's strong personality. The first was the Union Bank of Bangkok scandal, in which commander-in-chief of the Army Sarit

Thanarat (who would became prime minister in 1958) took over that commercial bank and through it conducted unfair foreign exchange transactions. Dr. Puey decided to pursue criminal charges against Sarit despite pressure from military leaders (Wanrak ed. 1996, 39–41). The second case involved the national currency printing house. Thailand had used the famous British company Thomas since 1901, but the director-general of the Police Department, Phao Sriyanon, requested the BOT to switch to an American firm closely linked to the CIA. Dr. Puey set up a special committee to investigate this case and finally rejected Phao's proposal on account of his personal connection with the CIA (Wanrak ed. 1996, 41–43). These two persons—Field Marshal Sarit and Police General Phao—were the top army and police leaders of the 1950s.

These episodes clearly demonstrated Dr. Puey's high dignity and technocratic competence in opposing the involvement of military rulers in economic affairs. Because of this opposition, he was dismissed from the cabinet after only seven months' service in the BOT and sent back to the Ministry of Finance as an economic adviser. From 1956 to 1959, he voluntarily stayed in London as an economic adviser attached to the Thai embassy. He apparently decided to leave for London in order to avoid needless friction with military leaders.

Economic Reforms of the 1950s

Before the 1958 military coup brought Field Marshal Sarit to power, three movements sought to reform Thailand's financial and economic systems. The first was based on the recommendations of a special team from the United States Public Administration Service (PAS), which visited Thailand to conduct a field study of financial and fiscal systems. The mission argued for the separation of budget planning from the ordinary activities of the Ministry of Finance. Dr. Puey was the local counterpart of this team, and this proposal led to the establishment of the Bureau of the Budget under the Prime Minister's Office in 1959 (Siri 1966, 24–25; Wanrak ed. 1996, 45). The second movement was associated with the committee chaired by American adviser John A. Loftus, then attached to the Ministry of Finance. The Loftus committee was set up primarily to propose reforms in macroeconomic management procedures. It submitted its first set of proposals to the government in June 1956 (Suphap 1974, 2–3; Muscat 1994, 52–54).

Dr. Puey was in London by that time and had no opportunity to collaborate with Loftus. However, the committee included three distinguished local representatives who were close to Dr. Puey. Bunma Wongsawan, the director of the Comptroller Department, was his good friend. Nukun Prachuapmo, secretary-general of the committee, was a young follower of Dr. Puey in the Ministry of Finance whom Dr. Puey had enthusiastically recommended for a post in the Permanent Secretary's Office when he graduated from Melbourne University (Nukun 1996, 33–34). Later, Dr. Puey advised Nukun to move to the Comptroller Department in order to cooperate with Bunma and Loftus (ibid., 36–39). Finally, there was Miss Suphap Yot-sunthorn, Loftus' secretary and co-author of the first well-organized textbook on economics written in Thai.[3]

The third movement was a one-year comprehensive research project (1957–1958) conducted by a World Bank economic team chaired by Paul Ellsworth of the University of Wisconsin. This team submitted a large volume of proposals to the government in 1958 (IBRD 1958) that had great influence on the economic reforms undertaken by the Sarit government. In February 1957, in response to the World Bank research, the Thai government set up a coordinating committee (Khanakammakan Ruam-mue Kap Khana Samruwat Setthakit khong Thanakhan Lok, or Ko. So. Tho.) to act as a local counterpart. This ad hoc committee included John Loftus and four Thai members: 1) Det Sanitwong as chairman (a vice-chairman of the National Economic Council and former governor of the BOT, 1949–1952); 2) Chalong Pungtrakun (first secretary-general of NESDB, 1959); 3) Bunma Wongsawan; and 4) Suphap Yot-sunthorn (chief of the Department of Research of the BOT) as secretary-general (Det 1975, 32–39). All members belonged to the reformist group led by Dr. Puey. In spite of the fact that Dr. Puey himself was not directly involved in this joint research, he continued to give advice and encouragement to the committee members.

Reviewing these processes, we see that the economic reforms advocated by Dr. Puey since the early 1950s were already embedded in the reform efforts of his comrades and followers. We also find that Dr. Puey appreciated the utility of appealing to the established power of foreign advisors and international organizations against the military rulers to develop his reform ideas into realistic programs.

Establishing BOT Autonomy

In October 1958, Field Marshal Sarit seized power through a military coup. He argued that his takeover did not constitute a military coup d'etat (*kan rattapraharn*), but a revolution (*kan patiwat*) that aimed to construct a modern state on the basis of Thai values and culture. In the field of economic policy, he employed two different approaches simultaneously.

He and his associates delegated authority to economic technocrats in non-rent-producing areas such as macroeconomic management, while attempting direct involvement in rent-producing areas such as licensing and allocation of quotas for rice exporters and tin miners. Military leaders also became chairmen, directors and shareholders of leading commercial banks and mining companies which needed licenses or concessions from the government.

Immediately after the "revolution," Prime Minister Sarit created an Economic Advisory Committee whose responsibility was to formulate overall economic policies for national development. He appointed Det Sanitwong as its chairman and invited distinguished technocrats such as Leng Srisomwong and Thawi Bunyaket to be members (Wanrak ed. 1996, 49). Det in turn requested Field Marshal Sarit to invite back Dr. Puey from London as he was the key person undertaking economic reforms in accordance with World Bank proposals. Since Dr. Puey was a mortal enemy of Sarit, the prime minister was reluctant, but he finally agreed to appoint Dr. Puey first director of the Bureau of the Budget. Dr. Puey initially rejected the invitation to join the Sarit government, but he too changed his mind and decided to work with Det's economic team to develop the financial and fiscal reform ideas he had planned from the mid-1950s. Soon after becoming director of the BOB, Dr. Puey was also appointed seventh governor of the BOT (June 1959). He was then 42 years old.

After Dr. Puey was empowered with full authority in both the BOB and BOT, he launched a series of institutional reforms in both the fiscal and financial sectors in accordance with global standards. The major reforms can be summarized in six points (Suehiro 2000, 70–71):

1. He initiated the enactment of the Budget Process Law of 1959, which aimed to separate capital expenditure for projects-based investment from ordinary expenditure for salary and facilities. This new law enabled the government to supervise the national budget process in accordance with the mid-term national economic plan which the NESDB planned to introduce in 1961 (Siri 1966, 22–23).

2. He transferred the authority of the Comptroller Department (Krom Banchi Klang), which supervised national revenue and formulated fiscal policies (including tax collection), from the Ministry of Finance to a new independent office in the BOB. Once the BOB began to improve the tax collection system and tax ratios, total revenues increased impressively from 6,800 million baht in 1960 to 8,600 million baht in 1963 (Silcock 1967, 196).

3. In 1961 he abolished the system of unlimited and arbitrary public borrowing from the BOT in order to fight the increasing fiscal deficit and introduced the system of setting a ceiling on government borrowing. At the same time, he changed the issuance of national bonds to recoup government borrowings from short-term to long-term (ten years and more) (Suphap 1968). This was the first attempt to control the money supply through the development of a long-term government bond market.[4]

4. Rather than revising a 1949 Act which was only implemented in 1959, Dr. Puey completed the enactment of a new Act for Commercial Banks of 1962. He accelerated its implementation and introduced a legal framework for licensing new banks, modernizing the banking business, and empowering the Ministry of Finance to supervise banks (Paul 1963, 142–154; Sommai 1993, 9).

5. He put the management of both the Fund for Foreign Exchange (FFE; later Exchange Equalization Fund, EEF) and the foreign reserves under the direct control of the BOT instead of the Ministry of Finance.[5] Originally, the military groups showed keen interest in foreign exchange and interest policy because these would have a direct impact on both private sector and military businesses such as weapons imports. To reap economic benefit from these policies, military leaders frequently requested the BOT to set up a National Foreign Exchange Control Committee or a National Financial Committee to which they would appoint themselves members. Dr. Puey rejected these requests, declaring that he would resign all posts if the government compelled the BOT to adopt such a system (Phatchari and Somchai 1995, 22).

6. Dr. Puey set up a new independent institution inside the Ministry of Finance to supervise and monitor overall fiscal policy. The Fiscal Policy Office (FPO) was established in October 1961, with Dr. Puey himself serving as first director after resigning as director of the BOB. The FPO was completely independent from the BOB and the Comptroller Department and was expected to play its own role in the fiscal sector. Later it was given the authority to supervise public external debt policies as well.

In addition to these six reforms, Dr. Puey devoted himself to the creation of the four core agencies system of macroeconomic management and the enhancement of BOT autonomy from the military government. He did this by relying on his personal networks. For instance, Dr. Puey appointed Sommai Hoontrakun, one of his most faithful allies and assistant governor of the BOT, to supervise foreign exchange rate (FFE) policy. When the government decided to take out a huge loan from the World Bank to construct the first modern hydro-electric dam (Yanhee Dam, later renamed the King Phumiphol Dam), Dr. Puey recommended Sommai to be the first governor of the Yanhee Electricity Generating Authority (later Electricity Generating Authority of Thailand, EGAT), further suggesting that the government give him overall authority to negotiate with the World Bank (Sommai 1993).

Similarly, when the World Bank requested the Thai government to create a new post of second deputy director in the Department of National Roads to monitor the management of a major foreign loan for the construction of a nation-wide first-class road system, Dr. Puey's comrade in the FPO, Nukun Prachuapmo, was appointed. He held the post for the next 11 years (1964–1974). Dr. Puey was initially reluctant to grant the request of Phot Sarasin, minister of National Development (Krasuwang Phatthanakan), to transfer Nukun to the new post, because the Department of National Roads would not be beneficial to Nukun's career as a financial technocrat, but he finally agreed (Nukun 1996, 45–48). Foreign loans are a typical source of political rent for the government and political leaders; Dr. Puey's comrades who occupied key posts overseeing the loans often ended up, intentionally or not, trying to protect the autonomy of these agencies.

When Dr. Puey became governor of the BOT, the leading posts of other major economic institutions were also occupied by his associates. Det Sanitwong was chairman of the NESDB and Chalong Pungtrakun its secretary-general. Dr. Puey selected Siri Pakatsiri to follow him as second director of the BOB; Siri was the person Dr. Puey trusted as the most qualified professional in budget administration. Indeed, Siri was a pure technocrat in budget administration, experience he gained as chief of the Budget Section and chief of the Budget Department in the Ministry of Finance before the BOB was established in 1959. Chalong, the second director of the FPO after Dr. Puey, was also his follower in the Ministry of Finance and an old member of the Puey reform group of the 1950s.

It is clear that the economic reforms of Dr. Puey's time were sustained by outstanding leadership and well-organized personal networks. Part of the success was also due to Dr. Puey's well-designed preparatory work aimed at enhancing the autonomy of both economic agencies and the BOT against the military rulers. Personal networks played a major role when Dr. Puey constructed the four core agencies system as well. In his memoirs, he noted the importance of cooperation among these agencies:

The relationship between the Finance Minister and the Governor of the BOT may be identical with that of a couple. Wife, i.e., Governor of the BOT, usually

should follow her husband, i.e., Finance Minister. But a wife also is expected
to improve her husband's way without hesitation if he tends to go astray (Puey
1966, 5).

Later in his memoir he wrote:

The BOB and the Ministry of Finance, FPO, may be comparable to a right
arm and a left arm. Accordingly, the two institutions cannot be separated
functionally because two arms belong to a single body (Puey 1960, 64).

As clearly expressed in his memoirs, Dr. Puey always strove for close
cooperation between the four core agencies and ensured their absolute
independence from political influence. Ironically, his efforts proved
effective during the period of military rule, but when Thai politics was
democratized after 1973, relationships among the four agencies would
change.

Conflict between Finance Ministers and BOT Governors

Welfare State-oriented Policies and Finance Minister Boonchu Rochanasathian

After the military government collapsed in the people's uprising of October
1973 and a new constitution was promulgated in 1974, the relationship
between finance ministers and BOT governors began to change. The
turning point was the appointment of Boonchu Rochanasathian as finance
minister of the Kukrit Pramoj government in March 1975.

Boonchu had been a student of Kukrit when he took his Master of Arts
in accounting at Thammasat University. After opening his own auditing
office, Boonchu was invited to the Bangkok Bank to modernize its auditing
system and was quickly promoted to assistant general manager in 1954,
then to vice president in 1963 (Suehiro 1989, 112–113). When Kukrit established a new political party, the Social Action Party, for the upcoming
general election, he invited Boonchu to be secretary-general. Boonchu left
the Bangkok Bank to join Kukrit. In January 1975, in the general election
conducted according to the new constitution, the Democrat Party won a
plurality of 72 out of 269 seats. Seni Pramoj organized a coalition government that survived for only two weeks before being forced to hand over
power to his younger brother, Kukrit. As the new prime minister, Kukrit
appointed Boonchu as finance minister. What is important is the fact that

Boonchu was the first finance minister in Thailand who did not belong to the group of economic technocrats; despite his business background, he was appointed because of his political party membership.

Due to the Social Action Party's minority position (18 seats) in a coalition government and Boonchu's unique ideas on party building, the new finance minister attempted to introduce a series of new policies favoring the interests of peasants and the poor. These policies included: a *tambon* (village) money circulation project in which the government granted an equal budget to each village in order to create new jobs in rural areas (2,500 million baht or 8 percent of total national expenditure in 1975); free medical service for the poor (650 million baht); free public mass transportation services (500 million baht); productions subsidies to paddy growers; and adjustments to income tax rates to favor lower income classes (Aphiwat 1982, 93–95, 108–109). Naturally such spending policies contributed to a quick increase in public expenditure. As Table 2-4 and Figure 2-2 show, the budget of FY1975 increased by 26 percent over the previous budget year; that of FY1976 increased again by 27 percent. As

Table 2-4. Revenue and Expenditure of Thailand's Central Government in million baht and percent growth (1972-1995)

FISCAL YEAR	REVENUE	EXPENITURE	BALANCE	REVENUE GROWTH RATE (%)	EXPENDITURE GROWTH RATE (%)
1972	23,090	30,149	-7,059		
1973	27,826	34,750	-6,924	20.5	15.3
1974	40,481	36,861	3,620	45.5	6.1
1975	40,419	46,298	-5,879	-0.2	25.6
1976	45,236	58,916	-13,680	11.9	27.3
1977	55,399	68,113	-12,714	22.5	15.6
1978	63,206	80,972	-17,766	14.1	18.9
1979	76,683	97,168	-20,485	21.3	20.0
1980	96,711	128,977	-32,266	26.1	32.7
1981	117,309	142,976	-25,667	21.3	10.9
1982	120,624	174,372	-53,748	2.8	22.0
1983	145,836	182,469	-36,633	20.9	4.6
1984	157,042	191,060	-34,018	7.7	4.7
1985	166,394	222,181	-55,787	6.0	16.3
1986	177,810	225,724	-47,914	6.9	1.6
1987	203,888	232,871	-28,983	14.7	3.2
1988	257,285	246,642	10,643	26.2	5.9
1989	323,481	268,749	54,732	25.7	9.0
1990	411,161	311,801	99,360	27.1	16.0
1991	486,029	366,715	119,314	18.2	17.6
1992	511,528	431,365	80,163	5.2	17.6
1993	572,921	506,558	66,363	12.0	17.4
1994	671,265	603,847	67,418	17.2	19.2
1995	780,824	657,973	122,851	16.3	9.0

Note: The fiscal year in Thailand starts on 1st October and ends on 30th September.

Sources: IMF; Government Finance Statistics Yearbook, various issues.

Figure 2-2. Revenue and Expenditure of Thailand's Central Government (1972–1995)

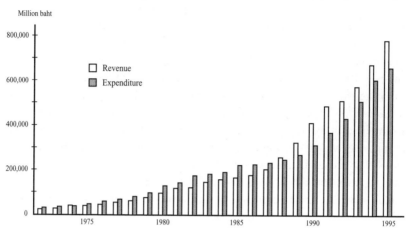

a result, a balanced budget turned into a deficit in FY1975 and worsened in FY1976.

Policies neglecting revenue sources apparently violated the basic discipline of the BOT, which called for a balanced national budget and stable money supply. In fact, the BOT opposed Boonchu's welfare state-oriented spending policies, but the finance minister simply ignored BOT objections. Instead he ordered the BOT to allocate a minimum 5 percent of outstanding commercial bank loans to farmers' groups or the agricultural sector (Bank of Thailand 1975, 40–41).[6] In addition to this quota system of agricultural credits, Boonchu introduced a new regulation obliging commercial banks operating in rural areas to allocate at least 60 percent of their total loans to local clients whenever they opened a new local branch.

The BOT staff was completely unfamiliar with monitoring agricultural credits, so it created a special section on agricultural credits that reported directly to the Ministry of Finance (Maxfield and Patchree 1992, 32). Boonchu had been a pioneer in developing agricultural credits during his directorship of the Bangkok Bank, and he began intervening without hesitation in the financial policies of the BOT in order to obtain farmers' political support for the government. Boonchu's new policies had a tremendous impact on cooperation among the four core agencies. The Ministry of Finance was empowered to borrow money from abroad without consulting the BOT (see the chronology in Table 2-5). The NESDB was requested to back up nation-wide projects such as the *tambon* project, while

Table 2-5. Changes in Thailand's Public Debt Policy, 1960–1992

YEAR	POLICIES
1960	Ceiling on public sector debt service ratio (DSR) set at 5 percent.
	Foreign debt service of public sector limited to less than 13 percent of forecast revenue.
1960	National External Debt Committee (NEDC) established to monitor and regulate foreign borrowing.
1964	Ceiling on DSR raised to 7 percent.
1976	Total public sector foreign borrowing limited to less than 10 percent of total government expenditure.
	Ministry of Finance empowered to borrow from abroad.
1977	Ceiling on DSR raised to 9 percent, of which 2 percent was reserved specifically for military borrowing.
	NDPC empowered to control public enterprises' foreign borrowing.
1984	Ceiling on DSR of 9 percent (plus 2 percent) set to include borrowing for the period 1984-1987 to accommodate refinancing program.
July '84	NEDP reorganized into the National Debt Policy Committee (NDPC) under the Ministry of Finance.
1986	A limit of total public sector foreign borrowing for all purposes established at 1,000 million dollars per year.
1989	Limit on public sector foreign borrowing raised to USD 1,200 million annually.
1990	Limit on public sector foreign borrowing raised to USD 1,500 million annually.
1991	Limit on public sector foreign borrowing raised to USD 2,000 million annually.
1992	Limit on public sector foreign borrowing raised to USD 2,500 million annually.

Sources: Warr and Bhanupong 1996, 94–95; for 1985–1992: Rangsan 1995, 36.

the BOB was forced to follow the tax reforms introduced by Boonchu. Collaboration between the BOT and the FPO also collapsed since policy making on public expenditure now shifted from the FPO to the finance minister himself.

In short, a democratized government began to challenge the autonomy of economic technocrats, and Boonchu's intervention politicized what was once an apolitical, professional process. The BOT view of the situation leading to the collapse of the four core agencies system was frankly expressed in its annual report of 1975:

It is to be noted that the previously used system for sorting out policies and operational economic plans had relied on the joint efforts of national organizations, i.e. the Ministry of Finance, the National Economic and Social Development Board, the Budget Bureau and the Bank of Thailand. Urgent consideration should be made on whether the previous system of economic management should be re-installed or abolished and replaced by a new system which should not, in any case, duplicate the work of various government agencies which are responsible for the actual implementation of operational plans (Bank of Thailand 1975, 101).

Dr. Puey did not have an official position at this time because when the Thanom Kittikachorn and Prapat government had dissolved parliament in 1971, he had resigned as BOT governor to protest military dictatorship. After his resignation, he was invited to become rector of Thammasat University (1972), moving up from the deanship of the Faculty of Economics (1964–1972). As the leader of several groups of intellectuals, he guided various movements to promote rural development and political democratization between 1973 and 1976 (Wanrak ed. 1996, 112–174). He had neither the intention nor the official channels to become directly involved with economic policies as a "super technocrat" in the new governments. And when the military again seized power after killing a large number of students and others rallying in the Thammasat campus in October 1976, Dr. Puey was forced into exile in London, where he stayed until his death in 1999. Since 1972, therefore, the core agencies lacked the key person who could re-establish their tight cooperation in macroeconomic management.

The Structural Adjustment Policies of the Prem Tinsulanon Government
The Kukrit government lasted only a year, and in 1976 the military once more seized power. From 1976 to 1988, when the Chartchai Chunhawan political party-based government was organized, governments supervised by the military (Field Marshal Kriangsak Chamanan and Field Marshal Prem Tinsulanon) again recruited financial or economic technocrats for the post of finance minister. Unfortunately, relations between finance ministers and BOT governors continued to worsen, reproducing the personal conflict between the top leaders first seen in the Boonchu era. When Field Marshal Prem, who had been commander-in-chief of the Army from October 1978 to August 1981, became prime minister in March 1980, the Thai economy was severely hit by world recession and domestic inflation arising from the second oil crisis.

To overcome this economic difficulty, Prem accepted a standby credit from the IMF in 1981 and agreed to World Bank conditions with a Letter of Intent (LOI) in exchange for structural adjustment loans (SALs) totaling USD 325.5 million in 1982 and 1983 (Chaipat 1992; Suehiro and Higashi eds. 2000, 24–28). The World Bank obliged the Thai government to conduct structural reforms according to its guidance, and the Thai government itself started to reassess existing national economic plans, focusing on growth and attempting to introduce self-designed "institutional reforms" in a Fifth Five Year Economic and Social Plan (1981–86).[7] On the basis of these original institutional plans together with external pressure from the World Bank, the Prem government launched a series of reforms. These included a new development plan focusing on economic stability rather than economic growth, reduction of income disparity between urban and rural areas, devaluation of the Thai currency and coordination between the public and private sectors.

To implement these policies, Prime Minister Prem ordered the cabinet to set up a National Economic Policy Steering Committee (NEPSC) that included the four core agencies (Sommai 1993, 155). The establishment of the NEPSC appeared to be a restoration of the four core agencies system of macroeconomic management (Muscat 1994, 177). But in actuality, this committee seems not to have played a significant role in undertaking economic reforms. Rather, according to the author's observation (Suehiro and Higashi eds. 2000, 34–35), four *new* institutions seemed to play more important roles in economic recovery. The four institutions are:

1. The *Joint Public and Private Sector Consultative Committees* (JPPCCs, or Ko. Ro. Oo), set up in August 1980. The JPPCCs included government representatives from related ministries and private sector representatives of three major organizations: the Thai Chamber of Commerce (TCC), the Bankers Association of Thailand (BAT) and the Federation of Thai Industries (FTI). These members held a joint monthly meeting chaired by the prime minister to exchange ideas and submit policy proposals on structural reforms to the cabinet (See Table 2-6) (Suehiro and Higashi eds. 2000, 41–43).

2. The *Coordinating Committee between the NESDB and the Ministry of Finance*, established in September 1983 to coordinate structural adjustment programs.

3. The *National Debt Policy Committee* (NDPC), a July 1984 reorganization of the National External Debt Committee (NEDC) empowered with full authority to manage external public debt policy (see Table 2-5). Although its committee members included the BOT governor, the NESDB secretary-general and the FPO director, 8 out of 15 members were appointed from among high-ranking officials of the Ministry of Finance (MOF). The finance minister chaired the

Table 2-6. Meeting Frequency of the Joint Public and Private Sectors
Consultative Committees (JPPCCs), by government, 1981–1999

GOVERNMENT	PERIOD	TOTAL MONTHS	NUMBER OF MEETINGS	MEETINGS PER MONTH	NOTES
Prem Government[a]	Mar '80–Aug '88	101	n.a.	n.a.	Principally, every month.
(Coalition Government)	Aug '81–July '86[b]	60	46	0.77	3 times for regional meetings; 9 times for overseas missions
Chartchai Government (Chart Thai)	Aug '88–Feb '91	19	11	0.58	7 times for overseas missions.
Anan Interium Government (National Peace and Order Keeping Committee)	Mar '91–Sep '92	19	1	0.05	
First Chuan Government (Democrat Party/ Coalition Government)	Sep '92–May '95	32	6	0.19	3 times for regional meetings
Banharn Government (Chart Thai/Coalition Government)	Jul '95–Sep '96	15	3	0.20	
Chawalit Government (New Aspirations Party/ Coalition Government)	Nov '96–Nov '97	12	4	0.33	JPPCC Office established within NESDB.
Second Chuan Government (Democrat/Coalition Government)	Nov '97–Nov '00	15	4	0.27	

Note:
a. former Commander in Chief of the Army
b. JPPCC held its first meeting in August 1981.

Sources: Prem and Chartchai governments: Anek 1992, 70, 74; Prem through second Chuan government: NESDB So. Ko. Ro. Oo. [JPPCC] 1998, 20–43.

committee, and the permanent secretary of the MOF acted as sec-retary-general (Suehiro and Higashi eds. 2000, 78–79).

4. The *Extended Meeting of Economic Ministers* (EMEM, or *khana kammakan rattamontri dan setthakit*), set up in August 1986. Unlike the cabinet, the EMEM was fully empowered to discuss and make final decisions on major national economic affairs.[8] What is important is the fact that EMEM members include not only economic ministers, the governor of the BOT and the director of the BOB, but also the chairman of the prime minister's economic advisory committee, the prime minister's secretary and a government spokesman. The JPPCCs and the NESDB served as the secretariat for the EMEM (Prasong 1989, 607–608).

In the management of these four committees, the NESDB and the Ministry of Finance—not the FPO alone—increased their roles in macroeconomic management in line with decline of the traditional four core agencies. For instance, the NESDB was the secretariat for management of the JPPCCs and the EMEM, while the Ministry of Finance together with the NESDB was empowered to supervise and control the NDPC. The role of the BOT was now confined to the area of monetary policy, while foreign exchange rate policy became the joint work of the BOT and Ministry of Finance. Concerning the changing relationship among the four core agencies, Muscat observed:

Between these secretarial functions, the responsibility for drafting the national development plans, and NESDB's role as coordinator of the preparation work for projects submitted for World Bank, Japanese, and other external loan financing, NESDB was in position to become a stronger center of policy influence and power than at any previous time in its history (Muscat 1994, 178).

Personal Conflict between the Finance Minister and the BOT Governor

In November 1979, Nukun Prachuapmo was appointed tenth governor of the BOT, and in March 1981, the Prem government invited Sommai Hoontrakun to become finance minister. While these two figures were long-time faithful followers of Dr. Puey, they were quite different in personality and policy orientation (Patchari 1995). Sommai was no longer a financial technocrat but a politician whom Prem fully trusted. He advocated a spending policy to help economic recovery and sometimes intervened in monetary policy on the basis of political judgment rather than economic rationality. In contrast, Nukun strictly followed the traditional policy stance of the BOT. He promoted policies focusing on monetary and economic stability and maintained that constraining inflation and stabilizing foreign exchange rates through market mechanisms was one of the most important targets of the BOT. That was the conventional position associated with Dr. Puey.

Therefore, Nukun frequently criticized Prem government policy in general and Sommai's position in particular. When Sommai decided to freeze petroleum prices to minimize the economic damage of the second oil crisis, Nukun fiercely criticized the policy, arguing that artificial price control would disturb and distort economic stability in the long run. He counseled that inflation should be constrained through sound monetary policy and market forces rather than political intervention in price mechanisms (Nukun 1996, 119–122). The conflict between the two leading figures ended abruptly when Sommai resorted to coercive means, dismissing Nukun in September 1984 and replacing him with Kamchon Sathirakun, director of the FPO. As Table 2-7 shows, there had been no previous dismissal of a BOT governor by a finance minister in 25 years. Since this time, a few finance ministers have experienced incompatibility of temperament with BOT governors against Dr. Puey's expectations.

Table 2-7. Resignation and Dismissal of BOT Governors and Deputy Governors, 1946–1998

No.[a]	NAME	DATE LEFT	POSITION	REASON	CAUSE
1	Wiwattanachai Chaiwan, Momluang	1946/10/16	Governor	resignation	Protested government policy concerning trade of gold.
4	Det Sanitwong, Momluang	1952/2/29	Governor	resignation	Protested government policy on foreign exchange rate for pound sterling
	Puey Ungpakorn	1953/12/24	Deputy governor	dismissal	Military pressure against Puey who levied criminal fines on Sarit's unfair trade in Union Bank of Bangkok.
5	Kasem Sriphayak	1958/7/23	Governor	resignation	Resigned over corruption of BOT staff.
6	Chote Khunnakasem	1959/5/3	Governor	dismissal	Military pessure against Chote who criticized change of printing house of national currency.
7	Puey Ungpakorn	1971/8/15	Governor	resignation	Resigned to protest Thanom's violation of democracy.
	Chalong Pungtrakun	1975/2/4	Deputy governor	resignation	Resigned over construction scandals concerning BOT's new head office.
8	Phisut Nimmanhemin	1975/8/23	Governor	resignation	Followed the government officer's retirement code calling for retirement at age sixty. Followed Chalong's precedent.
9	Sano Unakun	1979/10/31	Governor	resignation (dismissal)	Officially, resigned due to health problems. Actually, dismissed for the collapse of finance companies.
10	Nukun Prachuapmo	1984/9/13	Governor	dismissal	Dismissed by the finance minister for neglecting his orders.
11	Kamchon Sathirakun	1990/3/5	Governor	dismissal	Dismissed for concentration of power and failure to manage interest policy.
12	Chawalit Thanachanan	1990/9/30	Governor	resignation	Retired at age sixty.
	Ekamon Sririwat	1995/12/26	Deputy governor	resignation (dismissal)	Dismissed for illegal activity violating Commercial Banking Law and Securities Exchange Law.
13	Wichit Suphinit	1996/7/1	Governor	resignation (dismissal)	Dismissed for unfair trade in Bangkok Bank of Commerce.
	Chroeng Nukwan	1997/3/5	Deputy governor	resignation (dismissal)	Dismissed over Bangkok Bank of Commerce scandal.
14	Roengchai Marakanon	1997/7/28	Governor	dismissal	Dismissed over failure to manage currency policy.
15	Chaiwat Wibunsawat	1998/5/6	Governor	dismissal	Dismissed over illegal activity and inability to conduct duties.

Note: No. = Serial number beginning with the first governor.

Sources: Rangsan 1998, 280–281; Thanakhan haeng Prathet Thai 1992; The Nation Review.

Economic Expansion, Financial Liberalization
and the Collapse of the BOT

Economic Expansion Policy Led by Finance Minister Pramuan Saphawasu
Thanks to the implementation of structural reforms, Thailand began to show a gradual economic recovery from the mid-1980s. In addition, the 1985 G-7 agreement to adjust the Japanese yen (the Plaza Accord) paved the way for a rush of Japanese and other East Asian firms into Thailand and other Southeast Asian countries. The foreign direct investment (FDI) boom started in 1988, and FDI in 1990 alone (64.7 billion baht) exceeded the total accumulated FDI of the 16 years from 1973 to 1988 (64.6 billion baht). This dramatic increase contributed directly to the "economic boom" and unprecedented "stock boom" in Thailand beginning in 1988.

Along with the "economic boom," Thailand experienced a significant change in political structure. After the general election of 1988, Chartchai Chunhawan, the leader of the Chart Thai Party, was appointed prime minister and began organizing a working political party-based government that replaced the old quasi-democratic regime. After establishing a coalition government, he dramatically switched the policy target from structural reforms to economic expansion by improving economic relations with the countries of Indochina under the slogan "changing Indochina from a battle field to a market." He introduced policies aimed at attracting more FDI, lifted regulations on investment on heavy industries in the Eastern Sea Board Industrial Area and expanded public expenditure on economic infrastructure.

In order to promote these economic expansion policies, Chartchai empowered two actors with full authority: the prime minister's economic advisory team (the Ban Phisanulok) chaired by his eldest son, Kraisak Chunhawan, and the finance minister. He appointed as finance minister Pramuan Saphawasu, who as secretary-general of Chart Thai was responsible for party financing. Pramuan was a party member with a business background and the second person to come to the post of finance minister from a business circle after Boonchu Rochanasathian in 1975. Unlike Boonchu, however, who was a banker and expert in finance, Pramuan was completely unfamiliar with fiscal and monetary policies, given his background as the owner of a construction firm. He therefore immediately organized a special advisory team of seven members, including his own eldest son and his company's legal advisor.[9] Although this advisory team was a formal committee attached to the Permanent Secretary's Office of the MOF, its membership relied heavily on Pramuan's private connections (Somchai and Pathiya 1988).

After becoming finance minister, Pramuan asked Boonchu for policy advice as he had once been a member of Boonchu's Social Action Party. Boonchu suggested tax reforms and spending policies in favor of both the lower income class and business circles, polices that he himself had attempted during the Kukrit period. As a result, Pramuan moved to reduce individual income and import taxes, while increasing public expenditure to support economic expansion in accordance with Chartchai's political agenda. This policy naturally produced conflict with the BOT, whose main concern was economic stability.

One of Pramuan's most important targets was to finance the widening gap between savings and investment resulting from rapid growth in the investment ratio (from 27 percent in 1987 to over 40 percent in 1990) as against the slower rise in the savings ratio (from 27 percent to 32 percent in the same period). Pramuan introduced two major policies to provide incentives for savings while continuing to promote foreign capital inflow in the form of FDI and banking loans (Suehiro and Higashi eds. 2000, 28–30). He lifted regulations on deposit interest rates in May 1989 and granted tax incentives on so-called institutional savings, such as life insurance and pension funds inside private firms (BBRD June 1988, 229). In addition, he introduced important new measurements which had the result of intervening in BOT autonomy.

First, Pramuan expressed his intention to liberalize foreign commercial banking activities in Thailand, which had been prohibited under the 1962 Commercial Banking Act. In late November 1988, he invited representatives from nine major foreign banks of Japan, Canada, the UK, France and Holland to explain his new policy. He announced that he would admit new foreign-owned fully-licensed branches in Thailand as long as these would actively cooperate in introducing fresh money from abroad (BBRD December 1988, 495). This implied that the finance minister, if necessary, could exert his own power to supervise the commercial banking business according to government policy without consulting the BOT.

Second, Pramuan redefined one traditional role of the BOT as established by Dr. Puey—that of setting the interest rate ceiling for deposits and loans, an exclusive right exercised in consultation with the Bankers Association of Thailand (BAT). He argued that such a practice violated depositors' rights, as well as the economic interests of business, and called on the BOT to stop manipulating interest rates (Maxfield 1997, 85). This became official policy when financial liberalization was implemented in 1990.

Lastly, Pramuan raised limits on public sector foreign borrowing from USD 1,000 million to USD 1,200 million in February 1989. This decision was the crucial turning point in the government's neglect of the ceiling framework for public external debt that had been introduced in 1960. Indeed, the limit on public sector foreign borrowing was raised every year after 1989—to USD 1,500 million in 1990, USD 2,000 million in 1990 and USD 2,500 million in 1992. The official decision to raise the limit on foreign borrowing was an agreement reached by the four core agencies after several months of debate. However, a high-ranking officer of the BOT revealed that it was very reluctant to accept the finance minister's proposal due to anxiety about producing an overheated economic boom (BBRD March 1989, 101). So far as the government's progressive spending policies were concerned, by 1999 the BOT seemed not to be a good partner of the finance minister.

Financial Liberalization and the BOT Regional Financial Center Plan
Despite significant conflict between the BOT and the finance minister over fiscal policy, the two agencies were in agreement in promoting financial liberalization. In a 1990 interview, BOT governor Chawalit Tanachanan stressed BOT initiative in this area (Phu Chatkan 1990). The BOT planned the first Three Year Financial Institutions Development Plan (1990–1992), in collaboration with the Ministry of Finance, to deregulate foreign currency transactions, capital transactions and interest rates. Chawalit explained the main purposes of liberalization: to develop Thailand into a financial center in mainland Southeast Asia and thereby finance the widening gap between savings and investment ratios; to enhance the authority of the BOT to supervise and monitor local commercial banks and financial institutions; to develop and facilitate local bond markets to meet increasing demand for corporate finance; and to improve the operation of financial institutions in conjunction with the progress of information technology (ibid., 106–109).

Nevertheless, it is difficult to determine who were the actual promoters of financial liberalization from 1990. It is true that the BOT was the lead institution in introducing the policy, but in the late 1980s international organizations like the IMF and World Bank also dispatched special teams to study the financial market and financial institutions and submit policy recommendations to the Thai government.[10] Financial liberalization was apparently also beneficial to the expansion of the economic interests of Chart Thai MPs or cabinet members competing with traditional business groups whose power was based on monopoly and reliance on government regulations. It would be safe to say that financial liberalization was the combined product of three different movements: BOT initiative, external pressure from international organizations and the economic interests of politicians from business circles.

The year 1990 was important for the BOT because of the appointment of Wichit Suphinij as its thirteenth governor. Wichit was the first person who did not belong to the group of economic technocrats outside the BOT; instead, he rose through the ranks of the BOT staff (*luk-mo*). He was one of three promising staff members who received the first BOT scholarships Dr. Puey introduced in 1961.[11] After Wichit and up to the currency crisis of 1997, the government continued to appoint governors from among able persons who had received the BOT scholarship. Wichit was also an active promoter of the BOT plan to develop Thailand into a financial center in mainland Southeast Asia. He made Regional Financial Center Plan (Sun Klang thang Kan-ngoen nai Phumiphak) official in a September 1992 public address (Vijit 1992).

The Regional Financial Center Plan was originally designed by the BOT to enhance the financial position of Thailand in mainland Southeast Asia. Looking at the rapidly changing economic environment in Indochina—the Doi Moi policy in Vietnam in 1986, the New Economic System Policy in Laos in 1986 and the First Five Year Economic Plan in Cambodia in 1991—the BOT made an optimistic projection of economic growth in mainland Southeast Asia. Based on an estimation of Indochina's economic growth for the five years between 1988 and 1992, the BOT projected foreign trade to increase at least threefold and foreign direct investment to reach USD 1,200 million per annum by the end of the period (Nuwai Phatthana Rabop Kan-ngoen 1994, 14–15). There were also signs that potential competitors were heading in the same direction. Taiwan had already opened an off-shore money market, while the Malaysian government had started an off-shore finance service on Labuan Island in 1991. It was therefore urgent for the BOT to enhance Thailand's financial position to facilitate trade and investment within Indochina.

To achieve this goal, Wichit introduced two major new policies in the Three Year Financial Institutions Development Plan (1990–1992): the establishment of the Bangkok International Banking Facilities (BIBF) to serve as an off-shore finance service in June 1993 (Benjamas and Patira 1993) and tax incentives for "Non-resident Baht Accounts" to attract foreign investors into the Thai money market (Ruangrat 1993). These two policies were principally aimed at facilitating economic activity with Indochinese countries, with Thailand serving as a financial center to bridge the supply side in Asian money markets such as Singapore with the demand side from traders or investors with stakes in Indochina and Thailand.

In actuality, however, a large proportion of the money flowing into Thailand was mobilized exclusively for domestic markets rather than for Indochinese countries. For instance, by October 1993 (four months after the start of BIBF operations), outstanding loans through the BIBF amounted to 111,100 million baht, of which merely 1,800 million baht or 2 percent was mobilized for trade and investment with Indochina (Nuwai Phatthana Rabop Kan-ngoen 1994, 20). Likewise, while the gross inflow of non-resident baht accounts quickly increased from 576 billion baht in 1992 to 5,804 billion baht in 1994 and 10,370 billion baht in 1995, almost 100 percent was mobilized for short-term deposits or in the stock market to seek transaction profits, rather to facilitate foreign trade with Indochinese countries (Suehiro ed. 1998, 50).

This unexpected movement presented a serious dilemma for the BOT. The rapid inflow of short-term capital through the BIBF and the non-resident baht account combined to bring about "excess liquidity" in the Thai money market. The BOT was then requested to control the money supply through national bond operation, control of interest rates and automatic adjustment through foreign exchange rates. But the government prohibited the issue of new national bonds, even while liberalizing control on interest rates by 1993. Furthermore, it was impossible for the BOT to control the money supply by appealing to foreign exchange policy. This is because local firms depended heavily on dollar-based foreign debt, and depreciation of the baht would immediately damage repayment schemes for the private sector. The BOT was forced to protect the dollar-linked or quasi-fixed exchange system and not to float the system. This policy choice in the foreign exchange system accelerated the interest of shrewd foreign money market investors in Thailand, as well as the economic interest of international hedge fund groups such as Soros and Tiger Funds, who sought free-rider profit.

The Regional Financial Center Plan was the BOT's original attempt to adjust Thailand's financial sector to international changes such as globalization and liberalization. But shifting the BOT target from economic and monetary stability to financial sector reforms in support of economic expansion seemed to have produced new and serious problems, namely, unprecedented financial instability and an economic bubble.

Personal Conflict inside the BOT

The promotion of Wichit to governor in 1990 brought about another peculiar problem in the relationship of sections or departments within the BOT. As mentioned above, government had traditionally appointed BOT governors from outside, leaving little chance for someone from the BOT staff to be promoted to the highest post. Wichit's appointment changed that and encouraged competition for promotion among high-ranking BOT officials. The chance for promotion was now open to one deputy governor (increased to three persons in November 1996), three assistant governors and three directors of major departments (planning and analysis, banking and overseas affairs) (So. Po. Ro. or Nukun Committee 1998, 169–172). Hence, the more ambitious began to form cliques, as are seen in military groups, to enhance their own position. These developments reportedly included spy networks to watch rivals' activity (Rangsan 1998, 264–265).

What became problematic for the BOT was that some of these ambitious office seekers began to request political patronage from party leaders to cement their position. For instance, Wichit tried to approach the Chart Thai Party and established a close connection with its advisory committee members (the Ban Phisanulok). Wichit's rival Ekamon approached other political party leaders. As Ammar Siamwalla observed, "good macroeconomic performance was partly attributed to the presence of a highly competent technocracy insulated from the patronage politics that thrived in sectoral policies" (Ammar 1997, 64). In resorting to this kind of politicking, the top BOT leaders themselves began to destroy this sacred discipline and in the long run caused the disintegration of the BOT as a unified organization. The conflicts also exposed excess among high-ranking officials. Wichit was dismissed by the finance minister in July 1996 on suspicion of conducting illegal business in the stock market using private loans from the Bangkok Bank of Commerce Public Company, which was then under BOT supervision. Although he was an intimate follower of Dr. Puey, Wichit destroyed the discipline Dr. Puey had constructed in the 1960s. Dr. Puey instructed the BOT staff in 1960 that "if the BOT will attempt to maintain its autonomy under the condition of no legal empowerment, the staff must always evidence their high ability, distinguished morality and sincerity to the public" (Puey 1960, 60–61).

After Wichit's dismissal, Roengchai Marakanon was appointed fourteenth governor. With his selection, the appointment of finance minister seemed to follow the rule of seniority rather than ability. Roengchai had no experience in the field of international finance; as a result he could not adequately counteract attacks by international hedge fund groups on the Thai baht from 1996 to May 1997. In addition, there was reportedly neither communication nor information exchange between the two most important officials managing the foreign exchange, the administrator of the Exchange Equalization Fund (EEF) and the official responsible for buying baht and selling US dollars in the Department of International Finance (So. Po. Ro. or Nukun Committee 1998, 79–84). It became apparent that this paralyzed institutional functioning finally led Thailand to catastrophe in July 1997. On 28 July, Roengchai was dismissed for failure to manage exchange policy, and Chaiwat Wibunsawat, the deputy governor, replaced him (See Table 2-7).

The Collapse of the Four Core Agencies System

Crisis Management, the IMF and Finance Minister Tharin Nimmanhemin
The currency crisis of 1997 not only damaged the Thai economy but also led to the disintegration of the four core agencies system in the policy-making structure. The major developments under the second Chuan government (1997–2000) may be summarized as follows.

First, in May 1998, the government appointed Chatumongkhon Sonakun as the sixteenth governor of the BOT after dismissing Chaiwat Wibunsawat for his inability to deal with the crisis. Chatumongkhon was not a BOT staff member, but the permanent secretary of the MOF (Ministry of Finance), so with his appointment the governorship of the BOT returned to the traditional pattern of recruitment of an outside financial technocrat. Despite his institutional origins, Chatumongkhon hardly took MOF interests into consideration. Rather, he switched BOT policy targets back to the traditional monetary stability and strict inflation control. Contrary to the government's expectations, he sometimes strongly resisted MOF-initiated spending policies meant to support economic recovery. As in the eras of the Kukrit and Prem governments, the BOT and MOF sought different policy targets in managing the macroeconomy.

Second, immediately after the currency crisis, the government agreed to abide by IMF/World Bank conditionality in order to receive stand-by credits and structural adjustment loans totaling USD 17.2 billion. The amount of these external public loans was larger by far than the loans of the Prem government in the early 1980s. As a result, economic policy-making power became concentrated in two IMF-World Bank economic teams and the finance minister, Tharin Nimmanhemin, who was the key finance person in the Democrat Party and the former president of the Siam Commercial Bank Public Company (1984–1992). Unlike in the Prem government, there was no coordinating committee between the MOF and the NESDB. The finance minister became the most important figure in formulating and undertaking major reforms, despite the cabinet's December 1998 decision to appoint the NESDB as secretariat to coordinate various reform projects.[12]

Third, the FPO was forced into a diminished policy-making role. The Public External Debt Section was separated from the FPO and given independence to handle the growing loans from international organizations. Along with this organizational restructuring and transfer of several groups, the number of FPO staff was drastically cut from 250 to 150 by 1999. Decision making in major fiscal policy was moved from the FPO to the Economic Ministers Meetings (held every Monday ahead of the Tuesday cabinet meeting in the Chuan government) or to the finance minister himself. The most important changes that took place within government economic institutions after the currency crisis and during the second Chuan government may be found in the prominent decline of both the NESDB and FPO technocracy in policy making.

It is true that the four core agencies continued to cooperate in preparing the annual national budget plan. But these institutions could no longer affect the direction and implementation of structural reforms undertaken by the government in collaboration with the IMF and World Bank.

The Thai Rak Thai Party and the Thaksin Government

Such movement as we observed in the Chuan government becomes more apparent when we examine the policy-making structure of the Thaksin government established after the January 2001 general election. Prime Minister Thaksin Shinawatra was well known as an outstanding business leader in such newly emerging industries as computers and telecommunications. He started his business servicing rental computer equipment in 1973, while still director of the Police Department's Computer Center for Crime. Thanks to his distinguished entrepreneurship, strong personal connections with Thai politicians and American business circles and precious technical knowledge of government regulation of the telecommunications industry, he could quickly expand his business to control computer rental services, mobile phone services, TV broadcasting services, information services and satellite services. Indeed, when he was recruited as minister of Foreign Affairs, he disclosed to the public that his assets amounted to approximately 70 billion baht (Suehiro 1995).

Thaksin is quite different in political style from traditional political party leaders. When he established his own party, the Thai Rak Thai (Thai People love Thailand) Party in July 1998, he organized three major policy committees to engage exclusively in economic affairs, political affairs and public relations and appealed to the public by addressing their own policy agenda, including support for "Thai" big companies, promotion of small and medium-scale enterprises (SMEs) and promotion of small and medium-scale community economy (SMCE) without help from economic technocrats in government institutions.[13]

When Thai Rak Thai (TRT) won the general election with 50 percent of the vote, Thaksin launched a series of new policies to realize his political ideas. He appointed Somkit Chatusriphitak, a professor at the National Institute of Development Administration (NIDA), as finance minister. Somkit graduated from the Kellogg Graduate School of Management (KGSM) of Northwestern University in the United States. He was well known in Thailand as a translator of Michael Porter's famous book, *The Competitive Advantage of Nations*, and was co-author with his American advisor, Philip Kotler, of *The Marketing of Nations: A Strategic Approach to Building Nation Wealth*. He had served as a special managerial advisor since 1988 to the I.C.C. International Public Company, the core company of the SPI Group, and is strictly speaking better seen as a "corporate strategist" than an academic scholar.

From 1994, Somkit began to actively advance his ideas concerning the competitive advantage of the country, the vision (*wisaithat*) to be inspired by political leaders and a "core competence" in country management, publishing in such leading monthly economic magazines as *Phu Chatkan Rai-duwan* and *Corporate Thailand* (Phu Chatkan, April 2001, 64–103). These messages occasionally attracted TRT leader Thaksin's interest and Somkit was recruited as a key member of the Economic Policy Formulating Committee. Because of this personal connection with the prime minister, Somkit was appointed finance minister when Thaksin organized his cabinet in February 2001. As such a relationship between the prime minister and finance minister suggests, the Thaksin government seems to constitute a policy-making structure quite different from previous governments. Its major characteristics can be summarized as follows.

First, the Economic Ministers Meeting, to which the Chuan government gave top priority in formulating economic policies, was abolished and replaced by ad hoc "strategic committees" (*khanakammakan klan krong*) set up in accordance with specific targets. In this new organizational structure, the power of the prime minister was enhanced absolutely.

Second, the Economic Policy Team organized inside the TRT became the most important group formulating the outline of economic policies. Five core members of this committee—Phansak Winyarat, Suranan Wetchachiwa (Vejjajiva), Kittidej Sutrasukhon, Kitti Limsakun and Pramon Khunakasem—formally and informally began to have a major impact on even routine work at the ministerial level, as can be seen in the case of the Ministry of Industry.[14] It is safe to say that economic policies are now formulated and implemented by not government officials but by political party members.

Third, Finance Minister Somkit appointed an advisory team which was expected to exert influential power not only on fiscal policy but also on financial policy and trade and commerce policies. Members of this team were invited from three major groups—financial technocrats in the government sector, experts in the stock market and distinguished leaders of business (see Figure 2-3). The last group included Bunyasit Chokewattana, chairman of the SPI Group, and Thanin Chiarawanon, chairman of the CP Group (Phu Chatkan, April 2001). In contrast to the increasing importance of this advisory team, high-ranking government officers belonging to the MOF, the Ministry of Commerce and the Ministry of Industry saw an inevitable decrease in their policy-making influence.[15]

Economic advisory teams had played important roles in the Kriangsak government (1977–80), the Prem government (1980–88) and the Chartchai government (1988–1991) as well. What distinguishes the Thaksin government from its predecessors is that his advisory teams are closely associated with the political party in power. The Thai Rak Thai Party is therefore the first programmatic political party in the sense that it has a special committee or team to formulate its *own policy agenda* in order to present its ideas to the public.

Fourth, the rise of the party-based economic team contrasted with the declining influence of the four core agencies. Despite the fact that both the NESDB and the MOF jointly submitted mid-term economic plans on 28 items to the first mobile cabinet meeting held in Chiang Mai on July 17, 2001 (*National Economic Development Strategic Plan for Improvement of Quality and Sustainability of Economic Growth: 2001–2006*), it is apparent that the majority of policy programs faithfully follow the economic plans the TRT economic team presented to the public before the general election of January 6, 2001.[16]

Likewise, major macro- and micro-level programs are discussed inten-sively at regular "informal" meetings chaired by the finance minister rather than among the four core agencies. It is true that in these meetings, representatives of the NESDB, FPO, BOT and other economic ministries are invited, but the NESDB no longer plays a significant role in promoting micro-level projects, while the FPO has no notable influence in coordinating the work of each project at the macro-level.[17] All important projects actively initiated by the Thaksin government—the *tambon* project (*khrongkan kon thun muban*), the one village-one product project (*nung pharitaphan nung muban*), the 30-baht healthcare project (*khrongkan kon-thun prakan sukhaphap*), the People's Bank project (*Thanakhan Prachachon*), the SMEs promotion program—are now discussed mainly by the TRT economic team or

Figure 2-3. Policymaking Structure under the Thaksin Government, 2001–2002

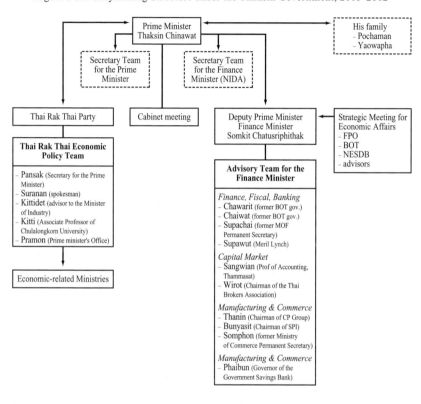

Sources: Depicted by the author on the basis of interviews with key persons in Thai Rak Thai (September 2001, March 2002, Bangkok); Phu Chatkan Rai-duan 18, no. 211 (April 2001).

among politicians rather than at the administrative meeting of the ministry concerned.

After the cabinet reshuffle in March 2002, the Prime Minister's Office replaced the Ministry of Finance and the NESDB as the headquarters of formulation and monitoring of all important policies undertaken by the government. And Prime Minister Thaksin completed an administrative reform in October 2002 that replaced coordination among ministers and economic institutions with a top-down system of decision making from the prime minister through the Thai Rak Thai Party and the Prime Minister's Office to each economic minister (Suehiro 2003, 100–105).

Finally, in contrast to the prominent decline of NESDB and FPO influence over economic policies, the BOT has seemed to recover its independence from the government. It is true that the government decided to replace the internally-promoted governor with an outside financial expert after the currency crisis. But, contrary to government expectations, new governors such as Chatumongkhon and Pridiyathorn Thewakun (Devakul) do not always follow the arbitrary spending policy of the government that targets economic growth. Rather, they seem to devote themselves to more traditional discipline focusing on strict monetary control and economic stability. Such policies seem to have contributed to the country's relative macroeconomic stability after 1999, as seen in the movement of consumer prices. Although the two governors have never been followers of Dr. Puey, they have attempted to reconstruct BOT autonomy. Therefore, the current policies of the MOF, which is based on the issuance of government bonds of large value, will likely become a crucial source of conflict with the more traditional BOT policy of strict control of the money supply. The debate over BOT autonomy will come to the fore again in the next five years.

Carefully examining these changes in the policy-making structure under the Thaksin government, we may conclude that the four core agencies system that Dr. Puey introduced in order to establish the autonomy of the economic technocracy from any power hegemony has almost completely disintegrated. Today, economic policy management has shifted from the four core agencies to the prime minister, the deputy prime minister, the finance minister and an economic policy team of the governing political party, who come together in the Prime Minister's Office. This movement may imply that the economic technocracy in Thailand now stands at the crossroads.

Concluding Remarks

In his critical examination of the currency crisis in 1997, Ammar Siamwalla reviewed the historical relationships between economic policy and the power structure and between economic performance and government policies in Thailand, making the following observation:

> Strictly speaking, the technocracy managing the country's macro economy consisted of officials from the Ministry of Finance, the Bank of Thailand, the BOB and the planning agency. This group emerged as a result of a major overhaul of the country's economic management system during the regime of Field Marshal Sarit Thanarat, a dictator who ruled Thailand between 1958 and 1963. Under him and his immediate successor, that is until 1973, this technocracy enjoyed considerable autonomy and managed to keep at bay the demands of the military who at that time occupied key political posts. The relationship between

the technocracy and its military rulers was far from smooth. The latter's need to expand government budget in general and the military budget in particular was a constant cause for conflict, as were some of their corrupt activities which entered the radar screen of the technocrats. But by and large, a modus vivendi was achieved, because both shared the vision that the economy needed to grow which for the technocrat was the desired aim, and for the military, was the means by which they could obtain greater spoils (Ammar 1997, 69).

The author mostly agrees with Ammar's argument, but would also like to stress the importance of Dr. Puey's distinguished leadership in constructing the four core agencies system. The ability of the four core agencies to protect the autonomy of economic technocrats against political groups in Thailand appears to have been guaranteed not only by well-established institutions or an *institutionalized decision-making process*, but also by the *notable leadership of a particular distinguished leader*. It is important for us to re-examine the role of distinguished leaders who are major players in a specific field, such as Dr. Puey in the financial sector. We can recognize the same pattern in the case of Dr. Adun Charunwichien in environment policy and Dr. Kosit Panpiamrat in the rural development program or Ko. Cho. Cho. (Suehiro and Higashi eds. 2000, Chapters 5 and 7).

Ammar (1997), Christensen et al. (1997) and Phatchari (1995) argued that political development or democratization does not always mean effective undertaking of economic policy in Thailand. At the same time, Muscat (1994), Warr and Bhanupong (1996) and Unger (1998) stressed the importance of the continuous development of social capital or institutional capacity of the technocracy in sustaining Thailand's long-term macroeconomic performance. But the author's survey focusing on relationships between finance ministers and BOT governors and cooperation among the four core agencies reveals two important facts—that technocracy-led policy making is crucially dependent on an individual leader and his/her personal connections and that the policy-making structure in Thailand has now shifted from the four core agencies-led system based on a "bureaucratic polity" to a political party-led system based on the prime minister's leadership. Which style will contribute to sustainable growth in Thailand in the future is another question.

Appendix

The appendix comprises Tables Appendix 2-1a to Appendix 2-2e.

Appendix 2-1a. Ministers of Finance: Birth Date, Cabinet, Academic Career and Puay Connection

Name	In post	Cabinet	Birth/ Death date	Bachelor	Master/Ph.D.	Puay Connection
1 Soem Winitchaikun	1958–58 1958–59 1965–68 1969–71 1972–73	Thanom Sarit Khana Phatiwat Thanom I Thanom II Thanom III	2/06/1907 *1985/7	Thai/Law School (Rongrian Kotmai), Ministry of Justice, 1929	France/Univ. of Paris: Ph. D/Law 1938	Superior in MOF
2 Chote Khunnakasem	1959–59	Sarit	1903/8/2; 1967/11/2	UK/Birmmingham Univ./Commerce 28	-	
3 Sunthon Hongradarom	1959–63; 1963–65	Sarit	23/08/1912	UK/Cambridge Univ./Economics	Cambridge Univ./MA: Economics	Superior in MOF
4 Bumma Wongsawan	1973–74	Sanya I	7/11/1917	UK/London LSE/Economics	London LSE/Ph.D. Economics.	Member of reforms
5 Sommai Hoontrakun	1974–75 1981–81 1981–83 1983–86	Sanya II Prem II Prem III Prem IV	1918/5/15 1993/6/30	Japan/Keio Univ./Economics	Keio Univ./MA: Economics, 1943	Member of reforms
6 Sawet Phiamphongsan	1975–75 1976–76 1976–76	Seni I Seni II Seni III	26/02/1911	Thai/Thammasat Univ./Accounting	-	
7 Bunchu Rochanasathian	1975–76	Khukrit	10/02/1922	Thai/Thammasat Univ./Accounting	-	
8 Suphat Suthatham	1976–77 1977–79	Thanin Kriangsak	22/07/1915	n.a.	Japan/Rikkyo Univ./MA: Commerce, 1941	
9 Gen. Kriangsak Chamanan	1979–80	Kriangsak II	17/12/1917	USA/General Staff School, 1954		
10 Amnuai Wirawan	1980–81 1996–97	Prem I Chawalit	22/05/1932	Thai/Chulalongkorn/Commerce	USA/Michigan Univ./Ph.D: Economics	Suboridinate in MOF
11 Suthy Singsaneh	1986–88 1991–92	Prem IV Anan I	22/07/1928	Thai/Thammasat/Accounting	USA/Illinois/Ph.D, Economics, 1957	
12 Pramuan Saphawasu	1988–90	Chartchai I	29/11/1927	Thai/Thammasat	-	
13 Wiraphon Ramakun	1990–90	Chartchai I	1/08/1943	USA/Univ. of Pennsylvania/Political Sc.	USA/Univ. of Pennsylvania/Ph.D: Economics	
14 Banharn Sinlapa-acha	1990–91	Chartchai II	20/07/1932	Thai/Bangkok Commerce College	-	

						Nepew
15 Phanat Srimasathian	1992–92	Suchinda (Military Government)	29/09/1932	Thai/Thammasat/Accounting	USA/Univ. of Illinois/Ph.D: Economics, 1958	Nepew
	1992–92	Anan II				
16 Tharin Nimmanhemin	1992–93	Chuan I	29/10/1945	USA/Harvard/Political Science, Business: 1968	USA/Stanford Univ./MBA, 1970	
	1993–94	Chuan Resh.				
	1994–95	Chuan Resh.				
	1997–98	Chuan II				
17 Surakiat Sathianthai	1995–96	Banharn	7/06/1958	n.a.	USA/Harvard/Ph.D: International Economic Law	
18 Bodi Chu-nanon	1996–96	Banharn	30/08/1935	Thai/Chulalongkorn/Commerce	USA/Wayne State Univ./MBA	
19 Thanong Phitthaya	1997–97	Chawalit	28/07/1947	Japan/Yokohama National Univ./Economics	USA/North West Univ./Ph.D: Business	
20 Kosit Panpiamrat	1997–97	Chawalit	28/05/1943	Thai/Chulalongkorn/Political Sc., 1963	USA/Marry Land/MA: Economics, 1965	

Note for Appendices 1a–1e and 2a–2e: Identification of persons related to Dr. Puey was made by the author with reference to Wanrak 1996.

Sources for Appendices 1a–1e and 2a–2e:

1. Cremation Books for: Some Winitchaikun (1985/10/19); Chote Khunnakasem (1968/2/28); Sommai Hoontrakun (1993/12/25); Leng Sirisomwong (1975/3/12); Det Sanitwong (1975/12/17); Kasem Sriphayak (1965/11/24); Suphap Yotsunthorn (1974/6/18); Phisut Nimmanhemin (1985/7/10); Siri Pakatsit (1966/9/15); Bandit Bunyapana (1993/9/1).

2. Krasuwang Kan Khlang 1992.

3. Who's Who (monthly); Who's Who in Business and Finance (monthly); Who's Who in Finance and Banking 1984.

4. Thammasat University 1963; Prachachat 1982; Who's Who Finance and Banking 1985–86 1985; Sita Sonsri ed., Business Elites Profile, 1988; Thawanya, A Who's Who Directory of Thailand Executives 1994, 1994; Bangkok Post ed., 50 Thais, Special Issue, August 1, 1996.

5. Bank of Thailand, Biographical Data of the Governor, various persons;

6. Daily newspapers: Bangkok Post, The Nation Review, Phu Chatkan Raiwan.

The entire survey was conducted by Akira Suehiro.

Appendix 2-1b. Governors of the Bank of Thailand: Tenure, Birth Date, Age, Academic Career, Puay Connection

Name	Tenure	Birth/ Death date	Age at Appointment	Bachelor	Master/Ph.D.	Puay Connection
1 Wiwattanachai Chaiwan, Praong Chao	1942–46 1948–48	1899–1990	42 49	UK/Cambridge Univ./History	-	Superior
2 Soem Winitchaikun	1946–47 1952–55	1907/6/2–1985/7/?	39 44	Ministry of Justice (Thailand) Law School	France/Univ. of Paris/Law, 1938	Superior in MOF
3 Leng Sirisomwong	1948–49	1900/9/5–1981/3/6	48	UK/Liverpool Univ./Commerce, 1925	-	Superior
4 Det Sanitwong, Mom Luang	1949–52	1899/2/18–1975/9/18	50	Germany/Bonn Univ./Political Economy, 1925	-	Superior
5 Kasem Sriphayak	1955–58	1903/12/30–1965/7/5	51	UK/Birmingham Univ./Commerce, 1925	-	
6 Chote Khunnakasem	1958–59	1903/8/2–1967/11/20	54	UK/Birmingham Univ./Commerce, 1928		
7 Puay Ungpakorn	1959–71	1917/3/9–1999/7/26	42	UK/London Univ. LSE/Economics, 1941	UK/London LSE/Economics, PhD, 1949	Principal
8 Phisut Nimmanhemin	1971–75	1915/5/23–1985/6/24	56	UK/London Univ. LSE/Banking, 1939	-	Member of reform group
9 Sano Unakun	1975–79	24/07/1931–	43	Australia/Melbourne Univ./Commerce	US/Colombia Univ./PhD, Economics	Junior
10 Nukun Prachuapmo	1979–84	25/07/1929–	50	Australia/Melbourne Univ./Economics, 1952	US/George Washington Univ./PhD, Economics, 1956	Junior
11 Kamchon Sathirakun	1984–90	10/08/1933–	51	US/Michigan Univ./Economics	US/Michigan Univ./MA, Economics	Junior
12 Chawalit Thanachan	1990–90	2/07/1930–	59	UK/Manchester Univ./Economics	-	
13 Wichit Suphinit	1990–96	14/07/1941–	49	UK/Manchester Univ./Economics, 1966	US/Yale Univ./MA, Economics, 1972	Junior/Subordinate
14 Roengchai Marakanon	1996–97	10/03/1942–	53	Japan/Keio Univ./Finance, 1967	UK/London Univ. LSE/MA Economics, 1970	Junior/Subordinate
15 Chaiwat Wibunsawat	1997–98	19/09/1946–	50	n.a.	US/MIT/PhD, Economics, 1973	Junior/Subordinate
16 Chatumongkhon Sonakun	1998–	28/09/1943–	54	UK/Harrow School	UK/Cambridge Univ./MA, Economics	Junior/Subordinate

Sources:
1. Cremation Books of available persons;
2. Thanakhan haeng Prathet Thai ed. 1992.
3. Records compiled by Department of General Affairs, Bank of Thailand.

Appendix 2-1c. Secretaries-General of the National Economic and Social Development Board (NESDB): Tenure, Birth Date, Age, Academic Career, Puay Connection

	Name	Tenure	Birth/ Death date	Age at Appointment	Bachelor	Master/Ph.D.	Puay Connection
1	Chalong Pungtrakun	1959–63	1920	39	n.a	-	Member of reform group
2	Phrayat Phuranasiri	1963–70	1910/9/13–1970/2/14	53	UK/Haileybury College	UK/Cambridge Univ./MA	
3	Renu Suwan-nasit	1970–73	17/06/1921	49	US/Minnesota University	US/Harvard Univ. Business School/MBA	
4	Sano Unakun	1973–75 1980–88	24/07/1931	43	Australia/Melbourne Univ./Commerce	US/Colombia Univ./PhD, Economics	Junior
5	Krit Sombatsiri	1975–80	7/10/1927	47	US/Butler Univ./Business Admin.	US/Michigan Univ./MBA	
6	Phisit Pak-kasem	1989–95	29/03/1934	55	US/Claremont Univ.	US/Pittsburg Univ./PhD, Economic Development	
7	Sumeth Tangtiwetchakun	1995–97	26/08/1939	56	France/Grenouble Univ./Diploma	France/Monteperie Univ./PhD, Economics	

Sources: Cremation Books for available persons; Who's Who (1987; 1994); newspapers

Appendix 2-1d. Directors of the Bureau of the Budget: Tenure, Birth Date, Age, Academic Career, Puay Connection

Name	Tenure	Birth/ Death date	Age at Appointment	Bachelor	Master/ Ph.D.	Puay Connection
1 Puay Ungpakorn	1959–61	9/03/1917–	42	UK/London Univ. LSE/ Economics, 1941	UK/London Univ. LSE/ Economics, PhD, 1949	Principal
2 Siri Pakatsit	1961–66	1910/6/17–1966/6/11	51	Thailand/Assumption High School	-	Junior
3 Renu Suwannasit	1966–70	17/06/1921–	44	US/Minnesota Univ.	US/Harvard Business School/MBA, 1950	Junior
4 Chan Angsuchote	1970–74	21/06/1914–	55	US/General Staff School, 1949; Military School 34th	-	
5 Buntham Thongkhaimuk	1974–76	24/12/1921–	52	Thailand/Thammasat Univ.		Junior
6 Suthi Sing-saneh	1976–83	22/07/1928–	48	Thailand/Thammasat Univ. /Accounting, 1945	US/Illinois Univ./ PhD, Economics, 1957	
7 Bodi Chunanon	1983–	30/08/1938–	47	Thailand/ Chulalongkorn Univ. /Commerce	US/Wayne State Univ./MBA, 1961	

Sources: Cremation Book of Siri Pakatsit etc; Who's Who (1987, 1994).

Appendix 2-1e. Directors of the Fiscal Policy Office: Tenure, Birth Date, Age, Academic Career, Puay Connection

NAME	TENURE	BIRTH/ DEATH DATE	AGE AT APPOINTMENT	BACHELOR	MASTER/ PH.D.	PUAY CONNECTION
1 Puay Ungkakorn	1962–67	9/03/1917–	45	UK/London Univ. LSE/ Economics, 1941	UK/London Univ. LSE/ Economics, PhD, 1949	Principal
2 Chalong Pungtrakun	1967–71	1920–	47	n.a.	–	Member of reform group
3 Charnchai Leethawon	1971–72	18/12/1927–	43	US/Illinois Univ./Banking, Monetary Policy	–	Junior
4 Sunthon Sathianthai	1972–75	10/10/1927–	44	Thailand/Thammasat Univ.	France/Univ. of Paris/ PhD, Economics, 1944	
5 Bandit Bunyapana	1975–79	1934/10/6–1993/7/8	40	Thailand/Bangkok Christian High School	–	
6 Kraisri Chatikawanit	1979–82	9/10/1930–	49	US/Miami Univ., 1953	US/Long Island Univ./MA, Marketing research	
7 Kamchon Sathirakun	1982–84	10/08/1933–	49	US/Michigan Univ./Economics	US/Michigan Univ./MA, Economics	
8 Manat Leewiraphan	1984–86	7/04/1933–	51	Canada/Economics, 1952	US/Univ. of California /MA, Economics, 1957	
9 Aran Thammano	1986–90	10/02/1935–	51	Thailand/Thammasat Univ. /Economics, 195	US/Oregon Univ./PhD, Economics, 1961	

Appendix 2-2a. Ministers of Finance: Career Formation in the Public and Private Sectors

NAME	TENURE	CAREER	MINISTRY OF FINANCE	BANK OF THAILAND	PRIME MINISTER'S OFFICE	OTHER
1 Soem Winitchaikun	1958–58; 1958–59; 1965–68; 1969–71; 1972–73	Lawyer; bureaucrat for finance	Permanent secretary, MOF: 1954–65	BOT governor, 1946–47; 1952–55	Committee Member of Royal Decree 1946–63; Chair, NESDB, 1972–80	Thailand's representative at the World Bank: 1952–59
2 Chote Khunnakasem	1959–59	Bureaucrat for economic affairs	-	BOT governor, 1958–59	-	President, Thai Military Bank: 1957–
3 Sunthon Hongradarom	1959–63; 1963–65	Bureaucrat for economic affairs	-	-	Chair, National Economic Council Chair, NESDB, 1980–88	Secretary-general, SEATO, 1969–74 Ambassador to UK and US
4 Bunma Wongsawan	1973–74	Bureaucrat for finance	Director, Dept. Comptroller, MOF: 1957–63	-	Chair, NESDB, 1988–89	President, Siam Cemen, 1974–76
5 Sommai Hoontrakun	1974–75; 1981–81; 1981–83; 1983–86	Bureaucrat for economic affairs	-	Assistant governor, 1963–72	-	Chair of negotiations for World Bank loans; president, Siam Commercial Bank; president, Siam Cemen, 1976–80
6 Sawet Phiamphongsan	1975–75; 1975–76	Bureaucrat for finance/politician	Dept. Comptroller of MOF: 1948–; deputy minister, MOF: 1954–	-	-	Leader of the Social Agriculture Party, 1974–
7 Bunchu Rochanasathian	1975–76	Banker/politician	-	-	-	Secretary-general, Social Action Party; deputy prime minister for economic affairs
8 Suphat Suthatham	1976–77; 1977–79	Bureaucrat for economic affairs	-	-	Audit and Accounting Office: 1934–61	-
9 Gen. Kriangsak Chamanan	1979–80	Military/prime minister	-	-	-	Supreme commander-in-chief in 1977 coup
10 Annuai Wirawan	1980–81; 1996–97	Finance/businessman/politician	Permanent secretary, MOF; 1975–77	-	Secretary-general, Board of Investment, 1967–71; chair, NESDB	Officer, Ministry of National Dev.; chair, Executive Committee of Bankgok Bank, 1983–
11 Suthy Singsaneh	1986–88; 1991–92	Bureaucrat for economic affairs	Deputy minister, MOF	-	Director, Bureau of the Budget, 1976–83	State Comptroller

12	Pramuan Saphawasu	1988–90	Businessman/politician	–	–	–	Owner of construction company; Leader of Chart Thai Party
13	Wiraphon Ramakun	1990–90	Scholar/politician	Deputy minister, MOF, 1991–92	Director, NESDB	–	Dean of Faculty of Economics, Chulalongkorn, 82–; Adviser to PM Prem, 83–
14	Banharn Sinlapa-acha	1990–91	Businessman/politician	–	–	–	Secretary-general, Chart Thai Party; minister of industry; prime minister
15	Phanat Srimasathian	1992–92	Bureaucrat for economic affairs	Director, Dept. Comptroller, MOF Permanent secretary, MOF	–	–	–
16	Tharin Nimmanhemin	1992–93; 1993–94; 1994–95; 1997–2000	Banker/politician	–	–	–	President, Siam Commercial Bank, 1984–92; Democrat Party
17	Surakiat Sathianthai	1995–96	Scholar/politician	–	–	–	Dean of Political Science, Chulalongkorn Univ.; Director, Law Development Institute, Chulalongkorn Univ.
18	Bodi Chu-nanon	1996–96	Bureaucrat for economic affairs	–	Director, Bureau of the Budget, 1983	–	–
19	Thanong Phitthaya	1997–97	Banker/politician	–	–	–	President, Thai Military Bank
20	Kosit Panpiamrat	1997–97	Bureaucrat for economic affairs	–	Deputy secretary-general, NESDB, 1986–92	–	Minister of agriculture, 1992–; chair, Executive Committee of Bangkok Bank

Note: MOF = Ministry of Finance; BOT = Bank of Thailand; PMO = Prime Minister's Office

Appendix 2-2b. Governors of the Bank of Thailand: Career Formation in the Public and Private Sectors

NAME	TENURE	CAREER	MINISTRY OF FINANCE	BANK OF THAILAND	PRIME MINISTER'S OFFICE	OTHER
1 Wiwattanachai Chaiwan, Praong Chao	1942–46	Bureaucrat for finance	Permanent secretary, MOF; finance minister twice	Founder, BOT	-	-
2 Soem Winitchaikun	1946–47	Bureaucrat for finance; lawyer	Finance minister four times	-	Chair, NESDB, 1972–80	-
3 Leng Srisomwong	1948–49	Bureaucrat for economic affairs	Assistant director, Dept. Comptroller; finance minister	-	Director, National Economic Development Board (NEDB)	Royal Railway scholarship; Manager, Siam Commercial Bank, 1942–44
4 Det Sanitwong, Mom Luangt	1949–52	Bureaucrat for economic affairs	-	-	Chair, NEDB, 1959–72	Chair, Coordinating Committee for World Bank (1957–58); Advisor to Sarit's Khana Patiwa
5 Kasem Sriphayak	1955–58	Bureaucrat for economic affairs	-	-	-	Royal Railway scholarship; minister of economic affairs
6 Chote Khunnakasem	1958–59	Bureaucrat for economic affairs	-	-	-	Royal Railway scholarship; President, Thai Military Bank, 1957
7 Puay Ungpakorn	1959–71	Bureaucrat for finance	Advisor to MOF; director, Fiscal Policy Office	Vice-governor, 1952	Director, Bureau of the Budget; Director, NEDB	Rector, Thammasat University
8 Phisut Nimmanhemin	1971–75	Bureaucrat for finance	Dept. Comptroller, 1940–42	Vice-governor, 1965–71	-	Chair, Exchange Equalization Fund (EEF), 1955–65
9 Sano Unakun	1975–79	Bureaucrat for economic affairs	Director, Dept. Comptroller, 1955–60	-	Secretary-general, NESDB, 1973–75, 1980–88	-
10 Nukun Prachuapmo	1979–84	Bureaucrat for finance	Director, Dept. Comptroller, 1978–79	-	-	Chair for negotiating World Bank loans for Dept of Royal Roads
11 Kamchon Sathirakun	1984–90	Bureaucrat for finance	Director, Fiscal Policy Office, 1982–84	-	-	Chair, Krung Thai Bank Reconstruction Committee
12 Chawalit Thanachan	1990–90	Bank of Thailand	-	Vice-governor, 1984–90	-	Minister of education; chair, EEF
13 Wichit Suphinit	1990–96	Bank of Thailand	-	Vice-governor, 1990	-	BOT scholarship 1; chair, EEF
14 Roengchai Marakanon	1996–97	Bank of Thailand	-	Vice-governor, 1990–96	-	BOT scholarship 2; chair, EEF
15 Chaiwat Wibunsawat	1997–98	Bank of Thailand	-	Vice-governor	-	BOT scholarship; chair, EEF
16 Chatumongkhon Sonakun	1998–2001	Bureaucrat for finance	Director, Dept. Comptroller; permanent secretary, MOF	-	-	-

Note: MOF = Ministry of Finance; BOT = Bank of Thailand; PMO = Prime Minister's Office

Sources: Cremation Books of available persons; Thanakhan haeng Prathet Thai 1992; Records compiled by the Department of General Affairs, Bank of Thailand.

Appendix 2-2c. Secretaries-General of the National Economic and Social Development Board (NESDB): Career Formation in the Public and Private Sectors

Name	Tenure	Career	Ministry of Finance	Bank of Thailand	Prime Minister's Office	Other
1 Chalong Pungtrakun	1959–63	Bureaucrat for finance	Director, Fiscal Policy Office, 1971–72	Vice-governor, 1972–75	-	-
2 Phrayat Phuranasiri	1963–70	Bureaucrat for finance	Chief, Revenue Section, 1934	-	-	-
3 Renu Suwan-nasit	1970–73	Bureaucrat for finance	Dept of Comptroller, 1951–52	-	Director, Bureau of the Budget, 1966–70	-
4 Sano Unakun	1973–75; 1980–88	Bureaucrat for finance	Dept of Comptroller	Governor, 1975–79	Secretary-general, NESDB, 1973–75, 1980–88	-
5 Krit Sombatsiri	1975–80	Bureaucrat for economic affairs	-	-	Specialist 1st, NESDB	-
6 Phisit Pak-kasem	1989–95	Bureaucrat for economic affairs	-	-	Deputy secretary-general, NESDB, 1982–89	-
7 Sumeth Tangtiwetchakun	1995–97	Bureaucrat for economic affairs	-	-	Deputy secretary-general, NESDB	-

Sources: Cremation Books for available persons; Who's Who (1987; 1994); newspapers.

Appendix 2-2d. Directors of the Bureau of the Budget: Career Formation in the Public and Private Sectors

NAME	TENURE	CAREER	MINISTRY OF FINANCE	BANK OF THAILAND	PRIME MINISTER'S OFFICE	OTHER
1 Puay Ungpakorn	1959–61	Bureaucrat for finance	Dept. of Comptroller, MOF	Governor, 1959–71	Director, NEDB	Rector, Thammasat University
2 Siri Pakatsit	1961–66	Bureaucrat for finance	Deputy chief, Budget Section, Dept. Comptroller, 1959–61	-	-	Engaged in Budget Section since beginning work in MOF
3 Renu Suwannasit	1966–70	Bureaucrat for finance	Dept. of Comptroller, MOF; permanent secretary, MOF	-	Director, Economic and Technical Cooperation, 1968–70; secretary-general, NESDB	-
4 Chan Angsuchote	1970–74	Ministry of Defense	-	-	Deputy director, National Audit Committee	-
5 Buntham Thongkhaimuk	1974–76	Bureaucrat for finance	Deputy chief, Budget Section, Dept. Comptroller, 1961–74	-	-	-
6 Suthi Sing-saneh	1976–83	Bureaucrat for economic affairs	Vice-minister, MOF twice; finance minister twice	-	Auditor, National Audit Committee, 1961–66	Chief auditor, Agricultural Cooperatives Dept., 1966–76
7 Bodi Chunanon	1983–	Bureaucrat for economic affairs	-	-	-	Internal promotion

Note: MOF = Ministry of Finance; BOT = Bank of Thailand; PMO = Prime Minister's Office

Sources: Cremation Book of Siri Pakatsit, etc; Who's Who (1987, 1994).

Appendix 2-2e. Directors of the Fiscal Policy Office: Career Formation in the Public and Private Sectors

	NAME	TENURE	CAREER	MINISTRY OF FINANCE	BANK OF THAILAND	PRIME MINISTER'S OFFICE	OTHER
1	Puay Ungpakorn	1962–67	Bureaucrat for finance	Economic advisor	Governor, 1959–71	Director, Bureau of the Budget, 1959–61; director, NEDB	Rector, Thammasat University
2	Chalong Pungtrakun	1967–71	Bureaucrat for finance	Advisor to MOF; Vice-minister of finance	Vice-governor, 1972–75	Secretary-general, NESDB, 1959–63	–
3	Charnchai Leethawon	1971–72	Bureaucrat for finance	Permanent Secretary's Office; director, Customs	–	–	Economic advisor to Thai ambassadors to UK and US
4	Sunthon Sathianthai	1972–75	Bureaucrat for finance	Economic specialist (Setthakan); vice-minister, Finance	–	Secretary-general, Board of Investment, 1982–2001	–
5	Bandit Bunyapana	1975–79	Bureaucrat for finance	Director, Inner Tax; director, Comptroller, 1982–86; permanent secretary, MOF, 1992–93	–	–	Economic advisor for UK and Europe
6	Kraisri Chatikawanit	1979–82	Bureaucrat for finance	Chief, Monetary Economy, FPO; director, Customs, 1982–	–	–	Economic advisor for UK and Europe
7	Kamchon Sathirakun	1982–84	Bureaucrat for finance	Chief, Customs Investigation, 1970–74	Governor, 1984–90	–	–
8	Manat Leewiraphan	1984–86	Bureaucrat for finance	Economic specialist (Setthakan)	–	–	–
9	Aran Thammano	1986–90	Bureaucrat for economic affairs	Director, Inner Tax; director, Customs, 1990–93; permanent secretary, MOF, 1993–	–	–	Ministry of Commerce, 1953–64; Ministry of Finance from 1964

Note: MOF = Ministry of Finance; BOT = Bank of Thailand; PMO = Prime Minister's Office

Notes

1 For a detailed story of the national budget process in Thailand, see Narong 1992, 57–64.

2 For a detailed history of Dr. Puey Ungpakorn, see his cremation book (November 4, 1999, in Thai) and Wanrak ed. 1996.

3 *Saphayasat*, written by Phraya Suriyanuwat (Koet Bunnak) in 1911, was known as the first textbook on economics in Thailand. It is true that this book discussed the country's economy systematically for the first time, but Phraya Suriyanuwat had no intention of introducing the theory and discipline of economics. From the mid-1930s, Thammasat University also published at least four textbooks on political economy (*Lat-thi Setthakit Kan Muang*), but these books did not touch on the real world of the Thai economy. Accordingly, *Setthasat Thai* (1955), by Dr. Puey and Suphap, was the first textbook to purposefully combine the discipline of economics with analysis of the Thai economy.

4 This new system is very important to the relationship between the Ministry of Finance and the BOT. Crucial points are discussed in Suphap's article, "Central Bank Involved in Development Policy" (*The Financial Times*, December 2, 1968).

5 It should not be overlooked that Dr. Puey had contributed as a Setthakan to abolishing the notorious double standard exchange system and introducing the Fund for Foreign Exchange (FFE) in July 1955 (Wanrak ed. 1996, 44).

6 According to *The BOT Annual Report* (Bank of Thailand 1975, 40), "in the past, agricultural credits accounted for only 2 percent of total commercial bank's credits and amounted to approximately B 1,300 million at the end of 1974."

7 In his public addresses, Sanoh (secretary-general of the NESDB) described the plan's strategy as "Growth plus Four," that is, growth with stabilization, diversification, decentralization and cooperation. While overall growth targets had little operational significance, they were important as a symbol that the government expected the economy to grow more slowly in this period than it had in all previous plan periods (Muscat 1994, 182).

8 The Extended Meeting of Economic Ministers changed its name to Economic Ministers Meeting after the Chartchai government, and it increased its role in decision making on economic matters in the era of the second Chuan government (1997–2000).

9 These seven members included Phanat Simasathian (permanant secretary of the Ministry of Finance); Puchon (former director of the
   Department of Comptroller and Pramuan's high school classmate);
   Ms. Nongyao (former rector of Thammasat University and Pramuan's
   friend); Choedchu (FPO Financial Policy Division); Siri (BOT
   Economic Analysis Division); Kamon (legal advisor to Pramuan's
   company); and Kopsak (Pramuan's son and the president of the
   Pramuan group company) (Somchai and Pathiya 1988, 62, 67).
10 For instance, in 1990, the World Bank published the report, "Thailand:
   Financial Sector Study."
11 Author's interview with Dr. Phaibun Wattanasiritham, governor of the
   Government Savings Bank, one of three other students who received
   the BOT scholarship. March 1999, Bangkok.
12 Author's interview with the secretary-general of the NESDB in January
   1999, Tokyo.
13 Author's interview with key persons of the Thai Rak Thai Party in
   Bangkok, March and August 2001.
14 Author's interview with key persons of the Thai Rak Thai Party, August and September 2001.
15 For instance, in 2001, SME promotion initiatives were shifted from
   the Ministry of Industry's departments of Industrial Promotion and
   Industrial Economy to Thaksin's advisory team.
16 Author's interview with key persons of the Thai Rak Thai Party,
   September 2001.
17 Author's interview with key persons of the MOF in Bangkok, August
   2001.

References

Ammar Siamwalla. 1997. Can a developing democracy manage its macro-
   economy? The case of Thailand. In *Thailand's Boom and Bust*, ed.
   Thailand Development Research Institute, 63–75. Bangkok: Thailand
   Development Research Institute Foundation.
Anek Laothamatas. 1992. *Business Association and Political Economy of
   Thailand*. Denver, CO: Westview Press.
Aphiwat Wannaphon. 1982. *Chiwit Phon-ngan lae Naew Khwam Khit khong
   Boonchu Rochanasathian* [Boonchu Rochanasathian: His achievements
   and way of thinking]. Bangkok: P.M. Book Center.

Bank of Thailand. 1975. *Annual Economic Report 1975.* Bangkok: Bank of Thailand.

Bank of Thailand. 1992. *50 Pi Thanakhan haeng Prathet Thai 2485–2535* [50th anniversary book: Bank of Thailand, 1942–1992]. Bangkok: Thanakhan haeng Prathet Thai, December 10.

BBRD (Bangkok Bank Research Division). Economic diary. *Bangkok Bank Monthly Review,* various issues.

BBRD. News roundup. *Bangkok Bank Monthly Review,* various issues.

Benjamas Rojvanit and Patira Suksthien. 1992. Bangkok international banking facilities. *Bangkok Bank Monthly Review* 33, no. 11 (November).

Bhanupong Nidhiprabha. 1993. Monetary policy. In *The Thai Economy in Transition,* ed. Peter Warr. Cambridge: Cambridge University Press.

Buntham Thongkhaimuk and Phaisan Chaimongkhon. 1960. Prawat lae Wiwatthanakan khong Samnak Ngop Praman [History and development of the Board of Budget]. In *Cremation Book of Siri Pakatsit.* Bangkok, September 15.

Chaipat Sahasakul. 1992. *Lessons from the World Bank's Experience of Structural Adjustment Loans (SALs): A Case Study of Thailand.* Bangkok: The Thailand Development Research Institute.

Chaipat Sahasakul. 1993. Fiscal policy. In *The Thai Economy in Transition,* ed. Peter Warr. Cambridge: Cambridge University Press.

Chaiyawat Wibulswasdi and Orasa Tanvanich. 1992. Liberalization of the foreign exchange market: Thailand's experience. Bank of Thailand *Quarterly Bulletin* 32, no. 4 (December).

Chatrudee Theparat. 1996. Dr. Sanoh Unakul: Master planner pursued economic and social goals in several key positions. In *Bangkok Post, 50 Thais* (August).

Christensen, Scott R., Ammar Siamwalla and Pakon Vichyanond. 1997. Institutional and political bases of growth-inducing policies in Thailand. In *Thailand's Boom and Bust,* ed. Thailand Development Research Institute. Bangkok: Thailand Development Research Institute.

Det Sanitwong. 1975. *Cremation Book of Momluang Det Sanitwong.* Bangkok: December 17 (in Thai).

Doner, Richard, and Daniel Unger. 1993. The politics of finance in Thai economic development. In *The Politics of Finance in Developing Countries,* ed. Stephen Haggard, Chung H. Lee, and Sylvia Maxfield. Ithaca: Cornell University Press.

Doner, Richard F., and Ansil Ramsay. 1997. Competitive clientelism and economic governance: The case of Thailand. In *Business and the State in Developing Countries,* ed. Sylvia Maxfield and Ben Ross Schneider. Ithaca NY: Cornell University Press.

Jansen, Karl. 1997. *External Finance in Thailand's Development: An Interpretation of Thailand's Growth Boom*. The Hague: The Institute of Social Studies.

Hewison, Kevin, ed. 1997. *Political Change in Thailand: Democracy and Participation*. London: Routledge.

IBRD. 1958. *A Public Development Program for Thailand*. Baltimore: The Johns Hopkins University Press.

Krasuwang Kan Khlang. 1992. *Anuson 100 Pi Krasuwang Kan Khlang*. Bangkok: Krasuwang Kan Khlang.

Maxfield, Sylvia. 1994. Financial incentives and central bank authority in industrializing nations. *World Politics* 46 (July).

Maxfield, Sylvia. 1997. The politics of changing central bank authority: Thailand. In *Gatekeepers of Growth: The International Political Economy of Central Banking in Developing Countries*. New Jersey: Princeton University Press.

Maxfield, Sylvia, and Patcharee Siroros. 1992. The politics of central banking in Thailand. In Annual Meeting of the Association for Asian Studies, 1–45. Washington, D.C., April 2–5.

Muscat, Robert. 1994. *The Fifth Tiger: A Study of Thai Development Policy*. Helsinki: United Nations University Press.

Narong Sachaphanrot. 1992. *Kan Chat-tham Anumat lae Borihan Ngop Praman Phaendin: Tharusadi lae Pathiwat* [Approval and implementation of the national budget: Theory and practice]. Bangkok: Bophit Kanphim.

NESDB. 1992. 42 Pi Samnakngan Khana Kammakan Phatthana Setthakit lae Sangkhom haeng Chat [42nd anniversary article: The National Economic and Social Development Board]. *Warasan Setthakit lae Sangkhom* 29, no. 1 (January–February): 1–64.

NESDB. So. Ko. Ro. Oo. [JPPCC], ed. 1998. *17 Pi Ko. Ro. Oo.* NESDB, September.

Nukun Prachuapmo. 1996. *Chiwit thi Khum Kha* [Valuable life]. Bangkok: Dokya Graphic.

Nuwai Phatthana Rabop Kan-ngoen, Fai Wichakan. 1994. Kan Phatthana Prathet Thai pen Sun Klang Thang Kan-ngoen nai Phumiphak [Development of Thailand into a regional financial centre]. Bank of Thailand *Rai-ngan Setthakit Rai-duwan* 33, no. 11 (November).

Pasuk Phongpaichit and Chris Baker. 1997. Power in transition: Thailand in the 1990s. In *Political Change in Thailand: Democracy and Participation*, ed. Kevin Hewison, 21–41. London: Routledge.

Pasuk Phongpaichit and Chris Baker. 1998. *Thailand's Boom and Bust*. Chiangmai: Silkworm Books.

Pasuk Phongpaichit and Sungsidh Piriyarangsan. 1994. *Corruption and Democracy in Thailand.* Bangkok: The Political Economy Centre, Chulalongkorn University.

Patchari Sirorot. 1995. Kan Muang Thai kap Thanakhan haeng Prathet Thai [Thai politics and Bank of Thailand]. *Warasan Setthasat Thammasat* 13, no. 2 (June): 5–39.

Paul Sithi-Amnuai. 1964. *Finance and Banking in Thailand: A Study of the Commercial System, 1888–1963.* Bangkok: Thai Watana Panich.

Phu Chatkan. 1990. Lang Chawalit: Khrai Cha Kaoi Phu-wa Baenk Chat? [After Chawalit: Who will succeed the post of the governor of BOT?]. *Phu Chatkan Rai-duwan* 7, no. 79 (April).

Pisan Suriyamongkol and James F. Guyot. 1985. *The Bureaucratic Polity at Bay.* Bangkok: Graduate School of Public Adminstration, The National Institute of Development Administration.

Prachachat Thurakit ed. 1982. *Tham-niap Nak-borihan: Phak Rattaban.*

Prasarn Trairatvorakul and Prakid Punyashthiti. 1992. Some structural changes and performances of finance and securities companies in Thailand during 1981–1990. Bank of Thailand *Quarterly Bulletin.* 32, no. 2 (June).

Prasong Sunsiri. 1989. *726 Wan tai Banlang Prem* [726 days of the Prem government]. Bangkok: Matichon.

Puey Ungpakon. 1960. Ngop Praman lae Chaonathi Ngop Praman (1960) [Budget and the duty of the Board of Budget]. In *Cremation Book of Siri Pakatsit.* Bangkok, September 15, 1966.

Puey Ungpakon. 1966. *Ruamsuntharaphot.* [Collected works of Dr. Puey]. Bangkok.

Puey Ungpakon. 1975. Botbat nak kan-muang kap Kan Phattana Setthakit [The role of politicians and economic development]. Reproduced in *Setthakit Thai: Khrongsang kap Kan Plianpleng* [The Thai economy: Structure and changes], ed. Klum Setthasat Kan-muang, 331–348. Dokya: 1979.

Rangsan Thanaphonphan. 1989. *Krabuwan Kan Kamnot Nayobai Setthakit nai Prathet Thai: Bot Wikhro Choeng Prawattisat Setthakit Kan Muang Pho. So. 2475–2530* [Determinants for economic policies in Thailand: Political economy analysis, 1932–1987]. Bankok: Samakhom Sangkhommasat haeng Prathet Thai.

Rangsan Thanaphonphan. 1995. *Setthakit Kan Khlang kap Botbat Rattaban Thai* [Fiscal economy and the role of the Thai government]. Bangkok: Klet Thai.

Rangsan Thanaphonphan. 1998. *Wikrittakan Kan Ngoen lae Setthakit Kan*

Ngoen Thai [Financial crisis and financial economy in Thailand]. Bangkok: Klet Thai.

Ruangrat Smanratanastien. 1993. The non-resident baht account. *Bangkok Bank Monthly Review* 34, no. 4 (April).

Silcock, T.H. 1967. Money and banking. In *Thailand: Social and Economic Studies in Development*, ed. T.H. Silcock. Singapore: Donald Moore.

Siri Pakatsit. 1966. Samnak Ngop Praman kap Kan Phatthana Nayobai Khwam Mankhong khong Chat [The Board of Budget and development of policies for national stability]. In *Cremation Book of Siri Pakatsit*. Bangkok, September 15, 1966.

So. So. Kho. (Samnakngan Setthakit Kan-khlang). 1991. *Samnakngan Setthakit Kan-khlang Khroprop 30 Pi* [30th anniversary book: Fiscal policy office]. Bangkok: Samnakngan Setthakit Kan-khlang Krasuwang Kan Khlang, 18 October 1991.

So. Po. Ro. (Nukun Committee). 1998. *Rai-ngan Phonkan Wikhro lae Winitchai: Kho Thetching kiaokap Sathanakan thang Setthakit* [Report on the examination of the truth of the economic situation]. Bangkok: So. Po. Ro.

Somchai Wongsaphak and Pathiya Chetnasen. 1988. Man Samong thi 2 khong Pramuwan [Pramuan's second brain group]. *Phu Chatkan Raiduwan* 5, no. 58 (July).

Sommai Hoontrakun. 1993. *Cremation Book of Sommai Huntrakun*, Bangkok, December 25, 1993 (in Thai).

Suehiro, Akira. 1989. Bangkok Bank: Management reforms of a Thai commercial bank. *East Asian Cultural Studies* (Tokyo) 28, nos. 1–4 (March).

Suehiro, Akira. 1995. Chinawat Krupu: Tai no Jyouho Tsusin Sangyo to Sinko Zaibatsu [Shinawatra Group: The telecommunications industry and the newly rising zaibatsu group in Thailand]. *Ajia Keizai* (Tokyo) 36, no.2, (February).

Suehiro, Akira. 2000. Zaisei Kinyu Seisaku [Fiscal and monetary policies]. In *Tai no Keizai Seisaku: Seido, Soshiki, Akuta* [Economic policy in Thailand: The role of institutions and actors], ed. Akira, Suehiro, and Shigeki Higashi. Tokyo: IDE.

Suehiro, Akira. 2003. 2002 nen 10 gatsu: Rekisitekina Shocho Saihen [October 2002: Historical reorganization of administrative offices]. In *Tai Kokubetsu Enjyo Kenkyukai Houkokusho* [Country study for Japan's Official Development Assistance to the Kingdom of Thailand], ed. Japan International Cooperation Agency (JICA) and Akira Suehiro. Tokyo: Japan International Cooperation Agency.

Suehiro, Akira, ed. 2002. *Tai no Seido Kaikaku to Kigyou Saihen: Kiki kara Saiken he* [Institutional reforms and corporate restructuring in Thailand: From the crisis to reconstruction]. Tokyo: IDE.

Suehiro, Akira, and Shigeki Higashi, eds. 2000. *Tai no Keizai Seisaku: Seido, Soshiki, Akuta* [Economic policy in Thailand: The role of institutions and actors]. Tokyo: IDE.

Suphap Yot-sunthorn. 1968. Central bank closely involved in development policy. *The Financial Times*, December 2, 1968. Reproduced in *Cremation Book of Suphap Yot-sunthon*, 99–103. Bangkok.

Suphap Yot-sunthorn. 1974. *Cremation Book of Suphap Yot-sunthon.* Bangkok. June 18, 1974 (in Thai).

Thammasat University, ed. 1963. *Khrai Pen Khrai Pho. So. 2506.* 2 vols. Bangkok: Thammasat University.

Thanakhan haeng Prathet Thai, ed. 1992. *50 Pi Thanakhan haeng Prathet Thai 2485–2535.* Bangkok.

Unger, Daniel. 1998. *Building Social Capital in Thailand: Fibers, Finance, and Infrastructure.* Cambridge: Cambridge University Press.

Vijit Supinit. 1992. Thailand in the 1990s: Economic prospect and future challenges: A speech at a breakfast meeting of the Asia Society, New York, 17 September 1992. Bank of Thailand *Quarterly Bulletin* 32, no.3, (September): 1–6.

Wanrak Mingmaninakhin, ed. 1996. *80 Pi Achan Puey: Chiwit lae Ngan* [Memorial book of Achan Puey at 80 years old: His life and works]. Bangkok: Thammasat University Press.

Warr, Peter G., ed. 1993. *The Thai Economy in Transition.* Cambridge: Cambridge University Press.

Warr, Peter G., and Bhanupong Nidhiprapha, eds. 1996. *Thailand's Macroeconomic Miracle: Stable Adjustment and Sustainable Growth.* World Bank Comparative Economic Studies. Kuala Lumpur: Oxford University Press.

World Bank. 1980. *Thailand: Coping with Structural Change in a Dynamic Economy.* Report no. 3067a-TH. Washington D.C.: The World Bank, September.

3

The Resurgence of US Government Influence on Thailand's Economy and Southeast Asia Policy

Ukrist Pathmanand

Past studies of Thailand's relations with the United States have mainly discussed American influence in terms of military strength, security and politics. Frank C. Darling (1967) and David A. Wilson (1970) typify this "traditional" approach, focusing on the post-World War II and Cold War period and examining how anti-communist policies in Indochina determined Thai-American relations. They highlighted the close relationship between Americans and their Thai counterparts in building the infrastructure deemed necessary to respond to the communist threat in the region: airports, military bases, seven army camps and several new strategic highways in Thailand's Northeast. The United States also provided military training assistance and stationed about 40,000 American troops in the country.

In a master's thesis submitted to Cornell University, Surachart Bamrungsuk explored another angle of this relationship, examining the US role in the establishment of militarism and authoritarianism in Thailand from the period after the Second World War to the October 6, 1976, massacre. While Darling and Wilson could best be described as liberal, Surachart approaches the issue from a Left perspective critical of "US imperialism" and Thai authoritarianism. His writings were influenced by the ideas of Thai radicals actively protesting the presence of US bases in Thailand, such as Pansak Winyarat, who was a contributor to the renowned radical journal *Sangkomsart Parithat*.[1] Nevertheless, Surachart's work (1985, 1988) does not differ dramatically from that of Darling or Wilson, although he does argue that Thai and US containment policies proved more beneficial to US leaders and Thai military dictators (Sarit Thanarat, Thanom Kittikachorn and Prapas Charusathien) than the so-called defense of democracy against communism policy.

These three studies are arguably significant in their emphasis on the political, military and security issues that largely defined Thai-US relations in the Cold War era. However, in the late 1980s, different approaches to the study of US-Thai relations began to emerge. The new studies reflected changes in the regional context that began with the Nixon Doctrine, when the United States began to reduce its military and political interest in Thailand and Southeast Asia. Taking a central role in the increasing trend of globalization, the US shifted its focus to trade with Thailand and the region. Promoting liberalization of trade, services and finance, the US also pressured Thailand to accept copyright laws regulating the use of computer software and drug patents and the surreptitious patenting of Thai Hom Mali rice. Eventually, in the face of the Asian economic crisis of 1997, the United States played a major role in channeling loans from the International Monetary Fund (IMF) to Thailand.[2]

Studies about these changes are far fewer and often more focused than works using the earlier approach. This author's master's thesis (1983) pioneered the study of increasing US economic influence on Thailand in the late 1950s and early 1960s. And Surakiat Sathirathai (1987) looked at trade problems between Thailand and the United States in his study of international trade law. But his study was written to serve the specific needs of business law firms, rather than in response to a body of academic knowledge and to the results of Thailand's international economic policies.[3]

Analyses of the United States' role in Thailand's 1997 crisis are equally few. These include the study by Nicola Bullard et al. (1998), which looks at the effect on Thailand of the IMF's larger economic rescue plan, and Pasuk Phongpaichit and Chris Baker's (2000) critical scrutiny of the US government's hand in the 1997 crisis as seen through the views and policies of high-ranking US officials.[4] The latter work nevertheless returns inevitably to the IMF, saying little about precisely how the Thai-US relationship influenced the IMF decision to provide support to Thailand.[5]

In this paper, I explore a number of areas that have not yet been given due attention in order to map the background of US economic influence on Thailand and to chart future trends of US political and economic policy toward Southeast Asia. The first is the extent of American influence on Thai economic policies during the Cold War, which can afford us a deeper understanding of the American presence in the region, and, relatedly, the specific role of the United States as a principal capitalist player in the confrontation and resolution of the 1997 crisis.

The second issue is the shift in Thailand's Southeast Asia policy after 1997. Following its acceptance of the IMF economic rescue program, the Chavalit Yongchaiyudh government (December 1996 – November 1997) was replaced by the second Chuan Leekpai administration (1997 – November 2000); this change had a tremendous impact on Thai policy making vis-à-vis Southeast Asia. The government of Chavalit Yongchaiyudh was known to stress regionalism in its relations with Southeast Asia (Funston 1998). The new Chuan government administration, which relied upon the financial and political support of the United States and the IMF, altered the country's Southeast Asia policy quite dramatically to embrace concepts and objectives never before seen in Thai foreign policy. These new concepts included democratization and human rights, which became the staple of Chuan's foreign policy from 1997 onwards, otherwise known as the Flexible Engagement Policy. How this shift came about is the second concern of this paper.

Economic Influence in the Anti-Communist Era

The US government's political and military policy in Thailand evolved from fear of communism into a series of bilateral treaties and agreements, notably the 1950 Agreement of Military Cooperation and the 1962 Thanat–Rush Joint Communique. However, while tied closely to anti-communist policies, one can also explain the increase in American attention as arising from economic interest. This perspective arose from a different set of assumptions based on new economic development philosophies that challenged existing nationalist policies against foreign trade and investment and Chinese business.[6] The new philosophies advocated the creation of national institutions for economic planning and stressed that economic growth and liberalization were not only sound and necessary, but also the only effective method of opposing communism in a sustainable manner.

The expansion of US influence on the Thai economy began unofficially, but was a systematic and stable process that grew from the de facto alliance against communism in Thailand and Indochina. Political leaders and policy makers on both sides saw its benefit; it particularly served Field Marshall Sarit Thanarat and his group, which would seize power in 1958.[7] During his stay in Washington, D.C., on an official visit and to undergo medical treatment in May and June 1958, Sarit met with several high-ranking US officials to discuss two main concerns.[8] The first was anti-communism; the US leaders expressed how strongly impressed they were by Sarit's proposed anti-communist strategy and signalled their support for its implementation once he returned to Thailand. The second concerned the development of the Thai economy; the state department official responsible for economic affairs proposed a framework of liberalism to the Thai leader.[9]

With Sarit's successful coup d'etat on October 20, 1958, Thailand's policies for economic development underwent drastic transformation at several levels.   At the level of policy, there was a marked shift from economic nationalism to economic liberalization and a new emphasis on private sector investments both locally and internationally. At the same time, the state assumed a bigger role in protecting local industries and facilitating basic infrastructure in the initial stages. At the strategic level, the first National Economic Development Plan specifically included economic liberalization as a long-term target, projecting as far as the third National and Social Economic Development Plan (1972–1976). Finally, at the institutional level, national agencies responsible for planning and monitoring economic development were established. The Office of the National Economic Development Board (which later became the National Economic and Social Development Board, NESDB) was created along with the Board of Investment (BOI). Both bodies were to oversee the promotion of private investment as a main component in liberalized economic development.

These policy changes continued well beyond Sarit's time and cemented close relations between the leaders of both governments. The correspondences of Presidents Dwight D. Eisenhower, John F. Kennedy, and Lyndon B. Johnson, for example, expressed approval for the Thai government's efforts to promote economic development, a sentiment that prevailed through the end of the Thanom Kittikachorn administration in 1973. Government advisors and personal friends of US presidents likewise expressed support. George B. Beitzel, a close advisor to President Eisenhower, visited Thailand to conduct a survey on economic issues, after which he submitted a series of positive reports aimed at promoting private investment as a vital element in Thailand's economic growth.[10] The World Bank also registered its approval with a report entitled "A Public Development Program for Thailand"; this report was used by the Thai government as a model for drafting the country's First Economic Development plan and for setting up the National Economic and Development Board.[11] In short, the Thai government's shift in economic philosophy produced a favorable response from the US government, which in turn helped legitimize and stabilize the Sarit and subsequent Thanom–Prapas regime. In winning American protection for Thailand's military dictatorships, economic policy should be seen as just as vital a component as political and military influence.

The 1997 Crisis and the Resurgence of US Influence in Thailand

When, on July 2, 1997, the government of Chavalit Yongchaiyudh announced the devaluation of the baht, the United States paid little attention. It refused to participate in plan devised by other countries in the Asia–Pacific region to put together USD 17.2 billion to save the Thai and Asian economies. American inaction was based on the belief that the crisis resulted from internal problems, notably economic mismanagement on the part of governments and graft and corruption in government and the private sector alike. Neither did high-ranking US officials subscribe to the theory that the contagion would spread globally, insisting that it would affect only Asian countries, particularly Japan. Finally, after the American government had provided a large sum of money to save Mexico from its 1994 crisis, the US Congress had imposed legal restrictions on such bailouts, limiting the amount of money available to assist the Asian economies in 1997 (Leaver 1999, 289). The United States did assist certain countries, notably Indonesia and South Korea, countries it deemed strategically crucial to US political and military interests in the region. Thailand was not one of these.

This insouciance began to change in early 1998 with the statements of the US deputy treasury secretary, Lawrence Summers, describing the US role in reconstructing the Asian region (Summers 1998b, 4–5). Presented by Summers as an act of philanthropy, the US began exporting the institutions and ideas that formed the basis of its own economic power. According to Summers, the Clinton administration's new Asian economic policy put pressure on the IMF to focus its economic resuscitation programs on macro-economic reforms aimed at reducing trade barriers, upholding labor standards, alleviating the social costs that arise from economic adjustments and controlling fiscal spending. In a later paper, Summers insisted that under US direction, the IMF had for the first time included conditions for tapping its resources, including trade liberalization measures and the revoking of direct government assistance and other discriminatory practices that distorted the market (Summers 1999).

These statements by a high-ranking official signified a drastic change from the earlier protectionist attitude of US leaders and reflected a new realization that the crisis could indeed impact US security and the

American economy (Rubin 1998, 1). In fact, they appeared after the release of a joint report by the departments of Treasury and Commerce outlining the severe economic damage that could result if the contagion was not stopped. It specifically showed the extent to which the economies of the American West Coast states were tied to Asia: the volume of Asia-bound exports of California, Oregon and Washington alone totaled more than half the entire volume of exports to Asia of all other states combined.[12] If the crisis spread to the American mainland, it warned, it would not only destroy these states' exports, but could cost the US more than 11 million jobs (Summers 1998a).

Henceforth, US policy makers became involved in implementing policies aimed at alleviating Thailand's economic problems. The minimal interest in Thailand shown during the term of Prime Minister Chavalit Yongchaiyudh was replaced by active American involvement during the Chuan Leekpai term of November 1997 to November 2000. President Bill Clinton, treasury secretary Robert E. Rubin, deputy secretary Summers, defense secretary William S. Cohen and secretary of state Madeleine K. Albright all issued statements and held meetings with Prime Minister Chuan, finance minister Tarrin Nimmanhaeminda and other key cabinet members at venues in Thailand, Southeast Asia and Washington, D.C., to discuss solutions to the crisis. [13]

At the same time, US policy makers emphasized the importance of Thailand's involvement in the IMF recovery program and its strict compliance with IMF conditionality. Deputy Secretary Summers made this clear during his first formal meeting with the Thai finance minister in Bangkok on January 14, 1998, when he encouraged Thailand to accept the conditions of the IMF's economic recovery program (US Department of State 1998a). In exchange, when Prime Minister Chuan visited Washington on March 13, 1998, the US offered economic assistance through the US Export and Import Bank and promised increased bilateral trade, enhanced security relations and assistance to law enforcement agencies involved in the interdiction of the drug trade. Most important, however, was the first part of the agreement, which illustrates the US government's confidence in the IMF. The US agreed to work closely with the IMF and other international financial institutions to help Thailand overcome the crisis, promising to play a vital role at each stage of the Thai recovery process by helping to facilitate the release of IMF stand-by credit of 4,000 million dollars and World Bank and Asian Development Bank loans of USD 1.5 and 1.2 billion respectively (US White House Press Secretary 1998).

Strict adherence to the IMF's economic recovery program resulted in two major changes in the Thai economic system. First, the power to determine economic policy was placed in the hands of the IMF, resulting in Thailand's loss of economic sovereignty. For each proposal submitted by the Thai government for an urgently needed loan, IMF officials would spell out conditions—policies the Thai government was required to implement before the IMF approved the loan. For example, the IMF mandated structural adjustments to alleviate the problem of current account deficits. These included imposing cuts in government spending and controlling the expansion of loans in the private sector by maintaining high interest rates and reducing excesses in the state sector. The value-added tax was likewise increased to 10 percent, expenditures in various economic sectors reduced and the price of utilities and oil products increased to generate revenues. Second, the American framework of values and interests became part of the IMF's program and were invoked as vital to Thailand's economic recovery, as exemplified by the Letters of Intent (LOI) submitted to the IMF. In LOI no. 1, the Thai government promised to carry out urgently the process of separating and closing down financial institutions to ensure stronger confidence in the financial system as a whole. It also promised to conduct structural reform in the finance sector through mergers and the injection of foreign funds (Thailand Government Spokesman Office 1997).

Operational plans for structural reform in Thailand's finance sector included in LOI no. 4 included increased funds for banks, specification of responsibilities for government banks, increased funds for financial institutions, structural guidelines for monitoring agencies and tax specification (Thailand Ministry of Finance 1998). This was exactly the kind of financial liberalization the US government had been pushing in various countries in Asia. In Thailand, the US was successful by virtue of the fact that if the Thai government had failed to include such proposals in their LOI, it would not have received the loans it needed to shore up its economy. Financial liberalization further expanded to allow 100 percent foreign ownership in financial institutions for as long as 10 years. Pressure from the IMF also led to amendment of laws concerning the conduct of business by aliens and permission for foreigners to purchase property in the country (Bullard et al 1998, 127).

As a result of the pressure imposed within the framework of the IMF recovery program, financial liberalization was carried out in haste. Several Thai banks were obliged to merge with foreign institutions: The Thai Danu Bank became partners with Singapore's DBS Bank, while ABN Amro of the Netherlands became the major shareholder of Asia Bank. Laemthong Bank merged with Singapore's UOB Bank, and Standard Chartered Bank became the major shareholder of Nakorndhon Bank. The government took over the Srinakorn and Siam City banks and immediately made plans to sell both to a foreign institution, a plan that failed. The remaining major Thai banks—Bangkok Bank, Thai Farmers Bank, Siam Commercial Bank and Bank of Ayudhaya—saw an increase in the number of foreign shareholders to the level of around 49 percent, far higher than the previously allowed 25 percent (Pathmanand 2001).

It is quite obvious that the trade and investment liberalization policies of the IMF were in tune with US trade policies, which demanded structural reform and accelerated privatization of major state enterprises in energy, transportation, public works and telecommunications. The Thai government, through the Ministry of Transport and Communications, complied by mapping out strategies for state enterprise conversions as early as June 1998. Unprecedented numbers of plans for financial, trade and investment liberalization were also prepared as a result of intense pressure that clearly served US interests. Since December 1997, the American Chamber of Commerce in Thailand openly called for the revocation of limits seen as obstructing foreign business interests in Thailand (Pasuk and Baker 1999, 24). Later, US trade representative Charlene Barshefsky frankly stated what the US expected in this time of economic crisis: "We expect these structural reforms to create new business opportunities for U.S. firms" (*Bangkok Post*, March 6, 1998).

The Economic Crisis and the Emergence of a New Southeast Asian Policy

Thailand's Pre-Crisis Southeast Asia Policy

Thailand's entry into the IMF economic recovery program and the replacement of Chavalit Yongcahiyudh by Chuan Leekpai led to significant policy changes in the government's Southeast Asia policy. Chavalit was known as a strong advocate of regionalism, but it did not originate with him. Regionalism had been the policy of several Thai governments of the late 1980s and through most of the 1990s. The regionalist perspective emphasized the importance of Southeast Asia in Thai development, and its the objective was to secure for Thailand both economic advantages and prominence in this rapidly changing region. Prime Minister Chartichai Choonhavan (1988–1991) called it "turning the battlefield into a marketplace," while the Anand Panyarachun administration (1991–1992) termed it Constructive Engagement. Under General Chavalit (December 1996 – November 1997), the policy became known simply as Regionalism.

The policy was formulated in the period when the "battlefield" of inter-communist wars in Indochina was drawing to a close. Thailand saw an opening to create a new dynamics of Southeast Asian diplomacy and economic revival through regional efforts and initiatives instead of foreign assistance from the West (Vatikiotis 1996, 275). Constructive Engagement displayed further regional vision by stressing the importance of Indochina and Burma as components of Thailand's new economic community. The policy became an effective diplomatic tool in penetrating the natural resources and trade markets of these regions (Raisser n.d., 3). When he came to power, General Chavalit continued the policy.[14]

The regionalist policies of these three governments were tied to the end of the Cold War: ideological and political conflicts in Indochina were ending; Thailand was attempting to redefine its diplomatic role; and distance was growing between Thailand and the United States. Since the 1980s, the US had been pulling out of Asia in accordance with the Nixon Doctrine and had also become an economic competitor of Thailand and other Asian countries. As a result, the US began its push for liberalized trade, putting particular pressure on Thailand to amend intellectual property laws governing computer software, medicine patents, agricultural machinery and bio-technology (Surakiat 1999, 122). At the same time, Thailand no longer attached much importance to the United States as a superpower and instead looked to China and Japan for long-term alliances. It even began to pay more attention to Australia, a country reaching out for a larger role in Asia. The first bridge across the Mekhong River, linking Nong Khai province and Vientiane, was constructed with funds donated by the Australian government during the Chartichai administration (1988–1991).

Subsequent Thai leaders also courted Burma, a country the United States increasingly considered a rogue state. In 1995, Thailand complied with the Malaysian proposal to offer Burma membership in ASEAN. Despite on-going border problems—especially regarding ethnic minorities—and the frequent eruption of armed conflict between the two countries, Thai prime ministers since General Prem Tinsulanonda have regularly paid official visits to Burma: Prem in 1987; Banharn Silpa-archa in 1995; Chavalit Yongchaiyudh in 1996; and Thaksin Shinawatra in 2001.

The Emergence of New Policies and Values

Surin Pitsuwan, foreign minister in the second Chuan Leekpai admin-istration, stated in early January 1998 that "conducting foreign policies in the midst of such conditions [of crisis] is challenging and most vital since this is a period whereby new directions are emerging to ensure survival amidst these changes. It all depends, therefore, on each country [and] the extent in which they are able to adjust themselves to these new global trends" (*Matichol*, January 2, 1999). The statement was a clear indication of a new direction in the country's Southeast Asia policy. No longer emphasizing Thailand's economic role in the region or regarding China and Japan as its main allies, policy makers adopted new values in accordance with the resurgence of US supremacy. These values were soon highlighted in the policy of Flexible Engagement, later renamed Enhanced Interaction. The two main principles of the new policy were, first, the termination of the principle of non-interference in the affairs of ASEAN member countries and, second, the use of foreign policy to solve the immediate economic crisis and in the long term to create a political economy conforming to the values of democratization and human rights.

Surin Pitsuwan was not alone in calling for an end to the principle of non-interference. It was a position that many new generation ASEAN leaders, like then-deputy prime minister Anwar Ibrahim of Malaysia, had come to believe in. Anwar proposed the principle of Constructive Intervention to enable ASEAN members to intervene in Cambodia's internal conflict (Ibrahim 1997). Jusuf Wanandi, of Indonesia's Center for Strategic and International Studies, also advocated exemption from the non-interference policy in the case of Burma, but proposed that it be done quietly within the ASEAN bloc. Surin's target was more direct: he attacked authoritarianism in Myanmar and Malaysia on the grounds that political problems in any nation that affected the stability of the region merited the intervention of other nations. Thailand's foreign minister argued for the termination of non-interference during the ASEAN Ministerial Meeting of July 1998 in Manila, saying, "If ASEAN fails in bringing up the questions of the Asian economic crisis, the challenge of globalization and interdependence, its dignity and the ability to support and protect the interests of ASEAN will diminish."[15]

But this was simply diplomatic rhetoric. In reality, the statement assailing the systems of government of Myanmar and Malaysia was in line with the United States' on-going criticism of these two countries' human rights violations. US criticism of Malaysia in particular had increased when the latter refused IMF assistance in the wake of the crisis.

From the onset of Flexible Engagement, both the foreign minister and his deputy endeavored to illustrate that democracy, political reform and human rights were conditions that had emerged from socio-economic change in various countries in Asia and around the world. Both leaders expressed confidence that the first two decades of the twenty-first century would see all Southeast Asian nations achieving economic growth, a rapid expansion of education and increasing integration into a global society characterized by greater knowledge and pluralism (Sukhumbhan 1998). But the need to enhance the country's capacity to cope with demands rising from rapid social change was highlighted to attract the sympathy and assistance of the IMF, the US and the world community.

Indeed, it has been demonstrated that Thailand has enforced policies, particularly its foreign policy, to cope with and adapt to such changing social trends. Similarly, high-level US leaders believe that an open political system, political participation and the promotion of human rights are vital bases for solving economic problems in the long run. They also believe that several of the countries affected by the crisis are in need of new leadership, a view shared and aired for quite a long time by high-ranking officials of the US Department of State.[16]

Conclusion

With the onset of the economic crisis in Thailand in 1997, American influence on Thailand's economic policies, exercised through the International Monetary Fund, became very pronounced. It was reflected in the stipulations attached to loans for economic resuscitation and the major economic structural reforms agreed upon in the various Letters of Intent. The prevalence of US economic influence is, of course, nothing new, but a revival in a different context and socio-political climate.

During the Cold War, US sway was exercised within the environment of containment of communism. At that time the United States pushed for the establishment of national agencies to be responsible for economic planning and promoting foreign investment and for the eradication of nationalist economic systems created by Southeast Asia's post-World War II leaders, which the US considered obstacles to foreign investment. Following a period of withdrawal from Southeast Asia, during which US leaders expressed little interest in its countries, the economic crisis that erupted in 1997 paved the way for the resurgence of US influence. After initially suggesting that the crisis was of Asian doing and should be solved by Asians alone, the United States, in its capacity as the world's capitalist leader, took the opportunity afforded by the crisis to accelerate the liberalization of economic systems in various countries, including Thailand.

This turnabout was the result of global ripple effects reaching American shores in the form of threats to US exports to Asia. US officials began to urge Asian countries to hasten their projects for economic reform. High-level US officials, from the president to the secretaries of Treasury, Defense and State, made frequent statements and visits with Thai leaders to push for reforms and adherence to conditions set by the IMF. Thailand's leaders responded more favorably to US policy influences than had been expected. In addition to strict compliance with IMF conditions, Thai policies towards Southeast Asia were adjusted. Regionalist policies placing Thailand's economy at the forefront, penetrating Indochina's natural resources and creating Asian alliances with China and Japan—policies Thai leaders had been advocating from the early 1980s—were dropped in favor of Flexible Engagement, which proposed the cancellation of non-interference and emphasized the promotion of democratic principles and human rights.

Theoretically, Thailand's new ideals of democratic principles and human rights were noble, but they were articulated to affirm US criticism of human rights violations in Burma and other countries in Asia. Like strict compliance with IMF conditionality, the new Southeast Asian policy emerged as a tool to win IMF and US support in addressing the economic crisis at home.

Notes

1 *Sangkomsart Parithat* was a radical publication which published writings by students and graduates from abroad. Its articles offered a critique on politics, socio-economic issues and foreign affairs that almost always opposed the position of the Thanom Kittikachorn regime.

2 Initially the US government and the IMF were interested mainly in South Korea, the 7th largest economy in the world and one of the main debtors of the US, and Indonesia, which as the fourth largest country in the world and the largest in Southeast Asia, which could significantly destabilize the region.

3 Surakiat Sathirathai emerged as a policy advisor in the government of General Chartchai Choonhavan (1988–1991) and was subsequently appointed minister of finance in the Banharn Silpa-archa administration (1995–1996), before becoming minister of foreign affairs in 2001 in the Thaksin Shinawatra administration.

4 The role played by the United States in the Thai economic crisis appears in the section "The Washington Version," which studies the statements, testimonies and speeches of the three giants in the US and world economy at the time: Robert E. Rubin, secretary of the Treasury Department; Lawrence Summers, deputy secretary of the Treasury Department; and Alan Greenspan, chairman of the board of governors of the Federal Reserve System. The book also analyzes statements and speeches delivered by other high-ranking US officials such as President Bill Clinton.

5 Special emphasis is obviously made in the chapter entitled "Dear Mr. Camdessus: Thailand and the IMF."

6 In Thailand, the governments of both Pridi Banomyong and Field Marshall Pibulsongkram (1947–1957) embraced these policies. See Phanit Ruamsilpa 1978 and Sungsidh Piriyarangsan 1980.

7 Field Marshall Sarit Thanarat made an official visit to the US between May and June 1958 with the additional purpose of undergoing surgery at Walter Reed Hospital. Cited in Ukrist 1983, 65.

8 Sarit met with President Dwight D. Eisenhower, defense secretary Neil H. McElroy, naval secretary Thomas S. Gates, Jr., deputy secretary of defense Donald A. Quarles, assistant secretary of defense Mansfield Spraque and deputy under-secretary of state for economic affairs C. Douglas Dillon. Documents on foreign co-operation in various projects in Thailand (1958–1966) from the United States National Archives are cited in Ukrist 1983, 69.

9 This is evident in Sarit's memoirs of his meetings with US leaders: "On May 15, 1958, I met with Mr. Dillon who enumerated the importance on investment by private foreign agencies that could help to develop the economy of undeveloped countries in addition to the financial assistance that the U.S. could allocate." Cited in Ukrist 1983, 69.

10 U.S.OM Bangkok, 1959.

11 At the first meeting of the National Economic and Social Development Board, Sarit proposed that the World Bank's economic report be used as a model. That board and its successor faithfully complied. Cited in the Minutes of the first National Economic and Social Development Board meeting, August 10, 1959.

12 The products exported to Asia from California, Oregon and Washington states are mostly agricultural produce, as well as electrical and electronic spare parts. See "Treasury and Commerce Release Analysis Showing Impact of Asian Crisis on Individual States." US Treasury and Commerce Departments 1998.

13 During the Chavalit administration, the US Treasury Department had issued only four brief statements dated August 5, 7, 11, and 20, 1997.

The statements mainly expressed US pleasure at the announcement made by General Chavalit and Dr. Tanong Bidaya, Minister of Finance, that Thailand would participate in the Credit and Economic Resuscitation Project (Rubin 1997).

14 Chavalit was the key person responsible for diminishing the role of the Communist Party of Thailand (CPT) through negotiation with and assistance from the People's Republic of China, a major CPT supporter. With China's help, he was also involved in aiding the Khmer Rouge and was instrumental in securing Thai government acceptance of the military government that seized power in Burma in 1988.

15 Surin Pitsuwan, "Thailand's Non-Paper on the Flexible Engagement Approach," July 27, 1998. Quoted in Thayer 1999.

16 The US State Department has its own long term commitment to demo- cratic and open states, a position it takes every opportunity to air. In the period of the Thai financial crisis, it was emphasized again during the meeting of Secretary of State Madeleine K. Albright and Thai Finance Minister Tarin Nimmanahaeminda in Washington on January 21, 1998 (US Department of State 1998b).

References

Bullard, Nicola, Walden Bello, and Kamal Malhotra. 1998. Taming the tigers: The IMF and the Asian crisis. CAFOD and Focus on the Global South. Reprinted in *Tigers in Trouble: Financial Governance, Liberalisation and Crises in East Asia*, ed. Jomo K.S. Hong Kong University Press, IPSR Books, Dhaka University Press, White Lotus, Zed Books.

Darling, Frank C. 1967. American and Thailand. *Asian Survey* (April).

Funston, John. 1998. Thai foreign policy: Seeking influence. *Southeast Asian Affairs 1998*. Singapore: Institute of Southeast Asian Studies.

Higgott, Richard. 1999. The international relations of the Asian economic crisis: A study in the politics of resentment. In *Politics and Markets in the Wake of the Asian Crisis*, ed. Richard Robison et al. London: Routledge.

Ibrahim, Anwar. 1997. Crisis prevention. *Newsweek*, July 21.

Jomo K.S., ed. 1998. *Tigers in Trouble: Financial Governance, Liberalisation and Crises in East Asia*. Hong Kong University Press, IPSR Books, Dhaka University Press, White Lotus, Zed Books.

Leaver, Richard. 1999. Moral (and other) hazards: The IMF and the systemic Asian crisis. In *Politics and Markets in the Wake of the Asian Crisis*, ed. Richard Robison et al. London: Routledge.

Pasuk Phongpaichit and Chris Baker. 1999. The Thai economic crisis: New ideals of liberalism and the reaction of Thai society. In *Articles Commemorating the Sixtieth Anniversary of Acharn Ammar Siamwala*, ed. Praipol Khumsap. Bangkok: Faculty of Economics, Thammasat University.

Pasuk Phongpaichit and Chris Baker. 2000. *Thailand's Crisis*. Bangkok: Silkworm Press.

Phanit Ruamsilpa. 1978. The policies of economic development in the Pibulsongkram period (1949–1954). Master's thesis, Chulalongkorn University.

Raisser, Gary. From conflict to cooperation: Thailand's rapprochement with its neighbors. Unpublished.

Rubin, Robert E. 1998. House Agriculture Committee. *Treasury News* (May 21).

Rubin, Robert E. 1997. Statement by Treasury. *Treasury News* (August 5, 7, 11, 20).

Sukhumbhand Paribatra. 1998. Preparing ASEAN for the 21st century. Speech delivered at the official dinner of the Institute of Southeast Asian Studies 30th anniversary Conference on Southeast Asia in the 21st Century: Challenges of Globalisation.

Summers, Lawrence. 1998a. American farmers: Their stake in Asia, their stake in the IMF. *Treasury News* (February 23).

Summers, Lawrence. 1998b. Opportunities out of crisis: Lessons from Asia. *Treasury News* (March 19).

Summers, Lawrence. 1999. Remarks to Senate Foreign Relations Subcommittee on International Economic Policy and Export/Trade Promotion. *Treasury News* (January 27).

Sungsidh Piriyarangsan. 1980. *Thai Bureaucratic Capitalism, 1932–1960*. Master's thesis, Thammasat University.

Surachart Bumrungsuk. 1985. United States foreign policy and Thai military rule 1947–1977. Master's thesis, Cornell University.

Surachart Bumrungsuk. 1988. *United States Foreign Policy and Thai Military Rule 1947–1977.* Bangkok: Editions Duang Kamol.

Surakiat Sathirathai. 1987. *Thailand and International Trade Law*. Bangkok: Sasin Graduate Institute of Business Administration, Chulalongkorn University.

Surakiat Sathirathai. 1999. Eleven economic laws: Reflections of the legislative process of Thai laws. In *Articles Commemorating the Sixtieth Anniversary of Acharn Ammar Siamwala*, ed. Praipol Khumsap. Bangkok: Faculty of Economics, Thammasat University.

Thailand. Government Spokesman Office. 1997. Letter of intent no.1. September 16.

Thailand. Ministry of Finance. 1998. Letter of intent no.4.

Thailand. Ministry of Foreign Affairs. 1998. Press release no. 227/2541: Thai–U.S. relations.

Thailand. National Economic and Social Development Board. 1959. Minutes of meeting on August 10, 1959.

Thayer, Carlye A. 1999. Southeast Asia: Challenges to unity and regime legitimacy. *Southeast Asian Affairs 1999.* Singapore: Institute of Southeast Asian Studies.

Ukrist Pathmanand. 1983. The United States and Thai economic policy (1960–1970). Master's thesis, Chulalongkorn University.

Ukrist Pathmanand. 2001. *Economic Crisis, Banking Employee's Massive Lay Off and Banking Restructuring in Thailand.* Research report submitted to Thailand Research Fund.

United States. Department of State. 1998a. Treasury Deputy Secretary Summers/Finance Minister Tarrin press briefing. Bangkok, January 14, 1998.

United States. Department of State. 1998b. News release: Madeleine K. Albright and Tarrin Nimmanahaeminda meeting in Washington, D.C., January 21, 1998.

United States. Departments of Treasury and Commerce. 1998. Treasury and Commerce release analysis showing impact of Asian crisis on individual states.

United States. White House Press Secretary. 1998. Fact sheet on U.S.–Thai relations. Washington, D.C. March 13.

Vatikiotis, Michael R.J. 1996. Shades of Suvanaphum: Thailand in the new regional order 1988–1996. *Proceedings of the 6ᵗʰ International Conference on Thai Studies.* Chieng Mai, Thailand, 14–17 October.

Wilson, David A., 1970. *The United States and The Future of Thailand.* New York: Praeger.

4
The Philippine Technocracy and US-led Capitalism

Teresa S. Encarnacion Tadem

During the period of martial law under Ferdinand E. Marcos (1972–1986), the economic technocracy was viewed as the third leg of the stool on which the dictatorship rested, along with the leadership's cronies and the military. The regime was heavily dependent on United States military and economic assistance, and the technocrats were the overseers of the policies that accessed this assistance. Their power became stronger in the late Marcos period as the dictatorship became more heavily dependent on external loans. After the 1986 People Power revolution, however, the technocrats appeared to lose their clout, but they never actually disappeared from the scene. Many observers argue that they have transformed themselves into advocates of neo-liberalism, the philosophy that underpins globalization.

This chapter traces the emergence of the technocracy during the Marcos and post-Marcos periods. It examines the ways in which the technocracy promoted US hegemony and the factors that abetted as well as opposed this process. Finally, it examines the transformation of technocrats from Marcos supporters to neo-liberals, a shift that enabled them to survive regime change and remain influential inside the state in the post-authoritarian period.

The Technocracy under Ferdinand Marcos[1]

The practice of hiring graduates of American universities in economics, law and business administration for high executive office began in the early 1960s and developed rapidly during President Marcos' first term of office (1965–1969) (Stauffer n.d. 189). Marcos recruited fresh graduates of top US schools of engineering, business, economics and public administration to staff agencies created to assist the executive branch in planning public policy. The most prominent of the Marcos recruits was Cesar E.A. Virata, a graduate of the Wharton School of Finance of the University of Pennsylvania. Appointed as a member of the Presidential Economic Staff in 1967, Virata became the country's finance minister in 1970 and held the post until Marcos was deposed in 1986 (WHO 1983, 8).[2]

The technocrats' economic policies reflected a bias toward export-oriented industrialization (EOI). National Economic Development Authority (NEDA) head Gerardo Sicat had been a student of the economist Gustav Ranis, who argued against developing countries' pursuit of heavy industrialization through import-substitution (ISI) and in favor of EOI. In EOI, he argued, they should enjoy the comparative advantage of abundant surplus labor and natural resources (Lichauco 1981, 78). The push for EOI also marked the entry of International Monetary Fund (IMF) and World Bank advisers who campaigned for a decontrol program to facilitate a return to free trade (Hawes 1984, 263). The technocrats, some of whom had trained at these financial institutions, were given freedom to change the structure of the country's economic policy. Heading offices like the Presidential Economic Staff and NEDA, they began to redirect the economy away from ISI and laid the foundations for the production of export goods and commodities for the world market. The integration of the local economy into the world capitalist market was furthered by Congress's passage of the Investment Incentives Act of 1967 and the Export Incentives Act of 1970 (Bello et al. 1982, 30). The 1960s, therefore, witnessed a blossoming technocratic presence in the state.

In 1972, Marcos declared martial law, ushering in a period of authoritarian control over Philippine society. This dictatorship was anchored in an alliance of Marcos and his close relatives, trusted business associates and political allies (the "cronies"), the Armed Forces of the Philippines (AFP), and the technocracy (Bello et al. 1982, 30). Technocrats like Virata and Vicente Paterno replaced the politicians who once held high positions in key developmental agencies and helped Marcos attract other technocrats from the private sector to join his "New Society" regime.[3]

The technocrats and the non-democratic regime found their association to be mutually beneficial. The internationally recognized economic expertise of the technocrats and their leadership in conceiving a credible development program endorsed by international governments, lending institutions and multinational corporations made them valuable assets to Marcos. They in turn found in authoritarian rule freedom from time-consuming legislative-executive debates that slowed the implementation of projects. This was a sentiment shared by the American government and the World Bank and IMF (Business International Research Division 1980, 99). And with labor's right to strike, picket, demonstrate and otherwise protest declared "subversive," a façade of political stability was created that the technocrats hoped would attract more foreign capital to the country.

The declaration of martial law began an intensified drive to open the Philippines to the world market, beginning with tariff reduction and the removal of restrictions on importing non-essential consumer goods (Hawes 1984, 277). To attract foreign capital, Marcos amended the Investment Incentive Act of 1967 and revoked laws against foreign participation in vital sectors like rice and corn and in "pioneer industries" like oil exploration. The Export Incentives Act of 1970 was amended as well, allowing foreign-owned firms to export 70 percent of their manufactured goods. The technocrats reorganized the financial system to enable greater foreign participation in banking; a presidential decree ordered banks to raise their capital, forcing small local banks to close or merge with larger, often foreign-owned, banks (Ibon 1985).

The IMF, World Bank, Asian Development Bank (ADB) and United States Agency for International Aid (USAID) assisted the government by providing and guaranteeing loans, insurance and other funding to assist the growth of the export sector (Shalom 1981, 49). Some of these loans went to the development of frontier lands, particularly those targeted for agribusiness and infrastructure development, including hydroelectric dams, power grids and road networks (Diokno 1980, 22). These projects inevitably strengthened ties between the technocracy and foreign capital. Sharing a Keynesian perspective and a bias in favor of hierarchical decision-making structures, technocrats and representatives of international financial agencies mutually supported each others' endeavors. Technocrats, for example, made use of the Ministry of Finance, Board of Investments and NEDA to launch IMF-World Bank programs (Lichauco 1973, 60) and regularly solicited advice from international consultants in formulating national economic policy.[4] The IMF/World Bank group rewarded technocrats with prominent positions in their institutions.[5] As members of such powerful bodies as the Consultative Group, for example, technocrats met in Paris, Washington and Tokyo to discuss the performance of the country's development program (Stauffer 1979). Most importantly, the Philippines enjoyed continued access to the "structural adjustment loans" that fueled EOI (Bello and Kelly 1981, 3).

The technocrat-foreign capital partnership helped Marcos enhance his own network politically and economically by providing the ruling elite access to funds brought into the country by the technocrats' efforts (Bello 1982, 105). Presenting themselves as critical brokers between government and foreign capital, these "bureaucrat-capitalists" (or "Marcos cronies," as they came to be known) entered into joint ventures with multinational corporations and availed themselves of foreign loans acquired by the state (Hawes 1984, 220–21). Their mediation was most appreciated by the technocrats and their foreign allies, but it eventually proved the alliance's undoing.

Opposition to the Technocratic Scheme of Development

The partnership between technocrats, foreign institutions and the Marcos family was not entirely devoid of conflict. One major source of tension was the surprising refusal of the technocracy and pro-Marcos elite to abandon ISI completely, despite their public pronouncement in favor of EOI (Business International Research Division 1980, 99). One reason was that some members of the elite were still involved in the ISI sector. And the regime's commitment to an ASEAN regional industrialization program involved a promise to pursue 11 major industrial projects aimed at developing a heavy industrial base—this was the very feature of ISI that the technocrats and IMF-World Bank group criticized. For the technocrats, however, ideological preference had to give way to perceived accountability to Marcos. Many quietly grumbled about the underhanded preservation of ISI, but in the end supported the president.

On the other hand, entrepreneurs and business associates of the Marcoses expressed discontent with certain policies pursued by the technocracy. As early as 1973, these local capitalists vehemently objected to the substantial concessions given foreign investors and the technocracy's backing for export industrialization. Both were perceived as part of a vicious scheme to eliminate the "national entrepreneurial class" (Bello and Reyes 1981, 114). Technocratic determination to produce an apolitical and pro-business atmosphere was also criticized as a vehicle for the state to destroy labor unions (Stauffer 1974, 173; Lim 1983, 19). At the community level, joint ventures between technocrat-managed state corporations and multinational corporations worsened existing social tensions, as communities were evicted and relocated from lands favored by these enterprises. The situation was aggravated because the joint ventures had little linkage with the communities, except for labor, and hence contributed little to their development. Soon, areas where communities had been dislodged in the name of development became recruiting grounds for underground cells of the Communist Party of the Philippines (CPP).

The Philippine Technocracy under Siege

By the 1980s, opposition to a technocratic development program for the country had grown, and the EOI strategy was deemed a failure. Critics ascribe the decline to three factors: inherent contradictions in the EOI strategy; increasing resistance from labor; and the absence of external conditions conducive to the continuing expansion of the export sector (Rocamora n.d., 2). Finance minister and chief technocrat Cesar Virata blamed the decline on the negative balance of payments, accumulating debts and low returns on capital (Bowring 1981, 50), but others pointed to the technocrats' idea of development itself as flawed from the start. The economic decline of some government corporations and other institutions headed by technocrats caused public confidence in the technocracy to further deteriorate (Galang 1985, 50).

Disillusionment spread even to the technocrats' foreign patrons. The immediate cause was an attempt in 1981 by Central Bank governor Jaime Laya to hide the country's worsening financial conditions from the IMF and the World Bank by "window-dressing" the country's international reserve figures (Galang 1985, 50). Although this generated public outrage, the technocrats' response was to borrow further, a reaction surprisingly condoned by IMF and World Bank officials. Their consent came after more promises to hasten the dismantling of tariffs and fully eliminate subsidies for local enterprises (Galang 1983, 72).

What probably damaged the technocrats the most was their relationship with Marcos and his cronies. Although they never approved of the cronies' use of ties with the regime to enrich themselves, they had accepted it as a necessary evil. But conflict rose over the question of whether export crops should become the center of state or private accumulation. The technocracy believed the state should play the leading role; the cronies believed otherwise (Hawes 1984, 220–21). This battle was most apparent in relation to the country's two major export commodities—sugar and coconut—which by the late 1970s had fallen under the respective control of Marcos allies Roberto S. Benedicto and Eduardo Cojuangco, Jr.. When Cojuangco convinced Marcos to impose a levy on coconut farmers, the technocracy decried it as double taxation. Virata also warned that the levy would further depress the already low price paid to farmers for their coconut products (Bowring 1981, 8). Virata wanted to end the intermediary role played by crony-controlled and state-created bodies in both the coconut and sugar industries. Conflict between technocrats and cronies also plagued the industrial sector, as world recession and the country's deteriorating terms of trade caused numbers of crony companies to fail. To prevent economic chaos, the technocracy stepped in to salvage some of these corporations and in the process stepped on the toes of many cronies, including those closely associated with First Lady Imelda Marcos.[6]

The technocracy's influence survived through the support of the IMF and World Bank, which blamed crony capitalism—fast becoming the symbol of government corruption—for discouraging foreign investors and fueling mass unrest. The IMF and World Bank applied subtle pressure on Marcos to lift martial law, and in 1981, he relented, formally replacing the martial law regime with a "New Republic." He appointed Virata prime minister. The IMF and World Bank had sought a greater technocratic presence at the center for several reasons. First, they wanted tighter control over the use of IMF-World Bank funds and regarded their technocrat allies as the only actors capable of assuming this responsibility. Second, fearing the regime was losing its political nerve in the fight against protectionism, the IMF-World Bank group hoped technocrats in the cabinet could prevent a reversal (Bello et al. 1982, 191). Third, the poor economic performance of the country and political instability of the government had made the Philippines a major credit risk. Only Virata's close ties with international banks enabled further borrowing. Finally, they believed that the technocrats' reputation as honest and credible public officials could improve the regime's image and bring some political stability.

The crony capitalists and Mrs. Marcos did not take kindly to the leadership's accommodation of technocratic priorities. They believed a technocrat-dominated cabinet would lead to tighter IMF-World Bank control over their activity. The cronies thus launched a nationalist attack on the technocrats for allowing undue IMF-World Bank influence on the economy, which they claimed undermined the country's sovereignty. In this they received unexpected support from local businesses whose interests were threatened by what they saw as blind loyalty to IMF-World Bank policies favoring foreign over local investors. They criticized the technocrats as "bureaucratic, arrogant and lacking in practical experience" (Bowring and Sacerdoti 1983, 54). And they voiced their resentment against the bailout of crony companies at the expense of those without government connections who therefore could not access rescue funds (Bello et al. 1981, 191).

These criticisms failed to prevent the formation of a "World Bank cabinet" and the strengthening of the political power of the technocrats. Virata, in his capacity as prime minister acquired the power to reverse presidential vetoes on legislation passed by the National Assembly. His appointment as chair of the cabinet's Executive Committee even put him in line as a possible successor to the presidency. On the other hand, Marcos was quite confident that despite newly acquired powers and IMF-World Bank backing, the technocrats lacked adequate clout to threaten his leadership. He was aware that they had no mass base, a prerequisite for any leader. And by retaining his power to issue decrees, Marcos ensured that final decisions on economic projects would still be his. This did not prevent the technocrats from becoming more vocal in their economic and political opinions.[7]

But it was late in the game. After 1983, the political crisis arising from the assassination of former Senator Benigno Aquino, Jr., eroded the alliance underlying the Marcos dictatorship. While the technocrats gained in power, so did opposition from the Marcos cronies, especially Imelda Marcos. The AFP began to break into factions, affecting its fighting ability in the countryside. Outside the regime, opposition to Marcos spread and deepened. Political polarization, infighting within government, and growing criticism within international institutions and the American government of Marcos' repression and mishandling of the economy eventually took its toll. Some technocrats became fed up and, like minister of Economic Planning Gerardo Sicat, left government. But the majority of the technocrats, Virata included, stayed on until Marcos was ousted in 1986. This is quite understandable, as even in the last days of the dictatorial regime, technocrats enjoyed economic and political powers unprecedented in history. Furthermore, despite criticism, they continued to receive the backing of the IMF and the World Bank.

The Technocracy in the Post-Marcos Era

After the 1986 People Power Revolution ousted Ferdinand Marcos, the technocrats suffered the consequences of their loyalty to the regime. They were treated as pariahs and Marcos' successor, Corazon Aquino (1986–1992), made a conscious effort not to appoint any associated with the IMF-World Bank group. This did not mean, however, that the economic policies advocated by technocrats waned in significance. The most important instance of this continuing influence was seen in the outcome of the public debate over the accumulated loans of the Marcos regime. The popular view was for debts associated with the Marcos family and its cronies to be repudiated, or at least that government declare a moratorium on debt payments until the economy had fully recovered. This position lost to a "pragmatic" commitment by Aquino to make all loan payments in full on time.

Aquino's unpopular decision was heavily influenced by her economic and financial advisers, who had close ties to foreign capital. These included Central Bank governor Jose Fernandez, who had also been Central Bank governor under Marcos and was a former president of the Far East Bank; Jaime Ongpin, Aquino's secretary of Finance and a former president of

Benguet Mining Corporation; and Jose Concepcion, Aquino's secretary
of Trade and Industry and head of a family-owned business conglomerate. Most of Aquino's advisers were members of the influential Makati
Business Club (MBC), a critic of the Marcos dictatorship and also a strong
advocate for a more open Philippine economy. These advisers feared that
anything less than full honoring of the debt would have severe repercus-
sions—not only from the IMF and World Bank, but from the international
banking community and foreign investors more broadly. They feared the
Philippines would lose access to loans they believed the country badly
needed. Nevertheless, Aquino's commitment to service the country's external debt led the administration "to borrow heavily from domestic financial
resources, forcing it to channel much of its budgetary expenditures for
repaying domestic and foreign debt obligations." A critic pointed out that
"from 1987–1992 debt service payments amounted to 50% of the budget,
putting the task of development on the sides" (Morales 2001, 16).

The lone voice against this policy in the Aquino Cabinet was that
of Solita Monsod, a University of the Philippines School of Economics
professor who was appointed director-general of NEDA. Monsod believed
that the Philippines should pursue a policy of selective debt repudiation.
Because of her views, Monsod was left out in the cold in decision making
relating to economic policies, especially in discussion of the country's
debt policy. She eventually resigned and Aquino replaced her with
someone more in line with the government's position. The new NEDA
director-general, Cayetano Paderanga, Jr., was known to favor the IMF-
World Bank prescription for economic recovery—further opening of the
market through EOI. The same technocratic solutions imposed during the
martial law period somehow returned under a democratic regime.

Despite the marginalization of their technocratic friends, the IMF and
World Bank had the best of both worlds under the Aquino administration.
Not only were their loans being repaid, but the new government's
economic policies were in tune with their principles and ideology.
After overcoming some resistance inside the Reagan administration by
friends of the Marcoses, the United States government also supported
Aquino, continuing its military and economic assistance and helping
defuse attempts by disgruntled elements of the AFP to overthrow the
new regime. However, after the coup threats were neutralized and the
situation stabilized, it became clear that there was still much to be
desired from the government's commitment to economic liberalization.
For one, crony capitalism persisted, albeit with a different set of actors.
Mrs. Aquino's natal family, the Cojuangcos, for example, continued to
monopolize the telecommunications industry through its Philippine Long

Distance Telephone (PLDT) Company, prompting the criticism that she was protecting her own crony network.

Neo-liberalism

Hopes of overcoming monopoly and crony capitalism, however, rose with the election in 1992 of Fidel V. Ramos as president. Although he was a second cousin of Marcos, Ramos was part of no political or economic dynasty. A graduate of West Point, he was regarded as a professional soldier committed to merit, not affinity, as the basis of success and one who valued the use of talent to move forward. He was the quintessential "middle class" president.

Ramos' presidency (1992–1998) came at an opportune moment. By the early 1990s, the economies of the Asian region were booming and the Philippines appeared to have overcome the crises of the 1980s. The spectacular growth of "tiger economies" South Korea, Taiwan, Singapore and Hong Kong meant the circulation of excess capital that the Philippines could tap for development. Indonesia, Malaysia and Thailand also displayed remarkable economic performance, meaning the potential availability of another source of capital. The Philippines looked forward to these broader options to make up for the lackluster inflow of capital from traditional sources like the United States and Europe. Ramos recognized this potential and moved immediately to break up the country's monopolies, signaling his commitment to market reform and full economic liberalization. This dovetailed with the third phase of the IMF-World Bank's structural adjustment program for the Philippines, involving rapid deregulation, privatization and liberalization of trade and investment (Morales 2001, 16).[8]

These developments came under the rubric of neo-liberalism. This "new" mantra of economic development attracted a broad group of actors—from government officials, the local and international business community and University of the Philippines (UP) economists to even non-governmental organizations (NGOs). Neo-liberals also became known as "free marketeers" whose admiration for the virtues of the market and EOI included criticism of crony capitalism. Unlike the technocrats of the 1970s and 1980s, the neo-liberal coalition of the 1990s advocated reducing the state's role in the economy, a popular sentiment given the sordid record of the recent past. The disarray of the Philippine economy was at this time blamed on the Marcos authoritarian state, which had intervened in the market for the personal gain of a few. Politically, the coalition also supported the notion of a "civil society" to act as partner to the limited state and the free market in the pursuit of development.

Neo-liberalism infected the politicians as well. In the Senate, a "growth coalition" was formed between Ramos supporters and the opposition, while in the House of Representative, a similar "rainbow coalition" insured the passage of economic reform measures that favored Ramos' program. The various opposition blocs in the lower house also announced their support for free enterprise, limited government and civil rights and liberties (Velasco 2002, 12, 16). Thus, while Ramos did restore the practice of hiring technocrats associated with the World Bank—notably, his secretary of Finance, Roberto de Ocampo—there was no need to bring in a corps of technocrats to push through liberalization measures. The politicians were doing it themselves.

One scholar has suggested that this remarkable concord indicated the emergence of a new generation of political elites. Renato Velasco points out that the social background of post-1986 party leaders differed from that of pre-1972 party elites. The latter had tended to be associated with the landed oligarchy; this group's rent-seeking activities and careers were anchored in state patronage and intervention. The post-1986 party elites came from a broader economic base and diverse career backgrounds, and they were more disposed towards free enterprise and limited government. Second, the new elites, having experienced the Marcos dictatorship and having joined forces against it during the 1986 people power revolution, were convinced of the virtues of democratic politics. This included their support for liberalization to counteract the flaws and costs of economic protectionism before 1973 and the adverse effects of crony capitalism during the martial law regime (Velasco 2002, 17). Third, with Ramos in power, "the political leadership could count on an economic administrative apparatus able to increase the state capacity for structural reforms." Finally, changes in the political economy had eroded the power base of the old landed elites, and the importance of export crops had declined as that of manufacturing and service industries markedly increased. Reinforcing this shift was globalization and information technology which induced growth in many sectors in the world economic and communication network (Velasco 2002, 22).

The Problem of Redistribution

Ramos's liberalization program led to the "privatization of profitable government enterprises like oil-refining and marketing firm Petron as were some vital services like the management of water supply." Government officials "became enthusiastic promoters of 'build, operate and transfer' (BOT) schemes in which projects were contracted out to the private sector with payments in the form of rights to manage the finished facility and rights to part of a stream of expected future income it would generate." (Morales 2001, 18). Restrictions on foreign investments were loosened considerably, with 100 per cent foreign equity allowed in all but a few sectors. The Philippines committed itself to free trade international coalitions like the ASEAN Free Trade Area (AFTA) and the Asia Pacific Economic Cooperation (APEC) and ratified the Uruguay Round of the General Agreement on Tariff and Trade (GATT) which obliged the country to reduce its tariffs and ban import quotas (Morales 2001, 18).

Liberalization was criticized, however, for failing to resolve a fundamental problem—the growing gap between a small, wealthy elite and the majority poor, both within the Philippines and internationally. The growing severity of public criticism against globalization compelled governments like that of the Philippines to commit themselves to resolving this imbalance and confronting its many consequences, the foremost of which was widespread poverty. Ramos therefore launched his Social Reform Agenda (SRA) as the anti-poverty program aimed at addressing socio-economic inequity. Among those who helped craft the SRA were Ramos' academic allies at the UP School of Economics and the National College of Public Administration and Governance (NCPAG) and NGOs identified with the moderate Left, which had supported Ramos' presidential campaign. Whether the SRA made any impact on social welfare continues to be debated.

Despite his relative success as an "economic reformist," Ramos could only work within the constitutionally-prescribed tenure of a six-year presidential term without possibility of re-election. He tried to get past this limitation by organizing a "popular clamor" to extend his presidency through constitutional amendment to a parliamentary form of government. The opposition—led by the Catholic Church and former president Aquino—proved too powerful. The business community supported Ramos, but its reluctance to shift to parliamentary politics compelled them to respect the constitutional process. This it did although business dreaded the coming electoral victory of Ramos' anti-thesis, vice-president Joseph "Erap" Estrada.

Joseph Estrada and the Resurrection of Crony Capitalism

President Estrada (1998–2001) won the presidency by the largest margin of victory in postwar history on a populist platform depicting him as a friend of the masses. Already popular from his days as an action movie star, Estrada's campaign slogan "Erap para sa Mahihirap" (Erap for the

Poor) touched a chord among Filipinos living below the poverty line. While there had been 7 percent GDP growth during much of Ramos' term, the poor did not feel it and some argued that there was no "trickle down." Then the 1997 economic crisis wreaked havoc on the Ramos program and raised questions about the viability of its neo-liberal policies. The majority of the electorate held fast to Estrada's promise to address socio-economic inequality through the redistribution of wealth.

Estrada's populism predictably raised alarms among free marketeers, who suspected the return of the Keynesian solution to poverty via active state intervention (Hall 2000, 385). Nor did his promise to redistribute wealth augur well with local elite, which felt they would be targeted. The United States was also suspicious of Estrada, since he had voted against the extension of the military bases agreement as a member of the 1991 Senate.

Still, there were those who did support Estrada, and this coalition was notable for its diversity. Among them were corporate clients of his vice-presidential running mate, Edgardo Angara, and members of the Filipino-Chinese business community who had supported Estrada's anti-kidnapping campaigns as vice-president and head of the Presidential Anti-Crime Commission (Velasco 2002, 14). Other Estrada supporters came from the ranks of Marcos cronies and martial law technocrats. One of his advisers was Cesar Virata. Finally, a fifth group consisted of former communists and leftwing UP academics, who helped craft social policies and organize popular mobilization for Estrada. This peculiar combination of allies would force Estrada to balance opposing interests while attending to his own patrimonial concerns, and his failure to find that balance led to his downfall. Despite his popularity and attempt to put order into his chaotic presidency in his second term, exposés of corruption and crony capitalism, not to mention Estrada's own un-presidential behavior led to his impeachment by the Congress. Moreover, while Estrada had brought the Marcos technocrats back to the political arena, he did not have the talent or sagacity of his predecessor in tapping their skills (Tiglao 2001, 9).

After his supporters effectively stopped his Senate impeachment trial from proceeding, Estrada was overthrown by "People Power II," a strange combination of a largely middle class-led "popular uprising" and de facto coup by the AFP leadership. His vice-president, Gloria Arroyo, duly took office. Her presidency has been described as an attempt to combine politics and technocratic management in one office.[9]

Arroyo: The Politician as Technocrat

Where Estrada boasted of being a college drop-out with little knowledge of the economy, Arroyo projected an image of intellectual competence backed by a PhD in economics from UP, a stint at Georgetown University (where former US president Bill Clinton was a classmate) and a commitment to neo-liberalism and professional governance. To boost her stature as a no-nonsense administrator, Arroyo assembled a technocratic dream team for her cabinet. Drawing on colleagues from the private sector, she appointed bankers to key institutions like the Department of Finance and the Central Bank. Many were American-educated and extremely familiar with the policies and practice of neo-liberalism and globalization (Hookway 2002, 14).

The background of one important player was representative of this powerful group. Secretary of Finance Isidro Camacho "worked for over 20 years as an investment banker after getting his Master's Degree in Business Administration from the Harvard Business School. Before assuming the Finance post in the Arroyo government he was an expatriate in New York, Tokyo, Hong Kong and Singapore working for Bankers Trust Company and then the Deutsche bank AG" (Quimpo-Espino and Domingo 2001, B1). Like Cesar Virata in the past, Camacho's connections with the international banking community made him indispensable to the government. An interesting difference, however, is that Camacho was trained not by the IMF and the World Bank but by private banks. This signified the growing importance of multinational banks in the era of globalization as compared to multilateral agencies such as the IMF and World Bank previously.[10]

Arroyo was also singular in openly advocating the "globalization of the technocracy" when she created a "high-powered board of international advisers" (Zamora 2002, 1). This group, which would offer her free advice, included Maurice Greenberg, chair and CEO of International Group; Paul Keating, former prime minister of Australia; Stephen Bosworth, former US envoy to the Philippines and dean of Fletcher School of Law and Diplomacy; Minoru Makihara, chair of Mitsubishi Corporation; and Junichiro Miyazu, president of Nippon Telegraph and Telephone Corporation (Zamora 2002, 1).[11]

A problem, however, was that Arroyo was seen by many as a "traditional politician" who lacked the moral stature of President Aquino. Her rise to power was the product of the patronage politics, mutual accommodation and backroom horse-trading that had long been the hallmark of the Philippines' cacique democracy. Necessarily, therefore, Arroyo's other priority was to distribute political spoils to her politician and NGO supporters and protect the AFP leadership that had made her presidency possible. As a result, her presidency did not look much different from Estrada's, although she proved a better manager.

The perception of Arroyo as more politician than technocrat was especially apparent in her attempts to gain the support of an important Estrada constituent groupt—the urban poor. Rather than tackling the problem of urban land distribution professionally, Arroyo preferred the dole-out, a tried-and-tested method of politicians to ensure votes on election day. Aggravating this image was the perception of her husband's "wheeling-and-dealing ways" and charges that Miguel Arroyo was involved in a shady deals. Soon, even Arroyo's "technocrat" image came under fire from the business community, which accused her of being arrogant, stand-offish and not the consultative president she had promised to be. The head of the Federation of Philippine Industries complained that "the President is a good manager," but at times of crisis, "the country needs a leader, not a manager" (Hookway 2002, 15). While this grumbling concerned mainly presidential condescension, it nevertheless represented a growing sense of Arroyo's inability to handle the perennial problems of the Philippine economy.

Arroyo had always made known her advocacy of globalization and the important role of foreign investment in economic development. As a senator, she pushed for the Philippines to join the World Trade Organization (WTO). As she began her presidency, however, the country was already dangerously saddled by the government's failure to deal with mounting debt obligations and liabilities, ineffective tax revenue system, massive graft and corruption and deteriorating peace and order due to weak security and police agencies. A "poor people's revolt" after Estrada's arrest on charges of economic plunder underscored her limited support among the majority of Filipinos. This made poverty and social welfare issues as important as market reform and trade liberalization. The challenge proved daunting, and Arroyo remained uncertain of her legitimacy.

The September 11, 2001, attacks in New York and Washington, DC, provided Arroyo the opportunity to seek a more stable and lasting basis of assistance from the United States. Immediately after the attacks, Arroyo made known to President George W. Bush that the Philippines would give all-out support to the US war on terror, including allowing US troops to assist the AFP in pursuing and eliminating "Islamic terrorist" groups like the Abu Sayyaf. In response, the US sent troops to southern Mindanao and increased military assistance to the AFP. Washington also promised to release "US\$ 20.2 million for development in the poverty-stricken Autonomous Region of Muslim Mindanao (ARMM)," and the World Bank followed suit with a pledge of USD 35 million in development assistance over the next five years.

As a result of this alliance, Arroyo's popularity rose. A 2002 survey conducted by private pollster Social Weather Stations found that 84 percent of respondents favored US assistance for the Philippine military in its war against the Abu Sayyaf (Hookway 2002, 16). There were those, however, who predicted that reliance on the US would eventually lead to her downfall. For inevitably, the gauge of success will be whether Arroyo and her technocrats can effectively reverse the country's perceived economic slide and its growing poverty and unemployment (over 4.2 million in 2002, Rivera 2002). The president herself admitted that the benefits of the country's recent economic growth had not reached the masses (Pazzibugan 2002, 1). Her critics assailed her for squandering the gains of "People Power II" and putting her own political interests ahead of the country. These criticisms coincided with a "growing cynicism" about the lack of major changes forthcoming under her presidency (Gonzales 2002, A1).

The technocracy has thus been resurrected by Gloria Arroyo, but it comes to a political economy far different from that of the 1960s when its predecessors first joined government.

Conclusion

This chapter has tracked the involvement and impact of technocratic participation inside the Philippine state. It showed how an elite corps of development experts helped US-led capitalism gain entry to the Philippine economy, mainly by acting as a conduit for the policies of the IMF and World Bank. These policies, relying heavily on foreign loans and investments and on export-oriented industrialization, were extensively implemented during the martial law regime of President Marcos, who saw the important role the IMF and World Bank-supported technocracy could play in bringing external assistance to his authoritarian government. But the technocracy also enabled Marcos cronies to tap the rich trove of foreign aid. Joint ventures between the cronies and foreign capital were initially welcomed by all, but as patrimonial plunder became more and more the norm, technocratic support for these ventures was replaced by growing criticism of "crony capitalism."

The country's official commitment to export-oriented industrialization did not guarantee that export-led growth would be accepted in practice. Elite factions whose businesses relied on import-substitution remained close to Marcos and, together with the Marcos cronies, led a counter-attack against the technocrats and EOI inside the state. Finally there was opposition from anti-Marcos groups, especially those who regarded the technocracy's preference for an apolitical and pro-business atmosphere as evidence of an authoritarian ethos. Moreover, the displacement of thousands of Filipinos by technocrat-supported projects added fuel to the growing communist insurgency in the countryside.

These factors, coupled with the absence of external conditions necessary for the EOI policy to succeed, limited the effectiveness of Marcos-era development policies. The technocrats tried to mask their failure by pointing to the excesses of the authoritarian regime, particularly crony capitalism and military repression. Marcos was therefore torn between the technocrats and his cronies. Because of the need for more loans to cope with a failing economy, Marcos opted to pacify the IMF and World Bank by giving technocrats more political power, but it came too late. In 1986 Marcos was overthrown and his technocrats marginalized. Their economic policies lived on through President Aquino's economic advisers, many of whom had close ties to foreign capital. While the economic players changed, the technocratic solution remained, now being pursued under a democratic dispensation.

The reality, however, was that technocratic solutions were not enough. The Aquino government was itself accused of nurturing cronies, showing that democratization did not spell the end of political and economic dynasties. The democratic space did allow some groups in the Left to become involve in "legal struggle," and engage the IMF, World Bank and ADB in discussions over the appropriate development thrust.

Under President Ramos, greater liberalization was pursued to take advantage of the economic boom in the Asian region. This thrust was couched in the language of neo-liberalism, a variation of the free enterprise philosophy which was not only adopted by policy-makers but by leading groups in "civil society." There seemed no need for technocrats in this period, as Ramos and his legislative coalition actively pushed the same liberalization and export-oriented industrialization policies that the technocrats had promoted during the Marcos era. Ramos' policy led to strong growth and strengthened the middle class, but critics questioned the ability of this growth to address socio-economic inequality.

The failure to address income disparity was used by Joseph Estrada to win the 1998 presidential election. Estrada's victory also came in the wake of the 1997 economic crisis, which highlighted the contradictions and problems of globalization and neo-liberalism. Although he campaigned on a strong social welfare platform, once in power Estrada continued the policies of his predecessors. This was understandable, as his advisers came from same business communities with the same extensive links to foreign capital. Estrada's economic program was also besieged by rampant crony capitalism and corruption that ultimately led to his downfall.

President Gloria Arroyo projected herself as the opposite of Estrada—competent and committed to market reforms and economic liberalization, but also to the elimination of inefficiency, corruption and patrimonialism inside government. Arroyo seemed fit to play the role, with her academic background, no-nonsense work-style and business-like way of governing. Her problem was that she was also a politician preparing for the 2004 presidential election. As such, she did what all politicians do in the Philippines—dispense patronage, engage in backroom dealing and craft temporary electoral alliances bereft of political philosophy. These habits were seen not only in the way Arroyo distributed government office to supporters after the fall of Estrada; they were also on display in her attempt to buy the support of Estrada's mass base among the poor.

The structural failings of the Philippine political economy, unremitting weakness of state institutions and Arroyo's shaky legitimacy went against her technocratic intentions. Her credibility was sinking until the US war on terror gave her a breathing spell and a new alliance. In an important sense, her reliance on the United States—to spur development or simply get out of an economic rut—as she prepared to run for her own term as president reaffirmed her technocratic birthright.

Notes

1 This section is based on Encarnacion 1985.
2 Pre-martial law technocrats included Gerardo Sicat (Massachusetts Institute of Technology), Alejandro Melchor (United States Naval Academy at Annapolis), Vicente Paterno, Arturo Tanco, Roman Cruz and Placido Mapa, Jr. (all Harvard University). With the exception of Paterno and Mapa, who come from wealthy families, all were middle class.
3 These were the following: Jaime Laya, Roberto Ongpin, Geronimo Velasco, Armand Fabella, Cesar Zalamea, and Manuel Alba.

4 An example of this was the Philippine Consultative Group, chaired by a World Bank official, whose membership included representatives from the IMF and major lending countries, large private bank consortia tied in with the debt package and the Asia Development Bank. The Consultative Group determined how public and private funds were to be spent and the country's financial strategy ranging from taxation policies to anti-inflation programs (Stauffer 1979).

5 Cesar Virata was chairman of the Development Committee of the IMF/World Bank (1976–1980), while Placido Mapa worked for the IMF in 1972 and served as executive director of the International Bank for Reconstruction and Development of the World Bank in 1979 (Stauffer 1979).

6 For example, Mrs. Marcos wanted to appropriate USD 2 million from cabinet and presidential funds to host a film festival in Manila. Mr. Virata vetoed this move and President Marcos agreed (Business International 1983).

7 Virata publicly suggested that elements in the government could have been involved in the assassination of Marcos opponent former Senator Benigno Aquino, Jr., in 1983.

8 The first phase (1980–1983) emphasized trade liberalization and the second (1983–1992), partly owing to the severe economic crisis, shifted to stabilization and debt repayment (Morales 2001, 15).

9 This paper discusses only Arroyo's completion of Estrada's term of office (2001–2004).

10 Camacho resigned from the government in 2003.

11 The others were: Andrea Jung, CEO of Avon; Marce Fuller, CEO of Mirant Corp; Dr. Laura Tyson, dean of the London Graduate School of Business and former economic adviser to US President Bill Clinton; Gerard Corrigan, managing director of Goldman Sachs; Dr. Victor Fung, chair of Li and Fung Group; Maarten van den Bergh, chair of Lloyds TSB Group; Dr. Stephen Zuellig, chair of Zuellig Group; and Anthony Burgmans, chair of Unilever, NV (Zamora 2002, 15).

References

Alikpala, Julie S. 2002. Yanks' arrival pours $60M into south. *Philippine Daily Inquirer*, March 2, A2.

Bello, Walden, David Kinley, and Elaine Elinson. 1982. *Development Debacle: The World Bank in the Philippines*. California: Institute for Food and Development Policy.

Bello, Walden, and John Kelly. 1981. Western patrons of the Philippine worried about the degeneration of the country. *Le Monde*, February 3.

Bello, Walden, and Severina Reyes. 1981. The logistics of repression. *Third World Studies Center, University of the Philippines Monograph Series.*

Bowring, Philip. 1981. A time to cry wolf. *Far Eastern Economic Review*, December.

Bowring, Philip, and Guy Sacerdoti. 1983. Time for a real debate. *Far Eastern Economic Review*, January 20: 48.

Business International Research Division. 1980. *Philippines 1983: Economic and Political Outlook for Business Planners.* Hong Kong: Business International Asia, Pacific.

Constantino, Renato, and Letizia Constantino. 1978. *The Philippines: The Continuing Past.* Quezon City: The Foundation for Nationalist Studies.

Diokno, Jose W. 1980. Tourism as subversion. *The Diliman Review* (November–December).

Encarnacion, Teresa S. 1985. The Filipino technocracy. In "Transnationalization, the State and the People," Working Papers of the United Nations University Asian Perspectives Project (Southeast Asia). Unpublished.

Galang, Jose. 1983. The financial wizards. *Far Eastern Economic Review*, December 15.

————. 1985. Economic husbandry. *Far Eastern Economic Review*, June 31: 46.

Gonzales, Stella O. 2002. Experts alarmed EDSA II gains 'being squandered.'" *Philippine Daily Inquirer*, February 4: A1 & A18.

Hawes, Gary. 1984. The political economy of transnational corporate investments in Philippine agriculture. PhD diss., University of Hawaii.

Hookway, James. 2002. All things to all people. *Far Eastern Economic Review*, February 7: 14–16.

————. 2002a. In the clutches of the eagle. *Far Eastern Economic Review*, February 7: 16.

Ibon Facts and Figures. 1985. Towards exports, no. 160/5 (April).

Lichauco, Alejandro. 1981. Notes on the political and economic situation: The struggle against underdevelopment in the Philippines. *Third World Studies Center, University of the Philippines Monograph Series* (February 16).

Lim, Linda Y.C. 1983. Multinational export factories and women workers in the Third World. *Third World Studies Dependency Papers, University of the Philippines*, Series No. 50 (November).

Morales, Natalia. 2001. Streams of neo-liberalism in Philippine reformist democracy. Paper presented in the Sixth International Conference on Korean Politics. Sangnam Institute of Management, Yonsei University, Seoul, Korea.

Paazibugan, Dona Z. 2002. GMA concedes masses don't feel benefits of economy. *Philippine Daily Inquirer*, March 12: A1 & A16.

Philippine Daily Inquirer. 2002. Millions of dollars in aid for RP after anti-terror war. February 2.

Quimpo-Espino, Marge, and Ronnel W. Domingo. 2001. Finance head spends his weekends counting sheep. *Philippine Daily Inquirer*, July 1: B1 & B10.

Quizon, Antonio B., and Violeta Q. Perez-Corral. 1998. *The NGO Campaign on the Asian Development Bank*. Manila: Asian NGO Coalition for Agrarian Reform and Rural Development.

Rivera, Blanche S. 2002. Pinoys lost jobs since January. *Philippine Daily Inquirer*, February 24.

Rocamora, Joel. Agribusiness, dams and counterinsurgency. *Southeast Asia Chronicle* 67.

Roxas, C. Edward. 1984. The role of the Filipino technocracy: A case study. In "Technocrats at Whose Services?" *IBON Databank* 31 October.

Shalom, Stephen. 1981. *The United States and the Philippines: A Study of Neo-Colonialism*. Philadelphia: Institute for the Study of Human Issues.

Stauffer, Robert B. 1974. The political economy of a corporation: Trans-national linkages and Philippine political response. *Journal of Peace Research* 15, no. 3.

———. 1979. Naming the new leviathan ruler. *The Circle*.

———. n.d. Political economy of refeudalization. *Third World Studies Center, University of the Philippines, Diliman*.

Tiglao, Rigoberto. 2001. The Virata, now the Angara syndrome. *Philippine Daily Inquirer*, January 10: 9.

Velasco, Renato. 2002. Parties, elections and democratization in the Philippines. Paper presented in Philippine Politics and Governance Textbook Writing Project Workshop, Department of Political Science, University of the Philippines.

WHO Magazine. 1983. The national drift.

Zamora, Fe. 2002. GMA has high-powered board of int'l advisers. *Philippine Daily Inquirer*, February 9: A1 & A15.

5

A State with "Seizable" Scale: A Political Economy Approach to Mahathir's Development Policies and Implementation Mechanism

Takashi Torii

Tun Dr. Mahathir bin Mohamad resigned as the fourth Malaysian prime minister (1981–2003) at the end of October 2003, transferring the premiership to his successor, Datuk Abdullah Badawi. Mahathir's 22-year tenure would be called the "age of development" in Malaysia, leading to the supposition that this power transition marked the end of the age of development. Mahathir's administration was notable for two features. The first was its strong promotion of development-oriented policies, or industrial policies in a narrow sense. His long-serving administration not only built visible mega-projects such as the Penang Bridge and the Dayabumi Building in the first half of his tenure and the Kuala Lumpur International Airport (KLIA) and the Putra Jaya administrative capital in the 1990s, but also pursued ambitious industrial policies like heavy industrialization, the Multimedia Super Corridor (MSC) and the K-economy. Mahathir's policies aimed to improve technological and industrial capability within a very short period in the service of the second notable feature of his administration: to realize the objectives of the New Economic Policy (NEP, 1971–1990), the primary of which was to raise the economic and social position of ethnic Malays, or *bumiputera* (sons of the soil). These two features can be expressed as industrialization with the development of a Bumiputera entrepreneurial class.

Although many studies have examined the content and impact of Mahathir's development policies, little is known about the formation process and implementation mechanism of these policies. The research that has been done on decision-making processes in Malaysia (Puthucheary 1990; Heng 1997; Ho 1988, 1992) has dealt not with ordinary day-to-day policy making, but with the formation of extraordinary policies, such as the NEP and the post-NEP plan. As far as policy implementation is concerned, Mahathir had quite a different style from his two predecessors. Both Tun

Abdul Razak (1970–1976) and Tun Hussein Onn (1976–1981) expanded the role of government through the establishment and expansion of public enterprises (Non-Financial Enterprises, or NFEs) and through direct intervention in private business activities. The Mahathir adiministration, however, selectively reduced the role of government in the process of economic development. And in the 1990s, his industrial development policy moved clearly away from government-driven and toward private sector-driven development.

Important topics related to economic policy making, such as the relationship between government, political parties and the bureaucracy, have received little scholarly attention. The aim of this paper is to analyze the formation and implementation of development policies, showing how Dr. Mahathir and his Prime Minister's Office accrued power to themselves in the process. I first survey Mahathir's development policies and the changes they underwent, dividing them into three phases. In the second section, the policy phase known as Malaysia Incorporated is discussed in detail, with special emphasis on the Second Industrial Master Plan, 1995–2005. Lastly, I show how Dr. Mahathir and the Prime Minister's Office used the terminology "nation with 'seizable' scale" to seize control of government agencies.

Overview of Mahathir's Development Policies

In contrast to his predecessors, who had emphasized the inter-ethnic redistributive features of the NEP, Mahathir put more emphasis on development-oriented policies. But the fact that Mahathir was not free from the imperatives of Malay politics can hardly be ignored. As president of the United Malays National Organization (UMNO), he had to be a strong protector of the Malay community. But he tried to reconcile his development orientation with the NEP's redistributive goals through the policies of heavy industrialization. Recognizing the limitations of redistribution depending on the oil-based national revenue and development system, he sought to transform Malaysia into a newly industrializing country (NIC) under genuine entrepreneurial *bumiputera* leadership (Felker 1998, 82; Jomo 2003, 1). Heavy industrialization had the aim of improving industrial technology while simultaneously creating a Malay capitalist, professional and middle-class that was later described as the Bumiputera Commercial and Industrial Community (BCIC). In giving Malays the opportunity to become substantive actors in industrial development—as engineers, technical workers and professionals—Mahathir broadened the original aim of NEP. From simply raising Malays' economic and social position, Mahathir put professional Malays (Malay enterprises in a narrow sense) in charge of Malaysian economic development.

Eventually, Mahathir entrusted the engine of economic development to the private sector through foreign direct investment and deregulation, while using the government to promote Malay entrepreneurs through the Ministry of Entrepreneur Development, established in 1995. (The changing role of the Malay community in industrial development can be seen through detailed analyses of successive five-year plans [Torii 2003]). It is important to keep in mind that Mahathir's development policies should always be understood to include both facets: the contents of industrial policies and their socio-economic effect on Malay communities. From this point of view, his tenure can be roughly divided into three periods.

Phase One (1981–1984)—Heavy Industrialization and Supporting Industries

The first phase ran from the beginning of Mahathir's assumption of power in 1981 to the end of 1984, when Malaysia began to experience economic recession. We can see its preparatory stage in Mahathir's tenure as minister of trade and industry in 1980, when he established the state-owned Heavy Industries Corporation of Malaysia (HICOM). As prime minister, Mahathir pursued heavy industrialization as the next step in import substitution, in order to lift the level of industrial capability from mere assembly operations to greater value-added secondary and tertiary processing.

Under HICOM, several large manufacturing joint ventures with Japan and other East Asian countries were established. Among these ventures, which included a motorcycle engine plant and steel and cement projects, the national car project company (Perusahaan Otomobil Nasional, henceforth Proton) has drawn most public attention. It is one of the most important HICOM projects for understanding of Mahathir's policy. The government's original intention for Proton was "to encourage the Bumiputera to join [the] automobile industry through Proton, acquire, accumulate the industrial technology, and establish auto-component industries." At the initial stage of Proton, the structure of the automobile industry was designed on the Japanese model, that is, a multi-layered structure of parts manufacturers, parts processors and material producers that is sometimes called a pyramid (Jamil 1983). As the final assembler of the automobile, Proton would be an umbrella under which *bumiputera* small- and medium-size businesses would become subcontractors. Furthermore, within Proton, *bumiputera* employees would be trained as substantive contributors to industrialization.[1]

Phase Two (1986–1990)—Deregulation and Bumiputera Entrepreneurship
After the economic recession of the mid-1980s, the Mahathir administration changed direction, placing more emphasis on economic recovery and expansion through private investment than on realizing the goals of the NEP. To promote private investment, the government amended the strict rules on foreign equity to permit 100 percent foreign ownership in projects in which at least 50 percent of output was exported (1986). New tax incentives for manufacturing and tourism investment were expanded under the Promotion of Investment Act (PIA) in 1986, replacing the Investment Incentives Act 1968. In addition, the range of manufacturing companies required to obtain a manufacturing license under the Industrial Coordination Act (ICA) was reduced twice, in 1985 and 1987.

These deregulation policies led to the changes in the role of *bumiputeras* under the NEP. Although the government continued to train and place them as technical workers and professionals in the private sector, a policy for *bumiputera* entrepreneur development was adopted. The privatization policy of May 1983 reduced state involvement in business and transferred state-owned enterprises to Malay entrepreneurs (furthering the creation of the BCIC) through Management Buy-Outs (MBO), Build-Operate-Transfer (BOT) arrangements and share listing on the Kuala Lumpur Stock Exchange (KLSE) (Jomo 1995).

Phase Three (Post-1991)—Quality-driven Industrial Development and the Promotion of Small Entrepreneurs
After the NEP expired in 1990, Mahathir released a much more development-oriented plan. Vision 2020 (Wawasan 2020) was unveiled at the inaugural meeting of the Malaysian Business Council (MBC) on February 28, 1991, as the government's mid-term development plan. In its concentration on industrial development, Vision 2020 was very different from policies of the NEP period.[2] It envisioned Malaysia becoming a fully developed nation by maintaining a real economic growth rate of 7 percent over the following thirty years. To realize this economic target, Mahathir set the new political and social goal of creating a Malaysian nation (Bangsa Malaysia) through cooperation and integration of the country's ethnic groups. The real agenda of this political goal was to mobilize the potential

of the non-Malay communities, which had had only a limited role under the NEP. In furtherance of Vision 2020, two new long-term development plans were introduced, the National Development Plan (NDP, 1991–2000) and the National Vision Plan (NVP, 2002–2010).

The Malaysian government continued its policy of private sector-led economic development and a limited government role in the operation of the economy. Even Proton, Mahathir's masterpiece of the heavy industrialization period, was privatized in 1995, together with its parent company HICOM.[3] A new industrial plan was also introduced. Under the Second Industrial Master Plan (2nd IMP, 1996–2005), the government emphasizes quality-driven development, or "total factor productivity" (TFP) (Government of Malaysia 1996). This reflects the attempt to move from input-driven industrialization to quality-oriented economic growth.

The effort to train *bumiputeras* as professional and technical workers to achieve quality-driven development continues (Torii 2003). At the same time, the BCIC has been promoted with the new concept, "Kelas Menengah Usahawan" (middle class entrepreneurs). In 1995, the Ministry of Public Enterprises was reorganized as the Ministry of Entrepreneur Development (MED). The MED's activities are twofold: an entrepreneurial promotion program and the training of contractors to take on government projects. The former consists of the Vendor Development Program (VDP) and the Franchisee Development Program (FDP) (MED 1997). The VDP, which originated in the Proton project, has expanded to other industries, including even the foreign-dominated electronics industry. To aid *bumiputera* entrepreneurs, the government has established a state-owned venture capital fund, the Perbananan Usahawan Nasional Berhad (PUNB, or National Entrepreneur Corporation).[4]

The Formation of Industrial Policy under Mahathir

As discussed above, Mahathir wanted to make the government's role in the economy smaller, selective and more strategic in comparison with the expanded role it played in the pre-Mahathir years of the NEP. Correspondingly, he wanted the private sector to be the major contributor to economic growth, especially in the manufacturing sector. Table 5-1 shows the changing capital structure of production companies during the course of the Mahathir administration. The private sector's share increased from 83 percent in 1989 to 93 percent in 1993. In contrast, the share of

Table 5-1. Equity Ownership by Ethnic Group in Production Companies (paid-up capital, by percentage and millions of ringgit)

	END OF 1980	END OF 1986	END OF 1989	END OF 1991	END OF 1997
Malaysian equity	60.2 (3,572)	68.5 (9,961)	52.8 (9,525)	49.2 (11,692)	42.1 (18,722)
1. Bumiputera	19.4 (1,151)	34.8 (5,058)	18.2 (3,288)	23.9 (5,568)	23.2 (10,311)
2. Public Enterprise	n.a.	n.a.	16.9 (9,525)	10.2 (2,419)	6.5 (2,912)
3. Chinese	25.1 (1,490)	20.0 (2,907)	17.2 (3,097)	14.8 (3,523)	12.1 (5,381)
4. Indian	00.7 (44)	00.6 (93)	00.5 (89)	00.3 (82)	00.3 (117)
5. Others	18.9 (1,200)	13.7 (19,03)	n.a.	n.a.	n.a.
Foreign Equity	39.8 (2,366)	31.5 (4,590)	35.5 (6,398)	39.5 (9,385)	46.4 (20,665)
Nominee Companies	n.a.	n.a.	11.7 (2,101)	11.3 (2,689)	11.5 (5,112)
Total	100 (5,938)	100 (14,551)	100 (18,025)	100 (23,766)	100 (44,499)

Note: Public enterprise data available only after 1989.
Source: Malaysian Industrial Development Authority

public enterprises decreased dramatically after 1989. It should be noted that within the private sector, foreign capital has continued to increase. Especially after the adoption of the deregulation policy, foreign capital's share has exceeded 40 percent of total capital, reaching 46 percent in 1997.

As a consequence of these changes, Mahathir needed a new framework to incorporate a growing private sector that had the potential to become a political threat to his administration.

Malaysia Incorporated: Original Idea and Institutionalization

The aim of the Malaysia Incorporated policy is to situate the growing private sector within Mahathir's development system. The policy originated in 1983, but lay dormant until the early 1990s (Abdullah Sanusi Ahmad 2003, 205). This is one reason it has not been researched adequately. Mahathir introduced the policy as a link between the public and private sector and to "offer useful information and guidelines of government policies" to the latter (Mohd. Nor et al. 1984). In Mahathir's words, "Malaysia should be viewed as a company where the government and the private sector are both owners and workers together in this company. In a company, all owners/workers are expected to cooperate to ensure the company's success. Only through the success of the company, will the owners' and worker's well-being be safeguarded and improved" (Jomo 1989, 9). In another statement, Mahathir likened the private sector to "the commercial and economic arms of the national enterprise, while the government lays down the major policy framework, direction and provides the necessary backup services" (Mohd. Nor et al. 1984, 1).

In short, the original aim of the policy was to build cooperation and share information between the sectors. The public sector was to improve the quality of services and facilities provided, while an important function of the private sector would be to provide feedback (industrial information) to the government. During its initial stage in the 1980s, however, no concrete progress occurred beyond an annual meeting held by the Ministry of Finance (MoF) and the Ministry of International Trade and Industry (MITI). MITI started the Annual Trade and Industry Dialogue in 1988 to meet representatives from each industry and each association in commerce and industry.[5]

In 1990, the Malaysian government took the first step to institutionalize Malaysia Incorporated when the Prime Minister's Office established the Malaysian Business Council (Felker 1998). In February 1990, the MBC was composed of ten representatives from the higher civil service and cabinet and fifty-five members from the private sector. Its purpose was to provide the prime minister with advice that had been distilled through discussion and sharing of problems and information about industrial development. In July 1991, the chief secretary of the Federal Government issued a Development Administration Circular requiring every federal ministry, state government and district office to "establish the consultation panel, which consists of the representatives of government and private sectors and to hold annual dialogue among them" (Ahamad Sarji 1996). The purpose of the panels was to "share information about government policies from both sides, and to manage public administrations more efficiently." Following this circular, the Ministry of Primary Industries, the Ministry of Agriculture and some state governments set up an annual dialogue panel. What should be noted is that the annual dialogue panels were given no decision-making power at this stage.

When the 2nd IMP was introduced in 1996, new industrial policy institutions were also established, making the Malaysia Incorporated policy part of the development apparatus. Before examining industrial policy formation under the 2nd IMP, a few remarks should be made about the formation of macro-economic policy in Malaysia. (Abdul Aziz Zakaria 1974; Samusudin Hitam 1993). It is roughly a four-step process. The first is policy drafting within the ministry, done through a planning council composed of relevant heads of department. The second step involves discussing, coordinating and adjusting the draft among the secretaries-general in the relevant ministries through the Inter Agencies Planning Group (IAPG).

The third step, the last within the bureaucracy, is to make final decisions on the draft in the National Development Planning Committee (NDPC). The head of NPDC is the chief secretary of Federal Government and its members are the secretaries-general of each ministry and the director-general of the Economic Planning Unit (EPU) of the Prime Minister's Office. The role and function of NPDC, besides formulating policy, is to implement, evaluate and allocate the development budget. After the NDPC is finished, the ministers, through the National Planning Council (NPC), and the cabinet meeting make any necessary decisions and adjustment.

Let us now return to industrial policy under the 2nd IMP. Industrial policy formation is divided into the same steps as economic policies, with some additional important mechanisms. In the first step, Public-Private Cluster Working Groups (CWGs) are set up for each of eighteen strategic industries; these allow the private sector to input information and proposals into policy drafts and to receive responses from the government sector. Even more important is a higher-level institution, the Industrial Coordination Council (ICC) at the ministerial level. The role and function of the ICC is "to review and check implementation of 2nd Industrial Master Plan" (Government of Malaysia 1996). Members of the ICC are the minister of MITI (chairperson of ICC), the secretary-general of economic ministries, the governor of the central bank, and fifteen members of private associations such as the Federation of Malaysian Manufacturers (FMM) and the Association of Chinese Chambers of Commerce and Industry of Malaysia (ACCCIM). Finally, at the prime minister's level, the Malaysian Industry-Government Group for High Technology (Might) was established in 1995 to achieve further development in high technology industries and in science and technology. It performs the same functions as the ICC.

Foreign-owned companies play a major role in the industrial sector, and Mahathir focused his administration's relationship on Japanese firms with his Look East Policy. The Japanese Chamber of Trade and Industry Malaysia (JACTIM) was approved to form the first foreign company-based chamber of commerce in Malaysia. The exceptional assistance given this effort by Mahathir made a highly favorable impression in Japanese business circles.[6] In response, JACTIM and the Japan External Trade Organization (JETRO) have conducted industry surveys on the operations of Japanese firms in Malaysia focusing on issues of local content, salary and environmental problems. Survey results, as well as requests from JACTIM members, are sent directly to the Prime Minister's Office and

MITI, or indirectly via the consultative councils by representatives of Japanese firms.

The Reality and Political Impact of the Malaysia Incorporated Policy

What has been the impact of this policy on the relationship between the domestic private sector and bureaucracy? The new organizations and institutions of the 1980s and 1990s, such as the annual dialogue, were not given decision-making power over industrial policy. Moreover, the individual proposals, opinions and interests of private companies were prevented from exerting strong influence by being channeled through the mechanisms of dialogue and chambers of commerce. Therefore, the initiative and control over the formation of industrial policy has not shifted to the private sector, but remained with the public sector. Despite the increasing contribution of the private sector following from deregulation in the late 1980s and 1990s, Malaysia Incorporated has protected the autonomous power of the Malaysian bureaucracy.

Have these mechanisms had any benefit for the private sector? They can be understood in the same context as consultative councils in East Asian nations, the so-called industry council or Shingikai, that promote cooperation between government and the private sector. However, they have greater political significance in ethnically-differentiated Malaysia because they provide non-Malay groups the opportunity to take part in policy formation. For example, representatives of the non-Malay business community can bypass political parties based on ethnic groups and contact the UMNO-led government directly. In other words, the function and meaning of these mechanisms is not simply cooperation between government and private sector, but institutional cooperation between the Malay-dominated public sector and the Chinese-dominated private sector.[7]

At the heart of this development was a shift in government's attitude toward business. From the start of NEP implementation in 1971 until Mahathir came to power, the government's attitude had been one of controlling and supervising the activities and progress of the private sector. In 1983, Mahathir first voiced the idea of Malaysia Incorporated, emphasizing partnership and cooperation instead—information sharing, gathering and inputting into the government machinery through interaction between government and business.

When in 1991 his administration turned to the promotion of inter-ethnic cooperation under Vision 2020, therefore, Mahathir easily adopted the same strategy in the industrial sector, the main venue for economic development. Under the 2nd IMP, MITI provides the private sector with more opportunity to take part in planning and coordinating industrial policy. In so far as the non-Malay community is still dominant in the private industrial sector, these mechanisms have an important political impact.

Lastly, to what extent do the mechanisms created under Malaysia Incorporated constitute institutionalization? It cannot be denied that organizations such as the MBC and Might *are* institutions. However, a closer look reveals that the core members of these organizations overlap and include businessmen close to Mahathir and Daim Zainnudin, his longtime economic advisor. This seems to indicate that organizations appearing to be official institutions may in reality have been based on Mahathir's personal relationships. The reason why they seemed to work effectively was Mahathir's role and attitude. Mahathir's pro-business attitude in the process of economic development was well known during his prime ministership. There is good evidence that Mahathir developed this attitude from his own experience. When he was expelled from UMNO after the 1969 general election, he served as chairman of the Food Industry of Malaysia (FIMA). He explained this experience in 1991: "Through my experience in FIMA, I have learned that we must have a thorough knowledge... [As chairman of FIMA,] I had to learn everything from the production process to accounting completely [my translation]" (Mahathir 1991).

Mahathir's pro-business attitude and his knowledge of relevant industries made favorable impressions on boards of directors, especially of parent companies of foreign firms represented in Malaysia.[8] His sincere attitude toward economic development was helpful in building strong cooperation with private sector leaders.

A Nation with "Seizable" Scale: Requirements for Centralized Power

Regularly held annual dialogues and good relations with the private sector are two elements of successful policy formation under the Mahathir administration. Another reason why these mechanisms function is that Malaysia is a nation with "seizable" scale. Malaysia is a comparatively small country among its ASEAN neighbors in terms of population, national territory and so on. This enables government machineries to more easily control various private sector activities as well as the impact of the national budget. Moreover, the country introduced a federal system after independence, reducing the activities and targets which are to be seized.

The significance of this point can be seen in the two kinds of development policies pursued under the Mahathir administration: NEP development for the Malay community and industrial development. In Malaysia, both the development budget and foreign direct investment for industrial development were "seized" by Mahathir's Prime Minister's Office.

The implementation of economic policies for Malay development was embodied in successive five-year plans. Both development planning, on the one hand, and implementation and evaluation of development projects, on the other, have been vested in the Prime Minister's Office. The Economic Planning Unit (EPU) is in charge of the former function and the Implementation and Coordination Unit (ICU) is responsible for the latter. The decision-making process is roughly divided into two levels. The bureaucratic level includes the National Development Planning Committee for planning and the National Development Working Committee for implementation. At the minister's level, these respective functions are performed by the prime minister-headed National Planning Council and National Action Council.

The real source of power of the EPU over the administration of planning rests in its influence over the allocation of development funds through the drafting of the five-year development plan. Moreover, the EPU can control foreign economic assistance for the development budget, such as technical assistance and government loans, through direct negotiation with foreign donors together with the treasury. During the Razak administration, power over the implementation and evaluation of development project was strengthened through the establishment of the ICU.

The relationship between the private sector and the Prime Minister's Office has changed as discussed above, but government policy on foreign investment has been consistently centered in that office. In the 1970s, when government controlled and supervised the private sector in order to carry out NEP objectives, its policy on foreign equity, including the manufacturing sector, was under the jurisdiction of the Foreign Investment Committee (FIC). The FIC was established in 1974 to "formulate policy guideline on foreign investment, monitor the progress and co-ordinate and regulate the acquisition of certain assets, or interest and mergers and take-overs of companies and businesses in Malaysia" to further the objectives of the NEP (Abdul Razak 1974). The FIC consisted of the secretaries-general of Treasury and the Ministry of Trade and Industry, the governor of Bank Negara Malaysia, the director-general of the EPU, the chairman of the Malaysian Industrial Development Authority and the

Registrar of Companies. The FIC Secretariat is located in the EPU and the chairman of the FIC is a special adviser to the prime minister.

During the period of deregulation after 1986, the private sector moved to the fore as the main contributor to economic growth and a partner to the public sector. As noted above, some prominent private sector leaders had strong personal connections to Mahathir that were facilitated by the mechanisms devised during his administration.

After the Asian Financial Crisis and Mahathir's Retirement

From the mid-1980s to 1997, Malaysia enjoyed strong economic development. This may be attributed to Mahathir's pro-business policy turn, as well as to East Asian economic circumstances more generally. The Mahathir administration constructed better relations with the private sector through organizations and policy mechanisms that seemed to be institutions, but the importance of these organizations was largely political, not economic. Their composition reflected the social structure of this multiethnic country, and some members were very close to specific UMNO leaders. It can not be denied that the significance of these organizations, especially the higher-ranking ones, was to be found in personal ties. They therefore helped Mahathir control and monopolize the decision-making process in industrial policy, even down to specific industrial projects.[9] His preference for a top-down system became stronger during the Asian financial crisis in 1997. In the process of Malaysia's economic recovery, Mahathir and the National Economic Action Council (NEAC), directly under his control, monopolized decision-making power.

After Mahathir's retirement from government, it is to be expected that the organizations and mechanisms he set up will not work in same way as before. But the system of strong control vested in the Prime Minster's Office has been left in the hands of his successor. Abdullah Badawi has two options for the future of policy planning and implementation. He may place his own contacts from the private sector into the system, following Mahathir's lead, or he make seek to institutionalize policy making in a real sense.

Notes

1 Interview with former chairman of Mitsubishi Company (1989).
2 In my understanding, however, most of the essence of Vision 2020 could

already be found in Mahathir's "New Elements for the 1980s," which was released soon after he assumed power. It would be better to regard Vision 2020 as the final attainment of Mahathir's developmentalism. On the other hand, the second point of Vision 2020, the creation of a Bangsa Malaysia, grew out of changes in ethnic relations in the 1980s.

3 The Yahaya Ahmad-led DRB group purchased 32 percent of paid-up capital of HICM in October 1995.

4 MED was established just after the 1995 general election. PUNB was set up in 1992 with paid-up capital of 200 million ringgit.

5 For instance, in April 1999, a six-day dialogue was held, at which 112 representatives from the private sector submitted 347 proposals to MITI.

6 Interview with former secretary-general of JACTIM in 1987.

7 Interview with board members of the ACCCIM and the Malaysian Associated Indian Chambers of Commerce and Industry in 1998.

8 On Mahathir's official and unofficial visits to Japan, he often visited factories and industrial areas, such as Tokyo's electrical town. When visiting factories of a parent company, he was able to discuss industry specifics with their directors. This ability impressed many of them with Mahathir's sincere attitude toward economic development (interview with Japanese directors involved in Malaysian national car project, 1996 and 1997).

9 For instance, Mahathir was regularly and directly briefed on the national car project, and he issued specific instructions on subjects presented in these briefings (interview with directors of relevant companies, 1998).

References

Abdul Aziz Zakaria. 1974. *An Introduction to the Machinery of Government in Malaysia*. Kuala Lumpur: Dewan Bahasa dan Pustaka.

Abdullah Sanusi Ahmad, Norma Mansor, and Abdul Kuddus Ahmad. 2003. *The Malaysian Bureaucracy: Four Decades of Development*. Kuala Lumpur: Prentice Hall.

Abdul Razak bin Hussein. 1974. Statement on guidelines for the regulation of acquisition of assets, mergers and take-overs of companies and businesses. Mimeo.

Ahmad Sarji Abdul Hamid. 1996. *The Chief Secretary to the Government*. Selangor: Pelanduk Publications.

Felker, Greg 1998. Political economy and Malaysian technology policy. In *Malaysian Industrialisation: Governance and the Technical Change*, ed.

Ishak Yusoff and Abdul Gahafar Ismail. Selangor: Penerbit Universiti Kebangsaan Malaysia.

Government of Malaysia. 1996. *The Second Industrial Master Plan 1996–2005*. Kuala Lumpur: Percetakan National Berhad.

Heng, Pek Koon. 1997. The New Economic Policy and the Chinese community in Peninsular Malaysia. *The Developing Economies* 35, no. 3.

Jamil (Tan Sri) bin Mohd. Jan. 1985. The role of HICOM and PROTON in the development of the automobile components manufacturing industry. Paper presented at Seminar on Automobile Components Manufacturing. Kuala Lumpur, May 14–16, 1985.

Jomo, K.S., ed. 1989. *Mahathir's Economic Policies*. Kuala Lumpur: Institute of Social Analysis (INSAN).

Jomo, K.S. 1995. *Privatizing Malaysia, Rents, Rhetorics, Realities*. Boulder, CO: Westview.

Jomo.K.S. 2003. *M Way: Mahathir's Economic Legacy*. Kuala Lumpur: Forum.

Ho, Khai Leong. 1992. Dynamics of policy-making in Malaysia: The formulation of the New Economic Policy and the National Development Policy. *Asian Journal of Public Administraition* 14, no. 2 (December): 204–27.

Khoo, Boo Teik. 1995. *Paradoxes of Mahathrism: An Intellectual Biography of Mahathir Mohamad*. Kuala Lumpur: Oxford University Press.

Mahathir Mohamad. 1991. *Watashi no Rirekisyo* [My personal history]. Nihonkeizaisinbun.

Ministry of Entrepreneur Development. *Annual Report*. Kuala Lumpur.

Mohd. Nor Abdul Ghani et al., ed. 1984. *Malaysia Incorporated and Privatisation Towards National Unity*. Selangor, Pelanduk Publications.

Puthucheary, Mavis. 1990. Malaysia: The shaping of economic policy in a multi-ethnic environment. In *Economic Policy Making in the Asia Pacific Region*, ed. John W. Langford and K. Lorne Brownsey. Halifax: Institute for Research on Public Policy.

Samusudin Hitam. 1993. Development planning in Malaysia. In *Development Planning in Asia*, ed. Somsak Tambunlertchai and S.P. Gupta. Kuala Lumpur: Asia and Pacific Development Center.

Torii, T. 2003. The mechanism for state-led creation of Malaysia's middle classes. *The Developing Economies* 41, no. 2.

6

Understanding "Democratic Transitions": Some Insights from Gus Dur's Brief Presidency in Indonesia

Vedi R. Hadiz

A Transition?

Since the fall of Soeharto in May 1998, numerous international conferences and workshops on Indonesia have been held, and papers or reports produced, that at least implicitly adopt the position laid out most clearly in the democratic transitions literature epitomized by O'Donnell and Schmitter's famous *Transitions from Authoritarian Rule* (1986). In this book, part of an impressive, much wider collaborative project, the authors state that they are dealing with:

> transitions from certain authoritarian regimes toward an uncertain "something else." That "something" can be the installation of political democracy or the restoration of a new, and possibly more severe form of authoritarian rule. The outcome can also be simply confusion, that is, the rotation in power of successive governments which fail to provide any enduring or predictable solution to the problem of institutionalising political power. Transitions can also develop into widespread violent confrontations...(ibid, 3).

The theory put forward by O'Donnell and Schmitter (and their collaborators) prominently highlighted "elements of accident and unpredictability, of crucial decisions taken in a hurry with very inadequate information..." (ibid, 3). It was premised on a largely voluntarist position which relied much on describing the "choices and processes" that present themselves in "indeterminate situations" that invariably characterize the demise of authoritarian regimes. Despite invoking "structural" factors from time to time, such a theoretical inclination could not avoid being heavily weighted toward the calculations and immediate reactions of political elites. Indeed, much emphasis was placed on elite "pacts" that emerge in the process of negotiating and crafting political transitions. Despite a chapter on "resurrecting civil society," this was an extremely actor- and elite-based approach, one in which social structures and forces were of secondary importance.

Much of the academic and political discussion of post-Soeharto Indonesia, whether undertaken inside or outside the country itself, has been equally elite-centered, actor-based and voluntarist. Scholars are typically overwhelmed by the rapid sequence of events and focus on detailing the dilemmas and choices of key personalities, but they sometimes forget to analyze them (Van Dijk 2001). Moreover, the idea that there could be a transition to "something" other than a liberal form of democracy has been somewhat lost in the recent Indonesian debates. In the euphoria of the fall of Soeharto after three decades of authoritarian rule, many initially assumed the unravelling of his New Order would usher in a benign period of democratic rule (Arief Budiman 1999; Van Klinken 2001). The conditions put forward for this to happen were generally technical in nature: guaranteed freedoms for political parties, "good" election laws and other legal and institutional reforms. Some would understand these, explicitly or not, in the context of achieving what is dubbed "good governance" in currently fashionable World Bank-inspired parlance.

Institutional reforms are clearly very important. Nevertheless, institutions and the ways they actually work are contingent on the outcome of contests between wider social forces and the interests embedded in them. Thus, following Bellin, I suggest here that the more fundamental task is to understand the specific constellation of power and interest and the way it affects the forging of political and economic regimes (Bellin 2001). In the case of today's Indonesia, which is commonly referred to as being in a stage of "transition" (e.g., Manning and Van Diermen 2001; Budiman and Kingsbury 2002), it is important to recognize that the salient forces shaping the post-Soeharto institutional framework were at least partly nurtured under the New Order. In other words, social, political and economic change is presided over largely by predatory interests incubated under the New Order, which are now learning to secure their ascendance through new and shifting alliances in an environment of greater political fluidity. This certainly does not mean that these interests escaped the Asian economic crisis or the fall of Soeharto unscathed. However, they clearly were not swept aside, as many expected, and have in fact remained ascendant in the post-authoritarian period in the absence of a coherent reformist challenge.

In adopting this position, this paper argues that the unravelling of the New Order has not been accompanied—and probably will not for some time—by the establishment of a democratic regime in which transparency, accountability, rule of law or social justice reign supreme. The "something" obtaining in Indonesia today cannot be associated with idealized notions of liberal democracy, but is rather a form of democratic governance powered by money politics, bossism, thuggery and violence, as practiced in Thailand or the Philippines (Arghiros 2001; Sidel 1999). Indeed, analysts now frequently compare Indonesia to societies in which post-authoritarian politics have only problematically been characterized as democratic.

What does all this say about the question of "democratic transition" in Indonesia? The old authoritarian regime has indeed floundered. But the currently highly volatile, angst-ridden state of Indonesian politics and society is not simply a transitional stage to a relatively benign liberal democratic regime. In fact, this may be no transition at all, in the sense that the patterns and essential dynamics of social, economic, and political power have been more or less established for the foreseeable future. In other words, the violence, vote buying, alleged political murders and kidnappings may not be growing pains toward an ultimately liberal democratic system, but fundamental elements of a "something else" that is already more or less entrenched.

This argument is pursued through a discussion of the bizarre rise and fall of Abdurahman Wahid—better known as Gus Dur—Indonesia's third president and a man once widely regarded as having impeccable credentials as a democrat and progressive thinker. A nearly blind, stroke-weakened, cleric-politician-intellectual and leader of the Nahdlatul Ulama, the largest Muslim organization in Indonesia, Wahid was hoped by many to be perfect to lead Indonesia to the promised land of benign democratic governance. After all, he was a prominent leader of the opposition to Soeharto as a founder of the Forum Demokrasi, a grouping of critical intellectuals and political figures, and was well known for espousing tolerance, equality and pluralism. Understandably, many viewed Wahid's ascension to the presidency as signalling the victory of the reform movement over the forces of the "status quo." Tragically, his tenure was almost incessantly mired in allegations of incompetence, corruption and nepotism, leading some—like the liberal economist and public commentator Sjahrir—to hold his government responsible for the "death" of reform.

What was the New Order?

One crucial factor in understanding post-Soeharto Indonesia—and the failure of the Wahid government—is the continuing legacy of the long-entrenched New Order. The institutional framework of power and control that Soeharto so masterfully crafted may have largely unravelled almost as soon as he fell, but its legacy will continue to influence Indonesia's post-New Order trajectory (Hadiz 2000).

Therefore, it is important to understand what the New Order actually was. Here I reject characterizations of the New Order as simply a military dictatorship, a bureaucratic polity or a case of sultanistic rule. The alliances that underpinned the New Order were clearly much too complex to characterize it as a military dictatorship or regime (Sundhaussen 1994; Caldwell 1975); in any case, the military-as-institution's real power was increasingly diminished in the last decade of Soeharto's rule. The New Order was also much more than a bureaucratic polity run by 1000 people insulated from public pressure and scrutiny (Jackson 1978)—this characterization overlooks the social forces, coalitions of power and interests that such powerful people represented. Moreover, though Soeharto's rule often appeared arbitrary, patrimonial and uncontested, it would be more accurate to think of him as a rapacious and ruthless capitalist rather than as a feudalistic sultan.

Together with Richard Robison, I have put forward the idea that at the height of the New Order around the 1980s—after its consolidation in the 1970s and before its crisis in the late 1990s—state power gradually evolved into the instrument of a "capitalist oligarchy." Fusing business and politico-bureaucratic interests, this oligarchy was led by families like the Soehartos, the Salims, the Bakries and the Kartasasmitas. Developing a social base outside the state bureaucracy itself, the key to the oligarchy success was its ability to appropriate state power and institutions and to develop a network of patronage based on control over state resources.

Along the same lines, I suggest here that the New Order was at least these three "things":

1. A capitalist oligarchy able to capture and "instrumentally"—not just "structurally"—utilize state power and institutions and the state's coercive capacities to further its own interests.
2. A system of state and society relations characterized primarily by the systematic disorganization of civil society groups and the dominance of state-created corporatist institutions.
3. An extensive and complex system of patronage, personified by Soeharto himself, the apex of which lay at Cendana Palace. This

system of patronage was pervasive and penetrated all layers of society from Jakarta down to the provinces, kabupatens, towns and villages. Underpinning this network was a huge amalgam of high state officials, petty local bureaucrats, national and local capitalists, political wheeler-dealers and fixers, informal local notables and military officers, as well as unofficial armies of hooligans and thugs.

Furthermore, I suggest that the capitalist oligarchy eventually transformed the apparatus of state into a virtual "committee" that presided over the protection of its interests (Hadiz 2001). Thus, less ambiguously than in contemporary advanced industrial countries, the Indonesian case was suggestive of Marx and Engel's well-known formulation of "the executive of the modern state" acting as a "committee for managing the common affairs" of the bourgeoisie (Marx and Engels 1998, 242). Indeed, harnessing state power and institutions for their purposes, these oligarchs, through their appropriation and direct colonization of key institutions of state power, were able to steer state policy in their interest. They did this even as Indonesia won plaudits internationally for its reorientation toward market-oriented policies, supposedly signalling state retreat from the economy. In reality, the process of economic liberalization was being hijacked and molded to consolidate oligarchic rule (Robison and Rosser 2000).

It is important to remember that the fall of Soeharto was not accompanied by the wholesale disappearance of this extensive system of patronage. As I shall argue further below, predatory interests nurtured by this system continue to appropriate state power, although necessarily within a format far more decentralized and diffuse than during the New Order.

But this is not the only "legacy" of Soeharto's three decades of rule. An equally important legacy has been the clinical pursuit of the disorganization of civil society characteristic of this long period. As has been well-documented, this aim was achieved through a variety of means: the forced fusion of mutually antagonistic political parties in 1973; the establishment of state-dominated corporatist institutions of interest representation; the entrenchment of Pancasila as state ideology; and the generous use of large doses of old-fashioned state repression against real and imagined opponents and such groups as organized labor.[1]

As is also argued below, the consequence of this approach was far-reaching. It essentially ensured that as the New Order teetered and floundered, coherent coalitions of social reformist forces were not able to emerge to effectively challenge well-entrenched predatory interests.

What Replaced the New Order?

The fall of Soeharto meant the old institutional framework of power was no longer viable. In order to survive, the interests that had been incubated and protected by his long rule had to reconstitute themselves within the new diffuse and decentralized political framework. Among the major characteristics of this new framework are:

1. The decentralization of power from the presidency to such institutions as political parties and parliament;

2. The rise of political parties, which rather than being held together by distinct, concrete social, economic and political agendas, are really just expressions of shifting power coalitions. Representatives of old predatory interests commonly populate these parties, with small reformist elements usually more or less marginalized within them;

3. The decentralization of power from Jakarta to the regions. Hence, the new importance of local offices such as that of *bupati* or town mayor, party branches and parliaments at the local level;

4. The emergence of decentralized, overlapping, and diffuse patronage networks built on the basis of competition for access to and control over national and local state institutions and resources;

5. The emergence of political fixers, entrepreneurs and enforcers previously entrenched at the lower layers of the New Order's patronage network;

6. The related rise of hooligans and thugs organized in party militia, paramilitary forces and possibly Islamic *lasykar*, many of which have taken over some of the functions of the military (for example, in intimidating labor and activists);

7. The replacement of overtly authoritarian controls by money politics and political violence and intimidation at the national and local levels;

8. The renewed importance of elections, including at the local levels, especially within the still ill-defined trend toward local autonomy;

9. The contested role of the military as an institution. Relegated to the position of "bodyguard" of the regime during the late-Soeharto era (Robison 1993), parties and politicians in the post-Soeharto period have not been able altogether to ignore the interests of the military.[2] A key issue of contention is the military's so-called territorial system, the basis upon which regional and local commanders have been able to enter into business and political alliances and wield influence at those levels, as well as the principle of military involvement in business through an array of companies and foundations (e.g., in forestry).

Interestingly, though the military's reputation clearly suffered in the immediate post-Soeharto period (Bourchier 1999) due to human rights violations and the like, fears are still commonly expressed that one day the military could reassume power, perhaps with the support of middle classes craving stability. In other words, that a military-dominated political framework which characterized much of the early New Order would—in old Soekarnoist parlance—"bury the parties" for the sake of national unity. But even in such an unlikely scenario, it is clear that the military would not be able to rule with a free hand; it would be forced to deal with the range of interests which entrenched themselves during the New Order and consolidated in the immediate post-Soeharto period. It is too difficult to turn back the clock that far.

Yet another important characteristic of post-New Order Indonesia needs to be added to the above list: the absence of an effective, genuinely reformist party. Indeed, rather than being formed on the basis of distinct agendas, the major political parties are mere expressions of tactical alliances within which predatory interests dominate. The experience of much party life in Indonesia today suggests that when reformers do fight for ascendance within these political vehicles, they tend to be sidelined. A good example was the departure from PAN, the National Mandate Party, of a group of liberal reformers led by economist Faisal Basri, who had been increasingly exasperated by the manoeuvrings of party chief Amien Rais. These included embracing such well-known New Order cronies as former Cendana "treasurer" Fuad Bawazier. The latter, a former Soeharto minister, was also a key official of the many Soeharto-headed *yayasan* (foundations) which functioned to siphon public funds to associated businesses and to bankroll Golkar, the state party.

This situation is an important legacy of New Order rule, which had made it extremely difficult for reformist elements within civil society to organize coherently and effectively. Thus, there is now a notable absence in Indonesia of, for example, a labor party that could push a social democratic agenda and social justice issues, or even a genuinely liberal party, which might advance a true "rule of law" platform. These sorts of agendas, if advanced forcefully and effectively, could threaten still ascendant predatory interests by pushing for the reorganization of corrupt state institutions and the revamping of a judiciary still incapable of pursuing cases of corruption and abuse of power by state officials and politically-connected owners of business conglomerates. As it stands, a number of major New Order business conglomerates, though damaged by the Asian economic crisis, managed to escape economic catastrophe through manoeuvring out of paying gargantuan debts at the expense of the state (see Robison and Hadiz 2004, especially chapter 8). It is believed that some have quietly gone on to repurchase previously taken-over assets at cut-rate prices.

Of all the new characteristics mentioned above, the most decisive might yet be the decentralization of power from Jakarta to the regions. Many analysts are aware that the fall of Soeharto has meant the emergence of local politics and coalitions of interests as a newly important factor in Indonesian politics and society. A related issue is the government's decentralization program—designed to delegate more power and authority to local governments—the exact form of which is still intensely debated. This contest is being closely watched; the stakes, which are supremely concrete and material, are tremendously high for the range of national and local interests involved.

But no matter how the issues are resolved, one thing appears certain: much of the local political dynamics have mirrored dynamics at the national level. The local contest is typically about control over the state machinery and developing potential bases for predatory networks of patronage and protection. Again, the major contestants are local interests nurtured within the New Order's vast system of patronage, though perhaps within its lower layers. Importantly, however, some local elites—especially in resource-rich areas—may be particularly successful in carving out relatively autonomous positions in relation to Jakarta.

The Rise and Fall of Gus Dur

Though lacking legitimacy, the B.J. Habibie government that immediately succeeded Soeharto's was able to design and implement a protracted plan of political change. This involved an extraordinary session of the *Majelis Permusyawaratan Rakyat* (MPR, People's Consultative Assembly) in November 1998, fresh parliamentary elections in June 1999, and another MPR session to elect a president and vice-president later that year. But rather than being the product of benign enlightenment, the democratic reforms Habibie initiated were forced concessions. Unable to wield the kind of control Soeharto had over the institutions of the state, he was not likely to survive within the same kind of framework. His only real option was to democratize, though he probably hoped the outcome could be controlled to ensure his election to the presidency.

What thwarted Habibie's plan was a "pact of mutual protection" (here I am indeed borrowing freely from the "transitions" lexicon) among political elites aware that his re-election could stimulate widespread discontent to manifest in mass protests. As Golkar high official Marzuki Darusman assessed in the month prior to Habibie's downfall, the "parties have to be aware of the possibility of a new radical movement, or people power. So we, the parties, have to sit down and talk together, negotiate with each other" (Bourchier 2000, 30). Significantly, the political party elites—now largely directing the process of political reconstitution—were also wary of a Megawati Soekarnoputri victory, which they feared would invite a backlash from sections of organized Islam. Expressed as a form of petty-bourgeois populism, Islam was becoming, like secular nationalism, an integral part of the ideological armory of the new alliances of predatory interests.

An Abdurrahman Wahid presidency therefore emerged as a compromise, although his People's Awakening Party (PKB) received only 13 percent of the national vote. This was unimpressive compared to the showing of Megawati's Indonesian Democratic Party for Struggle (PDI-P), which won 34 percent of the national vote, or even Habibie's own Golkar, which won 21 percent.

Accounts of Wahid's unexpected rise to power in October 1999 will note the backroom wheeling and dealing, the treachery of Golkar chair Akbar Tanjung (who organized a mass desertion of Habibie) and the cunning of Muslim politician Amien Rais. It is important not to lose sight, however, of what brought together the coalition supporting Wahid—the need to safeguard the access of new party elites to the spoils of state power, which required that mass politics be at least temporarily curtailed. In other words, the pact of mutual protection that brought Wahid to power should be viewed within the wider context of the reconstitution of predatory interests within a newly democratic political format.

Not surprisingly, the first step after securing Wahid's presidency was the division of the spoils. Wahid won the presidency, while Megawati received the vice-presidency. Amien Rais of the People's Mandate Party (PAN) and Golkar leader Akbar Tanjung claimed the speaker's positions in the MPR and the Dewan Perwakilan Rakyat (DPR, People's Representative Council), respectively. The epitome of this pact of mutual protection was Wahid's so-called National Unity cabinet, in which mutually antagonistic forces were well represented.

An important outcome of the pact was the preservation of a central New Order tradition—the absence of an effective political opposition. It was not ideological disagreement with the concept of opposition itself but the opportunities presented by access to state institutions and their resources that ensured its continuing absence. These were too enticing for interests incubated by such a predatory regime to readily accept any "outsiders." Thus, underlying the alliance was the concrete, material interest in mutually ensuring access to state institutions and resources, rather than any cultural propensity to cooperate in the name of national unity or harmony, as some might be tempted to suggest.

In spite of this mutual interest, the National Unity cabinet proved tenuous and ridden with contradiction. The actual problem was an intensifying contest among different coalitions for control over strategic state institutions, which, once achieved, would enable them to carve out distinct spheres of autonomy. It should have been of little surprise that Wahid would ultimately have great difficulty exercising authority over the vast and corrupt bureaucracy, the judiciary and the military and police forces. When he tried to exercise greater control in August 2000 by appointing a cabinet of loyalists and others bereft of a political base, it only antagonized those who brought him to power.

Indeed, almost as soon as Wahid attained the presidency, his administration was characterized by intense wrangling over control of strategic institutions by the component elements of the cabinet. Among the most important prizes being contested was the Indonesian Bank Restructuring Agency (IBRA), in control of taken-over private assets worth about Rp 600 trillion and widely regarded as vulnerable to abuse of power by its officials (*Jakarta Post*, April 20, 2000). Similar competition was seen over control of a number of state-owned enterprises (*Kompas*, December 31, 1999; *Jakarta Post*, March 22, 2000).

But Wahid, the Muslim cleric, also proved to be no saint. He was implicated in a number of scandals involving the illicit use of political funds, the so-called "Buloggate" and "Bruneigate" scandals. In the first, a political war chest was filled with money siphoned from the employees' fund of the state logistics agency; the second involved receipt of an illegal "donation" from the Sultan of Brunei. Also telling were his initial attempts to protect some debt-ridden tycoons from legal prosecution (*Kompas*, October 20, 2000). These all indicated the degree to which Gus Dur himself was sucked into the logic of a system in which money politics was increasingly crucial to the outcomes of contests over power—and to political survival. The irony, and tragedy, could not have been lost to those who had pinned their hopes on Wahid the reformer.

Wahid fell in July 2001, ostensibly because of Buloggate, Bruneigate and his dismissal of the national police chief without the consent of Indonesia's parliament (Suryadinata 2001, 182–191). Earlier he had hired and fired ministers representing different political parties seemingly arbitrarily. But the real matter was always the concrete struggle over control of state institutions and resources. In a further twist, Akbar Tanjung was later accused of utilizing funds originating from the same state logistics agency, Bulog, to fund Golkar's previous election campaign. It has transpired that virtually all political parties involved in that election—one of the few exceptions being the radical left-wing People's Democratic Party (PRD)—received some of these funds. In other words, legislators who persecuted Gus Dur for his misuse of Bulog funds were most likely silent perpetrators of the same offence.

Conclusion

Indonesia is not in a political transition. A form of democracy has now been established which is characterized by money politics and thuggery and in which interests nurtured in the many layers of New Order patronage are ascendant. The essential outlines, patterns and dynamics of this system are already quite well laid out. It does not ultimately not matter much which political personality takes center stage at any given point of time, nor what kind of power broking he or she engages in to function and survive. The point is that political actors must now operate within a particular kind of political framework created by the specific nature of the social forces contesting power after the fall of Soeharto in the absence of genuine effective vehicles of reform.

The brief Wahid presidency showed how difficult it is to expect genuine, far-reaching reforms toward rule of law, accountable government, transparency and social justice within this kind of framework. Following Wahid, another politician with reformist credentials—Megawati Soekarnoputri, whom Soeharto violently attempted to expel from the political stage in 1996—holds the reins of power. Or at least she occupies the Presidential Office. Her party, the PDI-P, is well populated by former Golkar apparatchik and operators, military officers and an assortment of New Order cronies and adventurers, some of whom have been mutually antagonistic. Moreover, much attention is being directed at her husband, Taufik Kiemas, a middle-level entrepreneur in the petrol station business with apparently big-time ambitions. No wonder—the kind of democracy run by money politics and intimidation ensures that the people of Indonesia remain susceptible to the ravages of alternating gangs of predators who, ironically, have found in the democratic institutions of political parties and parliaments the ideal vehicles to protect and further their interests.

This suggests that democracy can be no less useful to rapacious, predatory interests than overtly authoritarian and anti-democratic regimes, if they are able to capture and appropriate its institutions. It also suggests flaws in theoretical approaches—currently favored by such organizations as the World Bank—that view the crafting of institutions of "good governance" as a relatively simple matter of neutral, rational decision making, or as contingent upon the cultivation and accumulation of "social capital" (Fine 2001, chs. 8 and 9), while ignoring the key ingredients of conflict, power and interests.

Epilogue

In April 2004, the second parliamentary elections of the post-Soeharto period were held, followed in July by Indonesia's first-ever direct Presidential elections. The parliamentary elections delivered a huge blow to the PDI-P, whose share of the vote fell to only 18.5 per cent from its previous 34 per cent, leaving it in second place to a revitalized Golkar (more or less constant at about 21.5 per cent of the vote). The incumbency of Megawati Soekarnoputri was severely under threat—her main challengers for the Presidency being General Wiranto, the official Golkar candidate, and yet another general, the newly popular Susilo Bambang Yudhoyono. The latter had successfully latched onto a newly formed entity—the Democratic Party—and turned it into a successful electoral vehicle. While Wiranto personified the military in its function as the bodyguard of the New Order oligarchy—serving as Soeharto's adjutant as well as defence minister and commander of the Armed Forces—Yudhoyono is regarded as an "intellectual" general, who held such key positions as military chief of political affairs in the late-Soeharto period before serving in both the Gus Dur and Megawati cabinets. After the first round of voting in July, Megawati and Yudhoyono were left standing; in the runoff election in September, Yudhoyono won with over 60 percent of the vote.

The victory of Golkar, the emergence of two generals as major presidential hopefuls and the electoral victory of Yudhoyono indicate at least two things: first, the disenchantment of many Indonesians with the unfulfilled promise of *reformasi*—including the performance of the ineffective and corruption-ridden governments of Gus Dur and Megawati; second, a certain nostalgia for the "orderliness" and predictability of the

New Order, which is now "remembered" by some as guaranteeing a period of relative economic prosperity (a memory which entails conveniently "forgetting" that Indonesia's on-going economic troubles are the product of the rapacity of the New Order, especially its late period).

On the one hand, these developments underline the resilience of the old New Order forces—best symbolized by Golkar and the military. On the other hand, they underscore the necessity of even those at the core of the old centralized authoritarianism to adapt to the requirements of electoral politics. Even as a general captures the presidency of post-authoritarian Indonesia, the military-as-institution will still be required to deal with the new realities of a democratized society in which power is diffuse and decentralized.

Notes

1 On New Order labor controls, see, among others, Hadiz 1997.

2 During the late New Order era, Soeharto decided key military appointments in such a way that former adjutants and loyalists were on the fast track to promotion. This rattled many who attempted to preserve the autonomy of the military institution, including the feared General Benny Moerdani.

References

Arghiros, Daniel. 2001. *Democracy, Development and Decentralization in Provincial Thailand.* Richmond: Curzon.

Bellin, Eva. 2001. Contingent democrats: Industrialists, labor and democratization in late-developing countries. *World Politics* (January): 175–205.

Bourchier, David. 1999. Skeletons, vigilantes, and the armed forces' fall from grace. In *Reformasi: Crisis and Change in Indonesia*, ed. Arief Budiman, Barbara Hatley, and Damien Kingsbury, 149–171. Melbourne: Monash Asia Institute, Monash University.

Bourchier, David. 2000. Habibie's interregnum: *Reformasi*, elections, regionalism and the struggle for power. In *Indonesia in Transition: Social Aspects of Reformasi and Crisis*, ed. Chris Manning and Peter Van Diermen, 15–37. Singapore: Institute of Southeast Asian Studies.

Budiman, Arief. 1999. The 1998 crisis: Change and continuity in Indonesia.

In *Reformasi: Crisis and Change in Indonesia*, ed. Arief Budiman, Barbara Hatley, and Damien Kingsbury, 41–58. Melbourne: Monash Asia Institute, Monash University.

Budiman, Arief, and Damien Kingsbury, eds. 2002. *Indonesia: The Uncertain Transition*. Adelaide: Crawford House Publications and C. Hurst and Company.

Caldwell, Malcolm, ed. 1975. *Ten Years' Military Terror in Indonesia*. Nottingham: Spokesman Books.

Fine, Ben. 2001. *Social Capital versus Social Theory: Political Economy and Social Science at the Turn of the Millennium*. London: Routledge.

Hadiz, Vedi R. 1997. *Workers and the State in New Order Indonesia*. London: Routledge.

Hadiz, Vedi R. 2000. Retrieving the past for the future? Indonesia and the New Order legacy. *Southeast Asian Journal of Social Science* 28, no. 2: 10–33.

Hadiz, Vedi R. 2001. Capitalism, oligarchic power and the state in Indonesia. *Historical Materialism* 8: 117–149.

Jackson, Karl. 1978. Bureaucratic polity: A theoretical framework for the analysis of power and communications in Indonesia. In *Political Power and Communications in Indonesia*, ed. Karl Jackson and Lucien W. Pye. Berkeley: University of California Press.

Manning, Chris, and Peter Van Diermen, eds. 2001. *Indonesia in Transition: Social Aspects of Reformasi and Crisis*. Singapore: Institute of Southeast Asian Studies.

Marx, Karl and Friedrich Engels. 1998. The Communist manifesto. In *The Communist Manifesto Now: Socialist Register 1998*, ed. Leo Panitch and Colin Leys. New York: Monthly Review Press.

O'Donnell, Guillermo, and Philippe C. Schmitter. 1986. *Transitions from Authoritarian Rule: Tentative Conclusions about Uncertain Democracies*. Baltimore: The Johns Hopkins University Press.

Robison, Richard. 1993. Indonesia: Tensions in state and regime. In *Southeast Asia in the 1990s: Authoritarianism, Democracy, and Capitalism*, ed. Kevin Hewison, Richard Robison, and Garry Rodan. St Leonards: Allen and Unwin.

Robison, Richard, and Andrew Rosser. 2000. Surviving the meltdown: Liberal reform and political oligarchy in Indonesia. In *Politics and Markets in the Wake of the Asian Crisis*, ed. Richard Robison, Mark Beeson, Kanishka Jayasuriya, and Hyuk-Rae Kim, 171–191. London: Routledge.

Robison, Richard, and Vedi R. Hadiz. 2004. *Reorganising Power in*

Indonesia: The Politics of Oligarchy in An Age of Markets. London: RoutledgeCurzon.

Sidel, John. 1999. *Capital, Coercion and Crime: Bossism in the Philippines.* Stanford: Stanford University Press.

Sundhaussen, Ulf. 1994. The inner contraction of the Soeharto regime: A starting point for a withdrawal to the barracks. In *Democracy in Indonesia 1950s and 1990s,* ed. David Bourchier and John Legge. Melbourne: Centre of Southeast Asian Studies, Monash University.

Suryadinata, Leo. 2001. *Elections and Politics in Indonesia.* Singapore: Institute of Southeast Asian Studies.

Van Dijk, Kees. 2001. *A Country in Despair: Indonesia Between 1997–2000.* Leiden: KITLV Press.

Van Klinken, Gerry. 1999. How a democratic deal might be struck. In *Reformasi: Crisis and Change in Indonesia,* 59–67. Melbourne: Monash Asia Institute, Monash University.

7

Governing the Philippines in the Early 21st Century

Patricio N. Abinales

In early October 2000, a longtime crony, gambling partner and drinking companion of Philippine President Joseph Estrada, Ilocos Sur governor Luis "Chavit" Singson, revealed that he personally delivered a total of USD 8 million in illegal gambling money to the president over a 21-month period, plus an additional USD 2.5 million as the president's "cut" of the tobacco excise taxes allotted to his province (*Philippine Post*, October 11, 2000). This disclosure led to the impeachment of Estrada, the first Philippine president to be subjected to this process, and the mobilization of an anti-Estrada "movement" (*Philippine Daily Inquirer* [hereafter *PDI*], November 14, 2000). This conflict eventually led to the ouster of Estrada and the ascension to the presidency of Gloria Macapagal Arroyo. The latest in a series of political crises hitting the Philippines, Estrada's downfall brought to the fore the shortcomings of a new way of governing the country. I refer to the increasing use of alliance-based arrangements in support of candidates running for the presidency. These coalitions bring together forces from the left, right and center, which, in the event of victory, are apportioned their share of state agencies to run as they see fit.

The origin of this political pattern is fairly recent and can be traced back to efforts to form a coherent opposition to the Marcos dictatorship in the early 1980s. After the fall of Marcos, forces associated with the ousted dictator also ensured their survival in the post-Marcos era by taking part in such coalitional arrangements. Finally, the split in the communist movement and the integration of social democratic formations into post-Marcos governments led some members of the Left to join these alliances. Thus, in the early 21st century, coalition politics had become the convention in governing the country, participated in by practically all actors, groups and movements. Under political leaders capable of balancing the interests of these disparate forces, coalition politics benefited governing considerably.

Political stability through coalition-governing can be reinforced by what policy makers refer to as "sound economic fundamentals," activities in the national economy that mitigate a drain in resources due to corruption, mismanagement and other forms of patrimonial plunder. Such was the case in the last year in office of President Aquino and during most of the term of her successor, Fidel Ramos. But the marriage between coalition politics and stable governing also demonstrated its limits. Under less than competent leadership, a coalition can unravel and affect the ability of a regime to govern. Or, as appears to have happened under President Estrada, the coalition may survive at the expense of effective governing. It is therefore not enough to focus "personalistic" styles of leadership; we must also look at the nature of coalition politics itself and how it has affected governing in the post-Marcos Philippines.

The Institutionalization of Coalition Politics

The popular description of the ascension of Corazon Aquino to power as a successful case of non-violent action often glosses over a fundamental feature of 1986: because "People Power" was nonviolent, it never swept away the old order and replaced it with a new one. Not merely transitory, this Gramscian dilemma became a more-or-less permanent feature of post-Marcos politics, a malformed mixture of forces identified with the dictatorship and with its opponents (Elwood 1986). While Marcos was decisively ousted, his allies were never completely disempowered (Nemenzo 1988; *Kudeta* 1990). Instead, an extremely legalistic Aquino government tried to weaken their influence and power through the electoral process and the court system, on the assumption that popular animosity and legal inquiry would expose their unscrupulous character. These constitutionalist weapons hardly dented the forces of the Old Order. Former Marcos allies made use of the electoral process to revive their political bases at the provincial and regional level and took advantage of the deliberate and cumbersome procedures of the court system to slow down the government's quest for restitution. By the end of Aquino's term as president, Marcos forces were confident enough that even Imelda Marcos and her family could return home to run for public office.

The survival of the Marcos forces, however, was only one outcome of the peaceful transfer of power in 1986. Another was the re-appearance of anti-Marcos caciques who had been marginalized by dictatorship and the revolutionary opposition alike during most of the 1970s. The Aquino-led moderate opposition breathed new life into this group as it sought to create a national network to challenge Marcos. Aquino's people saw in the caciques necessary connections to the provincial and local levels, while they saw in Aquino a popular symbol who could strengthen their political comeback within their respective locales (Thompson 1995, 96–180). There were instances of anti-Marcos politicians imagining themselves as democrats, but in most cases their support for Aquino was a marriage of convenience—a tactical alliance that did not preclude them reaching out to Aquino's sworn enemies, the Marcos forces. One year after the ouster of Marcos, new coalitions involving erstwhile political enemies were born, prompting one political scientist to complain that the norms of the country's political elite were "ambiguous, inconsistent and opportunistic," adding that it was no surprise that "influenced by them, the nation at large seems to have a weak sense of right and wrong" (Abueva 1997, 25; see also Mojares 1993, 312).

At the local level, something comparable was taking place; "bosses," warlords, strongmen and political clans were the conspicuous symbols of the cacique restoration (Kerklviet and Mojares 1991). Here, the structure of the post-Marcos regime played a vital role in facilitating the return of these conservative forces. A 1991 local government code devolved certain powers previously held by the national government to the local, including the right to raise revenues and engage in business transactions with the private sector (Brilliantes 1997, 83–86). Allocations from the tax collection of the Bureau of Internal Revenue were also transferred to local governments. These measures helped many political clans consolidate control over their regions and provinces, especially when they had allies in the national center.[1] The shift of resources also created more intricate webs of corruption among officials permeating throughout the provinces, cities and municipalities (Gutierrez 1998; Parreño 1998, 45–47). By the time Fidel Ramos succeeded Aquino, these "rent-seeking" activities had become pervasive, resorted to even by the family of the new president himself (Florentino-Hofileña 1995; Weissman 1994).

Yet, the EDSA "revolution" also brought onto political center stage the various social movements which supported Aquino and which constituted the "left wing" of her coalition. Many of the leaders of these movements were recruited into the state agencies most responsible for social welfare and popular "empowerment" (Boudreau 1996). Others rode the popularity of Aquino and their ties with social movements to electoral office (Valencia 1993). Where they were most effective, however, was in putting their ideological and even philosophical mark on the new order. The 1987 constitution contains provisions promoting social justice and human rights, the role of women and youth in nation building, and the inclusion of party-list representatives in legislative elections (Diokno 1995, 92). Most important of all, the Constitution legitimizes the role of "people's organizations" (POs), defining these as "associations of citizens with demonstrated capacity to promote the public interest and with identifiable leadership, membership and structure."[2] Thus not only have these movements become part of governing, their discourse has become part of the language of state.

The split in the Communist Party of the Philippines (CPP) increased the ranks of the "pro-people forces" as cadres expelled by the Maoist faction in power reintegrated themselves to the political mainstream (Rocamora 1994, 107–138). Some joined electoral parties or organized autonomous social movements, while others founded non-governmental organizations (NGOs) to lobby for and act as social pressure on behalf of the dispossessed (Tigno 1997, 119). In short, NGOs, POs and the state found the proper mix to make programs work (Soriano 1993). In agrarian reform, for example, "social movements from below" combined with "reformist initiatives from above" to successfully implement land-to-the-tiller programs (Borras 1999, 61–70). In urban areas, where PO-NGO collaboration has had a long history, "popular forces" have successfully compelled local government officials to implement social welfare programs like public housing for the poor or land rights for urban poor communities (Angeles 1997). It was due to their lobbying that Congress passed the Local Government Code of 1991 devolving planning, regulation and revenue powers to the local governments, as well as the Urban Development and Housing Act, which legally recognized the rights of the urban poor, many of whom were "informal settlers" (Shatkin 1999: 34–35).

In electoral politics, NGOs and POs have availed themselves of a party list law to elect candidates to the House of Representatives to push for "pro-people" legislation and to challenge the dominance of "traditional" politics.[3] At the local level, clan power had been forced either to contend or cooperate with NGOs and POs, thereby putting a break—albeit limited—on their rent-seeking activities (*PDI*, April 18, May 20, 2000). The most effective tactic employed by these popular movements appears to be simply overwhelming local politicians and officials with their numbers (Tigno 1997, 124). The legal support for people's organizations further reinforced this popular presence by putting what one scholar calls "the legal infrastructure for the participation of nongovernmental organizations (NGOs) and people's organizations (POs) in the process of governance by making their membership in local special bodies mandatory" (Franco 1997, 292, 294–95, 347). As a result, candidates backed by these popular forces have won congressional seats despite strong resistance from local strongmen. During the Aquino period, anti-Marcos politicians lacking strong patronage networks were likewise able to win congressional seats by forming coalitions with many parties and POs (ibid., 319–20, 338–43). NGO and PO participation in "local governance" rose dramatically in the early 1990s, reshaping the political direction of many local governments, including those previously thought to be under cacique control.

Finally, while politicos continue to hold the upper hand by virtue of their control of government resources and rent-seeking actives, the NGOs and POs were not without their own sources of largesse. Funding agencies from the industrialized countries have been generous donors, providing NGOs and POs with the ability not only to pursue their populist projects but also to challenge and compete against cacique power. In 1986 alone, for example, NGOs in the Philippines received over USD 3.38 billion from the United States, Britain, Australia, Germany and Japan (Tigno 1997, 121). The Canadian International Development Agency (CIDA) likewise supported Philippine NGO projects amounting to CAD 46 million from 1987 to the early 1990s, while the Asian Development Bank poured 57.2 million pesos into the NGO sector in 1997 (Asian Development Bank 1998, 5).

All this prompted considerable optimism about the role of NGOs and POs, with one scholar proclaiming enthusiastically that a "quiet revolution is going on in the countryside proving that devolution is working. Though not as widely publicized it may be asserted that due to the increased powers and responsibilities of local governments, innovativeness and creativity at the local level was engendered by the Code. Not only were local governments taking up the challenge of devolution. Non-governmental organizations (NGOs) and people's organizations (POs) as well have been encouraged by the Code to be active participants in the process of governance at the local level" (Brillantes 1997, 93–95, 110–113; see also de la Rosa 1999). Another argued that these forces have "strengthened the state in small yet significant ways, helping it to attack entrenched socio-economic elite interests and helping the state to attract broad-based popular support for local and economic reform" (Clarke 1998, xvii).

With electoral politics the sole arena in which to pursue programs and interests, it was perhaps inevitable that the erstwhile protagonists, cacique and popular forces, would continue the practice they forged in the last days of Marcos—establishing alliances to win votes. For the NGOs and POs, especially those led by ex-CPP cadres, such coalitions offer the opportunity to hone their skills in once-hated "parliamentary politics" (de la Torre and Morales 1986; Ciria-Cruz 1992). For caciques, the mobilizing power of the NGOs and POs was a useful asset at a time when the traditional two-political party structure was replaced by a multi-party coalition-based system. The language of popular organizing was also an eye-opener for the politicians, introducing them to new ways of popular mobilization and adding to their traditional use of pork barrel and other largesse to gain votes and cement loyalties.

Reinforcing this *modus vivendi* was the surprising and steady decline of "factional election violence" in much of the post-Marcos period. A survey showed that after 1986, this type of violence declined due to the efforts of the Catholic Church to keep elections clean, as well as the steady withdrawal of the military from politics (see Table 7-1). This portrait may be too optimistic, yet it does suggest that the opportunity for long-term political equilibrium exists. While election fraud and violence still occur at the local level, especially in warlord-dominated areas, the kind of widespread fraud and violence characteristic of the Marcos era appears to be receding into the past. The hope is that national stability will trickle down to the local level with the institutionalization of the Church as election "watchdog" and the return of the military to the barracks. Conditions, however, remain fluid. An indication of how easily things can regress is the figures on political violence for 1998, the year Estrada was

Table 7-1. Violent Incidents and Deaths during Election Campaign Periods, 1965–98

Year	Type of Election	Violent Incidents	Deaths
1965	President, congress	69	47
1967	Senate, provincial	192	78
1969	President, congress	59	52
1971	Senate, provincial	534	905
1978	Congress	9	n.a.
1980	Provincial	180	71
1981	President	178	102
1984	Congress	918	154
1986	President	296	153
1987	Congress	48	50
1988	Provincial	127	98
1992	Synchronized	87	60
1995	Congress	97	73
1998	Synchronized	188	42
Total		2,982	1,959

Source: John Linantud, 1998, 300.

popularly elected to the presidency, which show a return to 1981–82 levels. Still, the May 1998 polls were hailed as "the most peaceful elections ever" (*Far Eastern Economic Review 1999 Yearbook*, 184).

This sanguine portrait must also be tempered by acknowledgement of structural limitations and the realities of political power. The decentralization of national power exposed the uneven ability of local governments to raise funds for their own operation, much less for the implementation of social welfare schemes (Shatkin 1999, 43). NGOs and POs must also contend with the power of the political clans in close alliance with their respective private sectors (Silliman and Noble 1999). And in certain cases, the temptation of local power and the opportunity of *becoming* a cacique hounded NGO and PO leaders (Gloria 1995). These limitations notwithstanding, it is a reality that NGOs and POs are now part of the political landscape.

The Practice of Coalition Politics

President Aquino was the first to try to govern via coalitions. Her "yellow revolutionaries" came from various shades of the political spectrum. The addition of the colonels of the Reform the Armed Forces of the Philippines Movement (RAM) further broadened the coalition, and Aquino came to power with a fuzzy center constantly pressured by two extremes. Because of the circumstances behind her rise to power, the Aquino coalition proved fragile and unsteady (Aquino 1990; Dahm 1991; University of the Philippines 1992–1999; Abueva and Roman 1993; Reid and Guerrero 1995). Fidel V. Ramos was more adept at coalition governing. Ramos was a joint candidate of the Lakas ng Bayan (LAKAS), a party formed to support Corazon Aquino in 1986, and the small National Union of Christian Democrats (NUCD). Lakas attracted the politicians who constituted Ramos's cacique flank while NUCD became the umbrella organization for NGOs and POs associated with the social democratic movement, with resources ensured by European linkages. Finally there were the business elites who supported Ramos for his "professionalism" and commitment to reforms. Backed by this atypical alliance, appropriating the language of the popular movements and with Aquino's "blessings," Ramos won the elections by a slim plurality (23 percent). He then proceeded to implement major economic reforms to free the market—deregulating the airline, telecommunications, banking and oil industries, privatizing the government-owned Manila Waterworks and Sewage System and, with the help of Congress, passing major health and housing welfare laws (Hutchcroft 1996).

In a decentralized constitutional system, however, reforms must rely on the cooperation of local and provincial officials who, after all, pass the laws and govern much of the country. Because his leftwing was miniscule, Ramos relied more on his cacique flank to push his projects (Boudreau 1993). Thus, despite his image as a reformist, Ramos was very much embedded in the cacique's world. Stories of pathbreaking reform stood alongside exposés of the use of pork barrel in exchange for legislative support. Ramos was also accused of turning a blind eye to sensational cases of corruption involving his closest advisers and allies ((Tordesillas and Coronel 1998; Coronel 2000b). Ramos' image as a military professional also suffered from waves of kidnap-for-ransom cases and when a Senate investigation indicted his political party for allegedly accepting a bribe of 2 billion pesos for a Manila Bay reclamation contract (*FEER 1998 Yearbook*, 185). Under Ramos, pork barrel allocations for legislatures "reached unprecedented proportions through congressional insertions shared by both administration and opposition parties in Congress" (de Dios 1999, 142–46). They unleashed "vast opportunities for corruption by many congressmen believed to be skimming off percentages from these allocations from suppliers, brokers, and all other sorts of individuals eager for a piece of the financial pie" (Gutierrez 1998, 59).

By the time Ramos left office, the deficit had reached P24.5 million, "in large part because of a budget bloated by a P54 billion allocation for pork barrel funds—a 189 percent increase from the 1997 pork barrel of P19 billion" (Gutierrez 1998, 61).[4] The government's plight worsened when the 1997 Asian economic crisis hit the country (*FEER 1998 Yearbook*, 7–10; Weissman 1994). Real GDP plummeted to −0.5 percent in 1998, reserves were reduced to USD 9 billion, over USD 3 billion left the country in the first four months of 1999) and unemployment rose from 7.7 percent in the first three months of 1997 to 10.6 percent in June 1999 (*FEER 1998 Yearbook*, 187). It was on the subsequent widespread disenchantment with Ramos that Joseph Estrada would launch his presidency.

If Ramos appropriated populist terms like "new politics," Estrada took from the Left its most popular word—*masa* (masses)—to reinforce his status as a movie star (*Asiaweek*, April 10, 1998). Business remained skeptical, despite his stated commitment to the deregulation and privatization programs, but its cynicism was offset by his appeal to the masses (Tanzer 2000). The coalition that formed around his presidential campaign was also much broader than that of Ramos. It brought together top Marcos cronies Eduardo Cojuangco, Jr., and Lucio Tan, alongside politicians, academics and former radicals of the communist movement. And these extreme flanks were much more powerful now—the cronies with their still unexpropriated billions, the radicals with a depth of organizing experience from the communist movement.

These factions were drawn to Estrada on the basis of friendship and opportunism. Academics who joined the campaign were attracted to the possibility of influencing policy on the assumption that the candidate knew little about governing. Many on the Left believed that he "was really for the people" (*FEER 1999 Yearbook*, 185). One sympathizer of the Left wrote that he "rooted for Estrada" because he disliked the elitism of Aquino and Ramos and their pretension of saving the nation though "nothing has been fundamentally changed in the past decades in the country's pro-rich economic structure" (*Sunday Times Inquirer*, October 29, 2000). A former CPP cadre justified his joining the Estrada campaign staff in these terms: "[The] key question is, is there a section of the political clans that the popular progressive movement can influence? This is the alternative to perpetual horizontal work or waiting for the new dawning of the new revolutionary elite" (Reid 2000, 75).

Estrada won the presidency by a comfortable plurality. In power, the new president's cabinet mirrored his diverse coalition, though he was seen to favor his cronies and friends (*FEER 1999 Yearbook*, 185–86). After a year in office, Estrada's popularity dropped significantly as reports of cronyism, factional infighting, feuds with the media, the apparent failure of his anti-corruption drive and the slow implementation of his anti-poverty programs increased public cynicism (*FEER*, August 26, 1999). A scandal in the stock market involving a presidential crony and Estrada's attempt to pressure officials at the Security and Exchange Commission to clear his friend reinforced the suggestion that practices associated with the Marcos dictatorship had returned (*Political Brief* 2000: 23–24).

Yet the government was not really a close approximation of the past dictatorship. Estrada's cronyism seemed to lack the same devastating impact of Marcos's. With the exception of two, his cronies were "engaged only in small or nonmainstream business." His families' wealth grew considerably after he became president, but most of their businesses were not in primary sectors and did not have the effect on the economy that the businesses of the Marcos family did (Coronel 2000a). And while Estrada still valued his friendships, he appeared to heed criticism, distancing himself from his cronies and trying to act more presidential (*Asiaweek*, February 18, 2000). Neither did he reverse the reformist course of his predecessor (Tanzer 2000, 3). A year into his presidency, Estrada tried to project an image of greater decisiveness. He dispelled the image of weakness by ordering the destruction of the Moro Islamic Liberation Front (MILF) camps and the takeover of Jolo island to destroy the Abu Sayyaf.[5] This military resolve briefly took the edge off relentless stories of cronyism, corruption and even insensitivity to his wife.[6] Most significantly, Estrada allowed his cabinet officials considerable autonomy in running their offices, intervening only in cases of "major developments" or "matters pertaining to the national interest" (FEER, June 17, 1999). Estrada had become "a savvy politician who governs through personal connections, a disdain for formality and, perhaps most surprising, some sophisticated cunning. They say that Estrada, by soliciting a wide range of opinions, manipulating powerful officials and tapping loyalists placed throughout the government, had found a way to get things done. In short: there's method in the madness. And it's keeping the government in working order" (FEER, April 15, 1999).

Granted their own spheres to operate, the various factions of the coalition pursued inconsistent policies and programs but to positive effect. And critics of Estrada conceded that sections of the government functioned well and delivered the goods.[7] Certain agencies of the government, some of which were under the management of ex-leftists, popular activists and academics, were thus compensating for the erratic leadership at the top. Except for its failure to deal with the Abu Sayyaf, the military had a more professional, less politicized officer corps (Ciron 1993). The effectiveness of the police force also improved by the appointment of a no-nonsense director who, together with Estrada, is credited with a sharp drop in kidnappings of businessmen (Tanzer 2000, 3).

Agrarian reform was another area in which government programs were working. Despite fierce resistance from landlords, the department managed to implement some land transfers and deal with rural poverty, thanks largely to the skill of its head, Leftist Horacio Morales, in getting different groups and sectors to work together (Morales 1999; The Philippine Post, October 10, 2000). In his two years in office, Morales irrigated more hectares of farmlands than his counterparts in the Aquino and Ramos administrations. This he managed to do by tapping "hundreds of millions of ODAs [overseas development aid]" with the help of the agrarian reform community (PDI, November 21, 2000). Another former radical, Leonor Briones, director of the Bureau of Treasury, was credited with bringing down interest rates and keeping these at levels beneficial to the middle class (PDI, October 30, 1999; Margie Quimpo- PDI, January

17, 2000). There were also reports of marked improvement in the Bureau of Immigration and the Civil Service Commission, two agencies hitherto notorious for inefficiency and massive corruption.[8] The government had become a "Jekyll and Hyde" character, where sometimes appalling governing practices (especially Estrada's) were offset by many respectable performances (Lozada 1998).

Complementing these "isles of efficiency" was an economy which, while still performing below expectations, had "sloughed off the 'sick man of Asia' label that had dogged it throughout the 1980s" (Asia Society and Asian Development Bank 1998). Estrada came to power at time when the economy showed signs of recovery. The Asian Development Bank wrote in its 1999 year-end report that GDP and GNP experienced positive growth, rising by 1.2 percent and 2.2 percent respectively in the first quarter of 1999. Agriculture contributed substantially to the recovery, "with a turnaround real growth rate of 2.5 percent against a drop of 3.8 percent in the same quarter last year" (Fabella 1999, 165). In 1999, the trade deficit also turned into a USD 4 billion surplus, resulting primarily from a 20 percent rise in exports, and the country's international reserves rose to nearly USD 15 billion, with new monies coming from a two-year IMF standby facility and bond financing on the international capital market (Asian Development Bank 2000, 108).

It helped, of course, that of all the economies in the region, the Philippines was the least affected by the Asian crisis. Having experienced a series of financial crises in the two decades before, the Philippine economy was not experiencing the same pattern of expansion and lending as others.[9] Prudent financial management by "risk-averse" policy-makers and its "underweighted" ranking by international fund managers were crucial in providing the Philippines with this "advantage" (Noland 2000, 5; Asia Society and Asian Development Bank 1998, 1). The country's ability to ride out the crisis was fortified further by its steady revenue base. One important "lifesaver" was the roughly USD 6 billion in remittances sent back to the country by the end of 1999 by over 5 million Filipinos working overseas (*FEER 2000 Yearbook*, 187; Coronel 1998, 64).

The other was the country's good export performance, especially in computers and electronics, which netted a return of USD 19 billion in the first year of Estrada's administration, a jump of 18.9 percent over the previous year (*PDI*, October 22, 1999; *PDI*, May 11, 2000). Electronics, in particular, have become the country's best revenue earner, constituting 62 percent of exports in 2000 (*PDI*, October 9, 2000). The Philippines had "quietly" become "the hottest site for chip assembly" with some fifty microchip assemblers and computer component manufacturers investing about USD 6.6 billion to tap a highly-skilled, low-priced labor force. Government incentives to privately-managed economic zones were quite attractive, including four-year exemptions from corporate tax (of 32 percent) with eight-year extensions, duty-free importation of equipment and exemption from export taxes. The entry of technology firms had, in turn, attracted companies providing support to these firms to establish their own assembly plants in the zones. The rise in exports was accompanied by increased employment for Filipinos (*FEER*, July 15, 1999). And high exports also allowed the central bank to build up reserves to "a record high" (*FEER 2000 Yearbook*, 187). All this led some observers to suggest that the Philippines' role in promoting information technology in Asia with its skilled, English-speaking labor force had more than offset the impact of the crisis. One analyst argued that including "intellectual input"—a "high value component" resulting from programs developed in developing economies—in GDP measurement would enable one to describe the Philippines as having a "new economy" (*Team Asia*, June 6, 2000: 3–4). The World Bank also declared the country as having "one of the world's most technologically advanced export structures" (*FEER*, July 15, 1999).

Both these factors—"isles of state efficiency" and a moderately "stable" economy—enabled the Estrada administration to cope with the lingering effects of the Asian crisis and withstand unremitting criticism of its leadership style (*FEER 2000 Yearbook*, 184–186). Yet it remained a "weak state," not, as one analyst puts it, a "model of economic rectitude," and many of its economic problems were "home grown" (Noland 2000, 5). Economic rebound was hampered by poor infrastructure and persistent corruption and mismanagement. The government "failed to capitalize on its relatively strong performance": as the Estrada government faced one financial scandal after another, Congress sat on the next series of economic reforms.[10] Most important of all, the latest events have shown the contradictions between coalition politics and governing, especially in relation to the economic crisis.

Crisis, Coalitions and Governance

The political gains Estrada registered in the first three quarters of 2000 were negated by the military's failure to deal decisively with its Islamic adversaries; this also took its toll on government coffers (*PDI*,

October 11, 2000). Unofficial estimates of the daily cost of war ranged from $500,000 to $2.3 million, forcing budget officials to divert monies from other programs to support the military (*Asiaweek*, June 2, 2000). Aggravating the government's woes were pervasive corruption and the persistence of cronyism. The World Bank called corruption in government "a factor that inhibits foreign and domestic investment and which may be eroding the country's competitive position" (Bhargava 1999, 1) Estrada himself admitted that 20 percent of funds allotted for government projects (roughly 24.13 billion pesos) were "lost to grafters," while the Office of the Ombudsman, the government watchdog, countered with its own estimate of 100 million pesos lost everyday to graft (*PDI*, July 10, 1999 and July 26, 2000).

Finally, drug trafficking and illegal gambling have become major economic activities at the expense of legitimate business ventures. Brisk smuggling and sale of crystal meta-amphetamine (*shabu*) generated about 250 million pesos for sales of 250 kilos per month by Filipino partners of Hong Kong syndicates (*PDI*, October 1, 2000). *Jueteng* (illegal gambling), however, was the centerpiece of the informal economy. A nationwide and popular operation based on betting on a combination of numbers, jueteng can net a local town "operator" as much as 1.2 million pesos and his provincial bosses 4.8 million pesos monthly.[11] Its profitability spawned a complex network of alliances between operators, politicians and law enforcement agencies from the national down to the village level. Politicians' campaign coffers and poorly-paid military officers alike came to depend on jueteng money. Very few passed up the chance to convert a 1 peso bet into a 400 peso winning.[12] It was no wonder, therefore, that a national leader wishing always to be resource-ready would dip into this large pool of money. Because the jueteng network was national, however, any crack in its highly centralized and well-protected structure could have serious national implications. Singson went public after Estrada set up a bingo network run by his own people to rival the jueteng organization and eat into its profits. In the ensuing fight, the presidency unraveled.

The jueteng controversy galvanized a broad anti-Estrada coalition that included the conservative Church and business sectors, "traditional" politicians belonging to the opposition parties, NGOs, middle class associations and different factions of the radical left. Estrada, however, was not without his supporters. The core of his alliance—the former Marcos cronies, provincial and town officials enriched by internal revenue allocations, Christian fundamentalist groups and former communists in his government—remained steadfast behind him (*PDI Sunday Magazine*,

November 19, 2000). What was remarkable about this confrontation was not so much its ferocity but the fact that both Estrada and his opponents relied on coalitions to project their power.

Coalitions did not make governance more effective, however. On the contrary, Estrada's image as the godfather of illegal gambling and the business community's open repudiation of his leadership virtually erased the prudent fiscal and economic policy that his economic managers had pursued. The economy entered a profound crisis as the peso lost over 22 percent of its value from the beginning of the year (*PDI*, October 16 and 31, 2000). Foreign capital avoided the country, and investments declined by 20 percent (*PDI*, October 18, 2000). The battle lines were drawn as Senate impeachment hearings headed into a crucial phase. But when pro-Estrada senators successfully blocked an attempt to open a crucial piece of evidence implicating the president, the battle shifted to the streets where anti-Estrada forces called for People Power II to force the president to resign. More than one million Filipinos returned to EDSA, led by a loose coalition of anti-Estrada politicians, the Catholic Church, the forces associated with People Power I and a wiser CPP. Estrada forces also began to mobilize to protect their president. The confrontation, however, never happened for the military leadership decided to force Estrada to resign (*FEER*, February 15, 2001). Vice-president Gloria Arroyo was sworn in as the new president and she soon ordered Estrada arrested on corruption charges.

The Quest for a "Strong Republic"

Estrada's arrest sparked a small uprising by his followers, dubbed People Power III. While easily squelched by the military, this "poor people's power" laid bare the worsening class contradiction in Philippine society (Doronila 2001, 254). Political battles after the Estrada period became more vicious, dividing parties, NGOs and POs and other civil society groups. Moreover, three uprisings, six coup attempts and "cacique democracy" had put enormous strain on the political system. In light of the polarizing consequences of Estrada's ouster, observers began to warn that "People Power as a method of political change and of ousting leaders...has made Filipino democracy volatile, unstable, and unpredictable. More dangerously, it has brought Philippine democracy to the edge of mob rule, even if exercised in the name of social change" (Doronila 2001, 256). It had taken a toll on the state's ability to govern "normally": administrative routines were repeatedly interrupted, offices experienced internal turmoil and frequent regime change made strategic policy planning uncertain. The dilemma that post-Marcos governments face—which became starkly apparent in the Estrada years—was how to strengthen the country's democratic foundations and govern effectively, given the fragile economy that has bred increasing class conflict.

This was the problem Arroyo faced upon her ascension to the presidency. While she promised a far different government from Estrada's, Arroyo spent her first year overcoming the trauma of People Power III and bolstering her legitimacy amid ongoing economic crisis as the coalition that brought her to power unraveled (*PDI*, October 16 and 18, 2000). There were criticisms as well that Arroyo was too dependent on the military.

As it turned out, the state did survive Estrada. Corruption may have worsened, but several state agencies continued to function reasonably well. The rise of a more professional cadre of municipal officials, city mayors and provincial governors, and the influence of intelligent, politically savvy and strategically minded "young turks" in the legislature also made their presence felt (*Newsbreak*, January 6/20, 2003: 16–18; 24–26). The state continued to display a Jekyll and Hyde character, where sometimes appalling governing practices were offset by many respectable performances (Lozada 1998: 1–4). Arroyo did nothing to alter this practice, but then her options were much more limited than her predecessors'. The economic slump persisted and unemployment remained high. The resurgence of communist rebellion and the Abu Sayyaf's kidnapping of tourists in Bornean and Philippine resorts indicated that consolidation might be fleeting. At the same time, Congress obstructed the implementation of the president's economic recovery agenda. In her second year, Arroyo responded by declaring her dedication to building a "Strong Republic." Unfortunately, this message was interpreted by the nationalist Left as an attempt to return to the Marcos era. Her communist opponents had a field day attacking her "Marcosian" intentions. Her support for the United States' "war on terror" allowed American troops back onto Philippine soil to work closely with Filipino soldiers in pursuit of the Abu Sayyaf—the first time since the 1992 withdrawal of US forces—providing yet more cannon fodder for her opponents. According to her critics, Arroyo was becoming "militaristic" and was returning to the days of Philippine servility to American strategic interests.

With her standing in the polls at an all-time low, Arroyo surprised everyone by announcing in January 2003 her withdrawal from the 2004 presidential race. She vowed to devote her remaining months in power to building the substance of a "Strong Republic," but by mid-2003, there were no signs she was succeeding. In the meantime, a rejuvenated communist movement continued to consolidate its presence in civil society politics by assassinating former cadres who were seen as organizational threats to its network.

Conclusion

This essay examined how coalitions became the foundation for governing the Philippines in the post-Marcos era. It was the result of the polarization of politics under Marcos and it has taken the place of political parties (both Right and Left) as the means for groups and individuals to aspire for and wield power. What is notable about coalition governing is that it brings together ideologically opposed groups. Either aware of their limited influence or pragmatic enough to realize the need for "tactical alliances," these opposing forces manage to set aside differences temporarily in order to work for a common goal—usually the election of a presidential candidate. The victorious candidate brings her supporting coalition into her presidency.

This means that while the apparatus of the state may be "dominated and penetrated by the political and economic elite, challenged by rebellion, weakened by private armies and organized crime, and evaded and ignored by many of its citizens" (Abueva 1997, 48–49), the very "softness" of the state also allows it to be penetrated by social and political forces with different interests from the politicians and patrimonial networks. These forces range from "reformist" businessmen seeking a more open, transparent market with less government interference, to anti-graft, pro-efficiency advocates from the middle classes, to former communists wanting to use the state to achieve social goals. The pre-eminence of coalition governing in the national capital has been replicated at the local level. While many provincial governments are still run by the proverbial warlord or landed family, others are managed by reform-minded politicians (some, ironically, heirs of the old elite) in alliance with popular organizations (McCoy 1993; Rivera 2000). This, again, renders a more complicated picture of governing—we see a mosaic of different regimes, from reformist to patrimonial and all shades in between.

The Philippine experience indicates that it is wrong to assume that weak states have no ability to govern even moderately.[13] A weak state with a long tradition of electoral and constitutional politics, which uses this tradition to construct coalitions of various political forces and constitute a ruling regime, is especially suited for this kind of moderately effective governing. This is what Philippine constitutional democracy is all about. Its antinomies and contradictions are precisely what keep it alive, even at the price of continued underdevelopment.

Notes

1 In 1998, each congressional representative received 30 million pesos for public works projects in his/her district. Of this nearly 6 billion peso total, nearly 2.2 billion pesos likely went to bribes. For every 1,000 pesos collected in taxes, only 250 pesos goes to actual operations. Parreño 1998.

2 Article XIII, Section 15 of the 1987 Constitution.

3 Republic Act 7941 was passed to strengthen the party list system.

4 The peso likewise depreciated and the government had to service a USD 21.8 billion external debt (*FEER 1998 Yearbook*, 188).

5 "Philippines: Pyrrhic Victory and Abysmal Defeat," *Asia Times* Online, July 13, 2000.

6 Three days of reporting by the *Philippine Daily Inquirer*, the Philippines' top newspaper, included a report on the "luxury" vehicles ordered by the secretary of education, the row between Mr. Estrada and his wife, Dr. Loi Estrada, over reports of his mistresses and their families enriching themselves, warnings of a "return" to martial law-style governing, efforts by Estrada friend Lucio Tan to shed his family's image as presidential cronies and, of course, the continuing military operations in Jolo island. See *PDI*, September 23, 24 and 25, 2000.

7 I asked three top Filipino journalists whether there were indeed "isles of state efficiency" in the government, and all three answered in the affirmative. E-mail conversations with Marites Danguilan-Vitug, Sheila Coronel and Rigoberto Tiglao, September–October 2000.

8 *PDI*, May 30, June 22 and August 26, 2000. On the Civil Service Commission, see "Three Agencies Use Prayer to Get Rid of Graft," *PDI*, December 12, 1999.

9 Estrada's trade and industry secretary put it well: "We fell from three stories; the others fell from ten stories" (Tanzer 2000, 1).

10 The most serious was the investigation of stock manipulation by a corporation owned by an Estrada crony. See Philippine Stock Exchange,

Inc., Compliance and Surveillance Group, "Investigation Report on BW Resource Corporation," February 11, 2000.

11 On jueteng revenues, see "Illegal Gambling Has a Grassroots Base," *PCIJ and Institute for Popular Democracy Reports*, December 4, 1995.

12 "Jueteng is Embedded in Local Society and Culture," *Philippine Center for Investigative Journalism and Institute for Popular Democracy Reports*, December 4, 1995.

13 Abueva defines a "strong state" (which is his ideal state) as one that can "in accordance with the Constitution, establish the rule of law, enforce its laws and rules on all concerned, and implement its policies and programs to benefit the people" (Abueva 1997, 48).

References

Abueva, Jose. 1997. Philippine democratization and the consolidation of democracy since the 1986 EDSA revolution: An overview of main issues, trends and prospects. In *Democratization: Philippine Perspectives*, ed. Felipe B. Miranda. Quezon City: University of the Philippines Press.

Abueva, Jose V., and Emerlinda R. Roman, eds. 1993. *Corazon C. Aquino: Early Assessments of Her Presidential Leadership and Administration and Her Place in History*. Quezon City: University of the Philippines Press.

Angeles, J. 1997. The role of the Naga City Urban Poor Federation in the passage of pro-poor ordinances and policies. In *State-Civil Society Relations in Policy-making*, ed. Marlon Wui and Glenda Gloria. Quezon City: University of the Philippines Third World Studies Center.

Aquino, Belinda A., ed. 1990. *Presidential Leadership and Cory Aquino: U.P. Assessment Project on the State of the Nation*. Diliman, Quezon City: University of the Philippines, Center for Integrative and Development Studies.

Asia Society and the Asian Development Bank. 1998. Financing Asian development: Growing opportunities in Asia's debt markets. Report of a study mission to the Philippines, Thailand and South Korea, May 20–30.

Asian Development Bank. 1998. Cooperation between the ADB and NGOs. Manila: Asian Development Bank Policy Papers.

Asian Development Bank. 2000. The Philippines. In *Asian Development Bank Outlook 2000*. Manila: Asian Development Bank.

Bhargava, Vinay. 1999. Combating corruption in the Philippines. World Bank report. Washington: D.C.: The World Bank.

Borras, Saturnino M., Jr. 1999. *The Bibingka Strategy in Land Reform Implementation: Autonomous Peasant Movements and State Reformists in the Philippines*. Quezon City: Institute for Popular Democracy.

Boudreau, Vincent G. At the margins of the movement: Grassroots associations in the Philippine socialist network. PhD diss., Cornell University.

Boudreau, Vincent G. 1996. Of motorcades and masses: Mobilization and innovation in Philippine protest. In *The Revolution Falters: The Left in Philippine Politics after 1986*, ed. Patricio N. Abinales, 60–82. Ithaca, New York: Cornell University Southeast Asia Program.

Brillantes, Alex B., Jr. 1997. Local government in a democratizing polity: Trends and prospects. In *Democratization: Philippine Perspectives*, ed. Felipe B. Miranda. Quezon City: University of the Philippines Press.

Ciria-Cruz, Rene. 1992. Why the Philippine Left must take the parliamentary road. *Debate: Philippine Left Review* 2 (March): 5–15.

Ciron, Ruben Fulgeras. 1993. Civil-military relations in the Philipines: Perceptions of PMA-trained officers. PhD diss., University of the Philippines.

Clarke, Gerard. 1998. *The Politics of NGOs in Southeast Asia: Participation and Protest in the Philippines*. London and New York: Routledge.

Coronel, Sheila. 1998. A long way from home. *Philippine Yearbook*.

Coronel, Sheila. 2000a. Erap and families. *I: The Investigative Reporting Magazine* (July–September): 5–10.

Coronel, Sheila S., ed. 2000b. *Betrayals of the Public Trust: Investigative Reports on Corruption*. Manila: Philippine Center for Investigative Journalism.

Dahm, Bernard, ed. 1991. *Economy and Politics under Corazon Aquino*. Hamburg: Institut fur Asienkunde.

Diokno, Maria Serena. 1995. Peace and human rights: The past lives on. In *Looking Back, Looking Forward 1996*, ed. Lorna Kalaw-Tirol. Manila: Foundation for Worldwide People Power.

de Dios, Emmanuel 1999. Executive-legislative relations in the Philippines: Continuity and change. In *Institutions and Economic Change in Southeast Asia: The Context of Development from the 1960s to the 1990s*, ed. Colin Barlow. United Kingdom: Edward Elgar.

Doronila, Amado. 2001. *The Fall of Joseph Estrada: The Inside Story*. Pasig, Metro-Manila: Anvil Publishing.

Elwood, Douglas. 1986. *Philippine Revolution 1986: Model of Non-violent Change*. Quezon City: New Day Publishers.

Fabella, Raul V. 1999. East Asia will again lead the charge. Will the Philippines keep apace? *The 2000 Philippines Yearbook*. Manila: The Fookien Times.

Florentino-Hofileña, Chay. 1995. The president's tribal grounds. In *Boss: Five Case Studies of Local Politics in the Philippines*, ed. Jose F. Lacaba, 121–23. Manila: Philippine Center for Investigative Journalism and the Institute for Popular Democracy.

Franco, Jennifer Conroy. 1997. Elections and democratization in the Philippines. PhD diss., Brandeis University.

Gloria, Glenda M. 1995. Makati: One city, two worlds. In *Boss: Five Case Studies of Local Politics in the Philippines*, ed. Jose F. Lacaba, 65–102. Manila: Philippine Center for Investigative Journalism and the Institute for Popular Democracy.

Gutierrez, Eric. 1998. The public purse. In *Pork and Other Perks: Corruption and Governance in the Philippines*, 56–80. Manila: Philippine Center for Investigative Journalism.

Hutchcroft, Paul. 1996. The Philippines at the crossroads. *Asia Update* (Asia Society) (November): 2–4.

Kerklviet, Benedict, and Resil Mojares, eds. 1991. *From Marcos to Aquino: Local Perspectives on Political Transition in the Philippines*. Quezon City: Ateneo de Manila University Press.

Kudeta: The Challenge to Philippine Democracy. 1990. Manila: Philippine Center for Investigative Journalism and Bookmark.

Linantud, John. 1998. Whither guns, goons, and gold? The decline of factional election violence in the Philippines. *Contemporary Southeast Asia* 20, no. 3 (December): 298–318.

Lozada, Becky. 1998. Jekyl and Hyde syndrome: Notes on the Estrada administration. *Philippine International Review* 1, no. 3 (Winter): 1–4.

McCoy, Alfred W., ed. 1993. *An Anarchy of Families: State and Family in the Philippines*. Quezon City: Ateneo de Manila University Press.

Mojares, Resil. 1993. The dream goes on and on: Three generations of the Osmeñas, 1906–1990. In *An Anarchy of Families: State and Family in the Philippines*, ed. Alfred W. McCoy. Madison and Manila: University of Wisconsin Center for Southeast Asian Studies and Ateneo de Manila University Press.

Morales, Horacio R., Jr. 1999. Prospects for poverty reduction under the Estrada administration. Paper presented at the public forum "The Estrada Administration amidst the Crisis: Can it Deliver its Promises to the Poor?," Utrecht, The Netherlands, April 23.

Nemenzo, Francisco. 1988. A season of coups. *Diliman Review* 34: 5–6.

Noland, Marcus. 2000. How the sick man avoided pneumonia: The Philippines in the Asian financial crisis. *Institute for International Economics*, Working Paper 00-5, May.

Parreño, Earl. 1998. Pork. In *Pork and Other Perks: Corruption and Governance in the Philippines*, 32–55. Manila: Philippine Center for Investigative Journalism.

Political Brief: A Monthly Digest of the Institute for Popular Democracy 8, no. 3 (March 2000).

Reid, Ben. 2000. *Philippine Left: Political Crisis and Social Change*. Manila, Sydney: Journal of Contemporary Asia Publishers.

Reid, Robert, and Eileen Guerrero, eds. 1995. *Corazon Aquino and the Brushfire Revolution*. Louisiana: Louisiana State University Press.

Rivera, Temario C. 2000. How fare the clans? Poverty and elite reproduction in the Philippines. Paper presented at the Third International Philippine Studies Conference, Manila, July 10–12, Quezon City.

Rocamora, Joel. 1994. *Breaking Through: The Struggle within the Communist Party of the Philippines*. Manila: Anvil Publishing.

de la Rosa, Romulo. 1999. Civil society and Mindanao 2000. *Kasarinlan* 14, no. 3–4: 17–183.

Shatkin, Gavin 1999. Community-based organizations, local politics and shelter delivery in Metro-Manila. *Kasarinlan: A Philippine Journal of Third World Studies* 14, no. 3–4.

Silliman, G. Sidney, and Lela Garner Noble. 1999. *Organizing for Democracy: NGOs, Civil Society and the Philippine State*. Quezon City: Ateneo de Manila University Press.

Soriano, J. Clark. 1993. *Selected Case Studies: NGO-PO-GO Interfaces in Local Governance*. Quezon City: Institute for Popular Democracy.

Tanzer, Andrew. 2000. The Ronald Reagan of the Pacific. *Forbes Magazine*, September 21.

Thompson, Mark R. 1995. *The Anti-Marcos Struggle: Personalistic Rule and Democratic Transition in the Philippines*. New Haven and London: Yale University Press.

Tigno, Jorge V. 1997. People empowerment: Looking into NGOs, POs and selected sectoral organizations. In *Democratization: Philippine Perspectives*, ed. Felipe B. Miranda. Quezon City: University of the Philippines Press.

Tordesillas, Ellen, and Sheila Coronel. 1998. Scam. In *Pork and Other Perks: Corruption and Governance in the Philippines*, 83–111. Manila: Philippine Center for Investigative Journalism.

de la Torre, Edicio, and Horacio Morales. 1986. *Two Essays on Popular Democracy.* Manila: Institute for Popular Democracy.

University of the Philippines. 1992–1999. *U.P. Public Lectures on the Aquino Administration and the Post-EDSA Government, 1986–1992.* Diliman, Quezon City: University of the Philippines Press.

Valencia, Ernesto M. 1993. National democratic movement and the electoral struggle. *Debate: Philippine Left Review* 8 (November): 51–59.

Weissman, Robert. 1994. The politics of economic chaos in the Philippines. *Multinational Monitor* (January–February).

8

Mahathirism After the Asian Crisis and Beyond Mahathir

Khoo Boo Teik

In discussing the topic of Mahathirism "beyond Mahathir," this essay does not provide a conjecture on when Mahathir, after almost 21 years in power, will depart from political office.[1] Instead, this essay focuses on what might be called the Mahathirist project which commenced under Mahathir's charge in 1981. When I coined the term "Mahathirism" in 1995, I had in mind several things. For a start, the term referred to a relatively coherent ideology and worldview articulated by Mahathir through his writings, speeches and polices, which supplied the ruling ideas of the Mahathir era. That ideology came to maturation with the statement of Wawasan 2020 (Vision 2020), which was first presented by Mahathir to the Malaysian Business Council in February 1991 (Mahathir 1991). Mahathirism also stood for a historical project of social and political transformation that had a backward linkage to the New Economic Policy (NEP), yet looked to the future by being more clearly defined as a state-led nationalist-capitalist venture of late industrialization inspired by the so-called East Asian model of development (Khoo 1995).

Looking back, the "Mahathir era" was a time of restless ambition exemplified by Mahathir's state-sponsored program of heavy industrialization. The ambition was driven by a mix of Malay nationalism and Malaysian capitalism, which coupled to conceive Mahathir's privatization and Malaysia Incorporated policies. The beginnings of the Mahathirist project were charged with the energy of the "2Ms"—Mahathir and his first deputy prime minister, Musa Hitam—and its principal goals sounded noble enough: Reform the bureaucracy! Modernize the economy! Change the Malays! Develop the nation! Compete with the world! The spiritual core of the project was to be built around a liberal "assimilation of Islamic values." In fact, the "Islamic values" identified and officially promoted were the sort of universalistic values which celebrated the qualities of learning, promoted the virtues of thrift and spoke of the dignity of labor. These were values that Mahathir thought Malaysians, and especially the Malays, did not embody in sufficient degree. They were the principal elements of an "Eastern work ethic" Mahathir wanted Malaysian society to imbibe and practice. Moreover, Mahathirist ideology contained many "paradoxes" which were attributable to Mahathir's personal impulses and experiences, but which also reflected major contradictions in Malaysian society (Khoo 1995: 9–10). Mahathirism's most exalted target was the creation of a Melayu Baru—a corps of "new Malay" capitalists and professionals—who would be progressive and competent enough to manage a modern economy and lead a unified Malaysian nation—Bangsa Malaysia—into the club of developed countries, not least by undertaking a conquest of foreign markets.

Mahathirism in a Time of Boom

Mahathir has always prided himself on being a visionary leader. But, as one can readily imagine, the success or failure of visionary projects of large-scale and far-reaching economic change and social transformation depends heavily on the resolution of social and political conflict. Just over one decade before the 1997 East Asian financial crisis, Mahathirism met its first major crisis in the combination of economic recession, intensified factionalism within the ruling party, UMNO, and heightened inter-ethnic disputes. Much of this crisis has been thoroughly analyzed (Kershaw 1989, Khoo 1992; Shamsul 1988; Tan 1990).[2] Here it is sufficient to state summarily that Mahathir triumphed very narrowly in UMNO's election of 1987 and afterwards managed to preserve political stability by repressive means. Economic rescue came via a relaxation of NEP requirements and an influx of foreign direct investment, especially from East Asia, from the late 1980s to the early 1990s. Consequently, Mahathirism recovered its appeal and reached its peak in the mid-1990s.

In political terms the signal achievement of Mahathirism was the landslide victory won by the ruling Barisan Nasional (BN, or National Front) in the April 1995 election. BN's victory came at the mid-span of a high-growth period (early to mid-1990s) and marked the close of an entire era of NEP politics of intense inter-ethnic disputes throughout the 1970s and 1980s. Ideologically, inter-ethnic recrimination was diminished by a sense of national unity envisaged in Vision 2020. One indicator of this new trend was the result of the February 1994 state election in Sabah. The combined Kadazan and Chinese opposition that from 1984 to 1990 had staunchly supported Parti Bersatu Sabah (PBS, or Sabah United Party) had been so eroded by 1994 that PBS was ousted from its ten-year hold on power by a combination of repression and defection to the UMNO-led BN.

A second and more telling indicator was the outcome of the 1995 general election, in which the large urban Chinese-majority constituencies, the definitive strongholds of opposition in the NEP era, significantly deserted the strongest opposition party, the Democratic Action Party (DAP).

Several factors contributed to the reduction in inter-ethnic recrimination. First, the economic boom and accompanying prosperity of the early 1990s assuaged the sense of deprivation and discrimination that had earlier provoked non-Malay opposition to government policies. Second, NEP's social engineering had sufficiently resolved the problem of Malay "relative economic backwardness" by creating a Bumiputera Commercial and Industrial Community (BCIC) which broadened the ranks of the Malaysian capitalist, professional and middle classes and, crucially, nurtured the rise of powerful state- or party-connected conglomerates (Gomez 1990, Searle 1999).[3] Third, Mahathir's policies offered economic solutions to several contentious cultural issues. For example, the partial deregulation of tertiary education and the rise of new private colleges removed much of the inter-ethnic disputation over ethnically determined quotas for admission into public universities. Few things captured the decline of inter-ethnic recrimination better than the increasing enrolment of Malay students in Chinese-language schools, a remarkable social development inconceivable during the NEP era.[4]

In that historical context, Malaysian society, broadly speaking, moderated its ethnic preoccupations and discovered a newer form of communitarianism evident in the popularization of Mahathir's Wawasan 2020 and Bangsa Malaysia[5] and in then-Deputy Prime Minister Anwar Ibrahim's multiculturalist slogan, *wo men dou shi yi jia ren* ("We are one family").[6] This was a communitarianism of competitive national capitalism and inclusive nationalist-populist ideology. To the extent that domestic politics was influenced by international events, the ethos of competitive national capitalism was alluring in the last days of the "East Asian miracle," while the inclusive nationalist-populist ideology was preferable to the ethnic wars of the collapsed Soviet bloc.

Equally important was the establishment of relatively cordial relations among the state, foreign capital and domestic conglomerates. Relations among these traditional centers of power were quite not so cordial during the NEP period of vigorous state interventionism, or even during the heavy industrialization drive of the early Mahathir administration. In 1991, NEP was replaced by a National Development Plan (NDP). NDP officially stressed economic growth rather than ethnically-based wealth redistribution, even if affirmative action favoring the *bumiputera* communities was retained in practice. The state's export-oriented industrialization policies continued to privilege manufacturing multinational corporations while financial liberalization facilitated the entry of speculative capital which arrived as part of the international money market's investment in "emerging markets." Domestic conglomerates still dominated the commodity and resource exploitation sectors but had also expanded into recently privatized areas of utilities, infrastructure, tourism and social services. Several of the conglomerates even began to "globalize" by investing in like areas—logging, tourism and gaming, for example—in countries less developed than Malaysia. In other words, the conglomerates now constituted a more self-confident national capital. The state had reason to consider that "Malaysia Inc." represented a stable tripartite balance of power among state, foreign capital and an ethnically-mixed domestic capital.

After the Asian Crisis

The second crisis of Mahathirism began in July 1997. In Malaysia, the impact of the East Asian financial crisis substantially depreciated the local currency, reduced the market capitalization of the Kuala Lumpur Stock Exchange (KLSE) and sent the economy into recession.[7] The currency and share price falls spared few, but the domestic conglomerates seemed destined to collapse spectacularly. Their dependence on external borrowings and stock market capitalization had exposed them to bloated loan repayments, plunging asset values and imminent insolvency. To rescue the conglomerates it had nurtured, the state was compelled to negotiate a new stance vis-à-vis the international money market. Mahathir's views counted most within the political leadership, and the conglomerates desperately needed his support. Mahathir refused to see July 1997 as marking the end of the East Asian model of capitalism. The international money market and the International Monetary Fund (IMF) insisted that crisis management required the remedies of currency floats, higher interest rates, restrained liquidity, market liberalization, financial sector reform and good governance. Mahathir ignored all these and chose to treat the financial crisis as a speculator's disease. He chose to cure it with a mixture of ad hoc regulation and state intervention. In a sense, he had no choice. Any of the "pro-market reform" remedies, properly applied, would have been bitter medicine for the conglomerates. Taken together, they would have been fatal to Mahathirism's critical pillar of Malaysia Inc.—the free market would govern a non-interventionist state! But state intervention via ad hoc changes to KLSE's corporate takeover rules and the selective rescue of well-connected conglomerates backfired and triggered a capital flight. Global capital refused to return to the Malaysian economy if the state, under Mahathir, could not be disciplined.

In their time, each of the policies of bureaucratic reform, heavy industrialization, privatization and liberalization, all part of the Mahathirist project, represented a significant step toward rationalizing Malaysian capitalism. This time, however, the impetus towards further capitalist rationalization—as a response to a fundamental shift in the global economy—came briefly from the "Anwar Ibrahim camp" (Khoo 2000: 224–228, 231–235). One critical component of this camp was made up of Bank Negara (the central bank), Treasury and other technocrats and regulators who sought an economistic return to fiscal and monetary "fundamentals." Another component was represented by a faction within UMNO that was superficially opposed to "kolusi, korupsi, nepotisme."[8] This faction wanted to exact Mahathir's departure and loosen the grip of some of the conglomerates as the political price of the economic crisis. For this amorphous and soon doomed "Anwar camp" there was some "market support," discreetly given by domestic businesses fearful of Mahathir's counter-productive confrontation with global investors, but loudly expressed by the guardians of the global money market (IMF officials, fund managers and the international media).

On September 1, 1998, the state via Bank Negara imposed foreign exchange and capital controls and pegged the ringgit to the US dollar.[9] One day later, Mahathir dismissed Anwar from all his government posts. Barely forty-eight hours later, Anwar was expelled from UMNO. Anwar's fall signaled that there would be no reforms of the kind that according with the money market's notion of what was needed to revitalize crisis-stricken Asian economies.[10] Instead, the regime opted for recapitalization of the financial sector using public funds, reflation to stimulate the economy and the rescue of imperiled conglomerates behind an "economic shield" of capital controls and currency peg.[11] The policy choices implicit in Bank Negara's measures and Anwar's dismissal did not merely involve a toss-up between adopting IMF-style structural adjustment (market-dictated governance) and allowing key economic sectors and strategic businesses to collapse. There was at least the option of tying rescue plans, bailout measures and reflationary policies to a critical disciplining of many of the politically most powerful conglomerates, for which there was a precedent of sorts. During the recession of 1985–86, in pursuit of Malaysia Inc. goals, Mahathir and Daim Zainuddin had forced a dose of fiscal discipline down the throats of a burgeoning and supposedly non-performing bureaucracy. In 1986, they suspended NEP's restructuring requirements, preferring "growth" over "redistribution." But perhaps there was the rub: both sets of measures favoured big Malay businesses over the bureaucracy and small Malay businesses. Now the Mahathirist project secured the survival of the conglomerates with an unreformed state protectionism. Malaysia Inc.'s framework of an alliance between the state and domestic conglomerates was preserved, but Mahathirism as the code for capitalist rationalization ended.

Had the state not acted, in the words of Bank Negara's acting governor, to "bring the ringgit back into the country" (*New Straits Times*, September 2, 1998), the currency would have collapsed. Instead, the capital controls halted the trend of capital flight, if only by trapping the remaining foreign funds for one year, and even reversed it, if only by forcing the return of offshore ringgit funds. The currency peg averted an imminent economic collapse by giving domestic businesses and foreign direct investment a measure of stability by which to plan, contract and manage. Meanwhile, Mahathir and Daim maintained a semi-autarkic regime of reflating the economy, relaxing monetary policy and resuscitating local business.[12] The state established three institutions to deal with the financial system. Danaharta, an "asset management company," took charge of "remov[ing] NPLs from the balance sheets of financial institutions," thus "free[ing] the banks from the burden of debts that had prevented them from providing loans to their customers" (Mahani 2000: 186). In 1999, Danaharta purchased RM 45.5 billion in NPLs from banks and financial institutions. Danamodal, a "Special-Purpose Vehicle," recapitalized the financial sector by giving "credit injections" totaling RM 7.59 billion to leading banks. The Corporate Debt Restructuring Committee (CDRC) managed 67 debt-restructuring applications involving RM 36.3 billion. CDRC's best known and most controversial applications came from the UMNO-owned Renong, the state-owned Bank Bumiputra and Sime Bank.

Recapitalization largely depended on three sources: public funds (notably the Employees Provident Fund and the reserves of the national petroleum company, Petronas), external loans (from Japan and the World Bank) and bonds that were eventually issued. Bank Negara increased liquidity and facilitated bank lending to the corporate sector while steadily lowering the banks' statutory reserve requirements from 13.5 percent to 4 percent between February and September 1998. From June to October, the base lending rate was reduced from 12.27 percent to 6.79 percent. The classification of NPLs was changed back from three months (March 1998) to six months (September 1998). Bank Negara also directed a higher target for bank lending. It made credit more easily available for private consumption (and on more favorable terms than pre-July 1997) to support key sectors such as the automobile industry and the property market.

The state's programs of recapitalization, rescue and reflation scarcely accorded with the reforms demanded by the money market of crisis-stricken Asian regimes.[13] Yet by late 1999, trade surpluses had built up the country's reserves and the economy had begun to emerge from recession. Share prices had recovered substantially with the support of domestic institutional funds. The regime claimed to have reversed "the wrong turns taken during the initial stage of the crisis"[14] (by Anwar, that is, in his last year as Finance minister). Critics of the regime's policies attributed the end of recession to a fortuitous growth in manufacturing exports. They insisted that the controls would not work in the long run and had harmed Malaysia's position as a destination of foreign investment.[15] But the capital controls had already been relaxed in February 1999 to permit the repatriation of foreign funds subject to a graduated exit tax. Some investment funds (notably Templeton) were adamant about staying away from Malaysia even after September 1999, when the "trapped" funds could exit without penalty. Still, the government and Petronas were able to raise bonds of USD 1 billion and USD 500 million respectively from the money market, albeit with Japanese backing and at punitive premiums. And Morgan Stanley Capital International reincorporated Malaysia into its index in 2000, paving the way for fund managers to re-enter KLSE. In short, the money market reached a rapprochement with the state despite disagreements in principle. Or, as an *Asian Wall Street Journal* editorial of June 23, 1999, cajoled Mahathir, "Now that the pressure of the Asian crisis has abated, it's time to declare victory and rejoin the global economy."

The rapprochement, and Barisan Nasional's return to power in the November 1999 election, might suggest that Malaysia could resume its developmental path under Mahathir and Mahathirism. But Malaysia had never been anything but integrated into the global economy. Nor has the turmoil kicked up by the Anwar affair abated, and the Malaysian political economy is not quite as delivered from crisis as appearances suggest. Indeed post-crisis Mahathirism faces different kinds of problems—economic, political and ideological—and often the three cannot be clearly disentangled or resolved separately.

Beyond Mahathir

One fundamental problem of political economy is whether the pre-crisis tripartite division of power between the state, foreign capital and domestic capital can be maintained. As the above-mentioned rapprochement suggests, it can, albeit with some changes. The state once governed the market in the mold of an East Asian developmental state, but now the state's scope of freedom has been curtailed. Foreign capital is not simply the manufacturing foreign direct investment welcomed by the state, but a globalizing speculative capital the state regards with a wariness that will not disappear, most definitely not before Mahathir departs from power. Domestic capital, too, is not pre-NEP "Chinese capital," but a conglomerate-dominated national capital whose ranks have been filled, however imperfectly, by the Bumiputera Commercial and Industrial Community. However, it is precisely the ambition but relative weakness of the BCIC has lain, and will continue to lie, at the heart of many political conflicts.

Leaving aside ethnic considerations, the state-sponsored creation of Malay capital that commenced with NEP was fundamentally dependent upon three factors. UMNO, as the dominant political party in government, supplied the political power to push through NEP's social engineering. The Malay-dominated bureaucracy provided the capacity for implementing NEP programs. And the performance of an incipient class of Malay capitalists had to vindicate the state assistance and nurture it received. However, the integrity of this party-bureaucracy-class axis was subjected to continuous strain, as the 1980s crisis had demonstrated. Influential and powerful coalitions emerged from the ranks of party, bureaucracy and class to claim state patronage and assistance. Yet, as resources were first controlled by bureaucrats but later privatized, as UMNO built itself an economic empire and as individual Malay capitalists emerged, these coalitions contended for power, access to resources and opportunities for accumulation. Over time, their agendas could less and less be amicably subsumed under NEP: all based their claims on ethnic wealth "restructuring," but each pursued its disparate interests. Mahathirism, with its pro-big business and anti-bureaucratic biases, helped to tilt the balance of power in favor of the rising class of Malay capitalists, who were nurtured by the state but maintained influential links to the party.

Many of the once wealthy and powerful Malay conglomerates, either UMNO-owned, or individually controlled, however, have been battered by the 1997 crisis. To this day, Mahathir claims that the conglomerates were doing well before the speculators caused their collapse (*New Straits Times*, March 9, 2002). But whereas these conglomerates once exuded confidence in taking on the world, as it were, they have since been clamoring for shelter from the challenges of globalization. Whereas privatization was once their ticket to influence, re-nationalization has become their path to survival, as witness the state's re-purchasing of troubled conglomerates. Among the most prominent of the re-nationalized conglomerates are the

Malaysian Airlines System, the light rapid transit companies, PUTRA and STAR, and the waste disposal services company, Indah Water Konsortium. As before, the state defends its support for the conglomerates with the nationalistic rationale of protecting them from foreign acquisition and maintaining Malay control (*New Straits Times*, March 9, 2002).

The credibility of this rationale has been wearing thin since September 2, 1998, when the Anwar affair erupted. Anwar's fall exposed UMNO's factionalism, which has since NEP reflected the deep fault lines along the party-bureaucracy-class axis. UMNO emerged by bearing the historic mission of Malay nationalism. Today it is seen as largely pursuing its corporate mission of fostering Malay capitalism, taking advantage of privatization under the aegis of Malaysia Inc. The conflicts that emerged within UMNO and its economic empire became such that UMNO's internal politics could no longer be limited to manageable policy differences, personality clashes, power struggles or leadership succession. Increasingly, UMNO's factionalism was all these at once—an indication that the party had approached a state of systemic failure. The Anwar affair so traumatized the Malay community as to draw major Malay reinterpretations of Malaysian politics that recast issues such as Malay economic nationalism in the derogatory terms of "rescue of Malay cronies." In the November 1999 general election, UMNO probably won less than half the Malay popular vote. For the first time ever—it had happened in none of UMNO's previous crises—half the Malay community was prepared to contemplate an "alternative" government not led by UMNO. As a result of this deep and broad Malay dissent, Mahathir and Mahathirism has been forced to grapple with challenges from two different but sometimes overlapping sources—Islam and populism.

The challenge of the Islamic opposition is well known and can be quickly reviewed here. In the 1999 election, riding the anti-UMNO swell among the Malays, Parti Islam (PAS) made substantial electoral gains. PAS increased its parliamentary representation threefold and became the strongest opposition party. At the state level, PAS retained control of Kelantan and won back Trengganu state, which it last controlled in 1962. As things stand, UMNO can scarcely hope to overturn PAS's massive winning margins in those two states in the next election. Indeed, UMNO has been put on the defensive in other states of the "Malay heartland," such as Kedah,[16] where PAS's influence has grown. Presently, PAS's 14 percent share of parliament and control of two state governments do not place the party close to any imminent assumption of power across the country. However, PAS poses genuine obstacles to UMNO's attempt to reconstitute its hegemony over Malay society. The UMNO-led federal government's hostility towards Kelantan and Trengganu leaves PAS with the unattractive option of building Islam in two impoverished states. But the same hostility, together with police repression of the opposition, undercuts UMNO's appeals to "Malay unity" and Malay economic nationalism.

As the situation in 2000 showed, UMNO's desperate and chauvinistic calls for "Malay unity" were hollow without PAS support. Cut off from federal funds, the PAS governments in Kelantan and Trengganu can only hope to demonstrate the superiority of Islam in pietistic ways, that is, via PAS's morally conservative policies. PAS's moral conservatism unsettles non-Muslims, who fear the party's commitment to an "Islamic state," as well as "liberal-minded" Muslims, who fear it no less. This was so even before September 11, 2001. But PAS's moral conservatism is allied to the widespread Muslim belief that Anwar could not have been convicted under Islamic law in a *syariah* court. That is sufficient to make Mahathir's former policy of Islamization count for little and that is perhaps why, ideologically, no Mahathirist today still talks of the "assimilation of Islamic values."

The populist challenge is a putative one that can be best discussed with reference to what Anwar today stands for, despite scepticism and uncertainty as to whether he can ever make a serious return to politics, let alone power, even after Mahathir departs. In a thirty-year career of activism and politics, Anwar may be said to have gone through four phases. During the first phase in the late 1960s, he was a student at the University of Malaya. There he led the Persatuan Bahasa Melayu (Malay Language Society) and Persatuan Kebangsaan Pelajar-pelajar Islam (National Muslim Students' Society). His Persatuan Bahasa Melayu image and activities drew him to some politicians, like Mahathir, who were admired by many Malays then as "Malay nationalists" and feared by others, especially non-Malays, as "Malay ultras." The second phase came in the 1970s when Anwar founded Angkatan Belia Islam Malaysia (ABIM, or Malaysian Islamic Youth Movement) and built it into a powerful vehicle of Islamic resurgence, all the more powerful for being the voice of a new generation of Malay-Muslim youth. The third and longest phase, 1982–98, found Anwar in UMNO and government. Anwar rose from being co-opted into the early Mahathir regime to being "anointed" as Mahathir's successor. Indeed, he rose with a dizzying rapidity that alarmed many of his party rivals. The present and potentially decisive phase is post-September 1998, when Anwar reinvented himself as the icon of *reformasi*.

One thing is immediately striking. In three of his four phases, Anwar was an anti-establishment figure. To put things simply, he was anti-Tunku Abdul Rahman after 1969, anti-Barisan Nasional in the 1970s and has been anti-UMNO and anti-Mahathir since 1998. Only during that third and long UMNO phase was Anwar a leading figure of the establishment. His ideological commitments in the anti-establishment phases seem varied enough when taken separately. Anwar's 1960s Malay nationalism was associated with the promotion of Malay as the national language, but it also took in NEP-type issues. It is well known that Anwar was a campus ally of Mahathir, who let him read drafts of what was later published as Mahathir's *The Malay Dilemma*. In the 1970s, Anwar's Islamic commitments were initially expressed via various Yayasan Anda activities in aid of Malay-Muslim students and the nascent campus *dakwah* (propagation of the faith) movement both at home and abroad. Later, Islam became the fount from which Anwar drew his moral criticisms of government policies and their outcomes. Anwar's positions on poverty, economic inequality and social dislocation under NEP led him to Baling, Kedah, to support the 1974 demonstrations. He was thereafter arrested and sent to the Kamunting Camp for a stretch of detention under the Internal Security Act.[17] In the final years of Anwar's Islamic phase (before he joined UMNO), ABIM led a coalition of societies—what would be known as non-governmental organizations (NGOs) today—in a big campaign against the Societies Act. Finally, between September 2, 1998, when he was sacked, and 20 September, when he was arrested, Anwar inspired a movement for democracy, reforms and social justice.

Anwar's ideological commitments in his anti-establishment phases have never been fully spelt out, which is one reason he was often thought to be malleable, if not opportunistic. Yet, viewed collectively, those commitments contained several notable threads. One thread was drawn from the ethnic strands of the different phases. It began with the campus Malay nationalism. It was modified by ABIM's brand of "non-ethnic" civil activism. It was grafted onto *reformasi*'s experiment in multiethnic politics. This first thread captures Anwar's shift, albeit a gradual one, to a position on ethnic relations that was most liberally called multiculturalism in the 1990s. A second thread grew from ABIM's critiques of economic inequalities, social injustice and restrictions imposed on civil liberties. Over time, they expanded from the defence of the Baling farmers to the national campaign against the Societies Act. After Anwar's fall, those critiques were dusted off from the shelves of his UMNO days and meshed with the opposition of the Barisan Alternatif (BA, or Alternative Front, the anti-regime coalition that sprang up in 1999) to "cronyism, corruption and nepotism."

There is an important third thread. It was not formed by what Anwar stood for, so much as whom he most comfortably stood with, and who, in his moments of tribulation, would stand most firmly by him. These were students, youth and civil society. Students and youth featured prominently in all phases of Anwar's anti-establishment activism, and civil society featured in his Islamic and *reformasi* phases. After September 1998, this thread allowed Anwar to reinvent himself as an activist and establish an old affinity with groups and people who, in social and political terms, make up floating, transient and marginalized constituencies. Spun together, the three threads were likely to produce a fabric with cultural motifs, the concerns of civil society and aspirations for moral renewal. This was precisely the intellectual fabric of *The Asian Renaissance*, the book Anwar published at the peak of his establishment phase.

Almost from start to finish, Anwar's UMNO phase was marked by contradiction. By joining UMNO, Anwar split ABIM. By taking part of ABIM along with him, he helped to split UMNO. For him, Islam had nourished a moral critique of society under capitalism. Now he fell in with Mahathir, for whom Islam meant a work ethic to serve Malaysian capitalism. Anwar left civil society to enter the state but he liked to speak as if the state should behave like a "caring civil society." However, reasons of state seemed to leave no room for his idealism and personal promises. Anwar justified his co-optation by Mahathir as a mission to "change things from inside." But nothing could be changed "from inside"—not the Societies Act, Sedition Act, Internal Security Act or Official Secrets Act.

Speaking politically, not spiritually, Anwar might have thought he could carve a niche for himself by negotiating between unstoppable political imperatives and unattainable personal impulses. For example, Anwar could not alter the course of Mahathir's program of late industrialization, but he could try to put a benign face on it. He could not prevent all kinds of injustices, but he wanted to offer sympathy to their victims. He could not control the rapacity of the corporate bosses, but he could spare a thought for the common man. Sceptics call this hypocrisy. A neutral take is to regard it as the politics of an uneasy conscience, most often practiced by former dissidents or critics of a regime who become "part of the system" but believe they have not "sold out." One plays this political game at the apex at one's peril. In good times, one sounds like a wimp. In tense situations, one is called a non-team player. When the chips are down, one becomes a turncoat. *Mahu makan taukeh ke?* ("Are you trying to eat up the boss?"), they ask in UMNO parlance.

Anwar had watched (and maybe helped make) Musa Hitam fail in this game between 1981 and 1986. Yet the point was, Anwar, like Musa, never quite shared Mahathir's vision of building Malay capitalism, at least not with the same resolve and purpose. Mahathir apologized to no one for devoting himself to the hardnosed preoccupations of the corporate world, money market and global economy. He changed from being a "man of the people" to being a patron of the movers and shakers of the domestic scene. For him, people were moved by boundless ambition, ceaseless competition and actual achievement, or they were destined for failure. Anwar seemed to apologize, so to speak, on Mahathir's behalf by dabbling in a vague moral economy, a sort of "Anwar's agenda." Basically Anwar's agenda contained not much more than a hope that a helping hand from the state might stop the devil from taking society's hindmost. No one kept a tally of the real achievement of this agenda as opposed to the rhetorical satisfaction it gained from "being concerned with" low-cost housing, low-cost healthcare, helping the poor and assisting the dislocated. After July 1997, for example, while Mahathir and Daim tackled the problems of the conglomerates, Anwar was left to tend to the little guys of the industrial system—the small- and medium-size industries—but without much to offer in the way of available funds.

One final matter tells something novel. Whereas Mahathir urged the Malaysian conglomerates to conquer markets in far-flung places, Anwar seemed excited about sending Yayasan Salam, an incipient Malaysian "peace corps," to poor places. That was like spreading ABIM's Yayasan Anda across the world! It tells us that Anwar's common threads were perhaps woven across his UMNO phase, as it were, in a coexistence of pro- and anti-establishment sentiments. In the early to mid-1990s, Mahathir wanted an East Asian Economic Caucus and spoke an authoritarian language of "Asian values." Anwar wrote *The Asian Renaissance* and acquired the idiom to go with his moral economy: civil society, universal values, empowerment and sustainable development. All this should not make us overstate the policy differences between Anwar and Mahathir (and Daim) that combined with personal considerations to force their showdown after July 1997 (Jomo 2001: xvii–xxi). It is sufficient, though, that Anwar's ideological threads had garnered a perspective on globalization that allowed for "creative destruction" where Mahathir only saw conspiracy and speculation. Seen in this light, Anwar was a putative anti-Mahathirist even before the roof collapsed on East Asia.

In the first days of September 1998, Anwar's hour of need, the politicians and corporate bigwigs who had jostled to rub shoulders with Mahathir's "anointed successor" were conspicuously absent from his side. But just when everything seemed lost for Anwar, thousands and thousands of ordinary people—unnamed students, youth, and members of civil society—rallied to his cause. Anwar recounted this in his home town of Permatang Pauh, Penang, when he launched *reformasi*. He declared that he finally knew who his real friends were. They were not the rich corporate and powerful political types whom he had helped but who abandoned him at the drop of a hat. His real friends, he said, were the common folk whose support allowed him to reinvent himself.

It was fashionable in *reformasi* quarters to call him "DSAI" (short for Dato' Seri Anwar Ibrahim). In political terminology, we can call him a populist. Populism is notoriously difficult to define since populists come in many shades and shapes. Some of them project latent fears and prejudices that can be quite outlandish and disheartening. The more promising populists purport to articulate the basic interests of "the peo-ple," "grassroots" and "communities," in opposition to big business and insincere government, but without demonizing others, such as foreigners or minorities of one kind or another. It is possible to interpret part of Anwar's pet "caring civil society" project as an expression of his pop-ulism: to offer assistance to the poor, compassion for the disadvantaged and guidance to "lost youth." In the present circumstances, another part of Anwar's populism lies in his anti-establishment criticisms of corrup-tion, authoritarianism and lack of respect for human rights, which today find its broadest appeal in *reformasi*. In all, these are the concerns of "the people" —including the students, youth and civil society who stood by him.

The point here is not whether Anwar can make a serious political comeback, let alone return to the pinnacle of power.[18] The issue of Anwar's putative populist challenge is the loss of legitimacy suffered by Mahathirism as a result of the twin crises of July 1997 and September 1998. In its salad days, Mahathirism had a hegemonic appeal. It was common knowledge that privatization had exacerbated the politicization of business and the commercialization of politics, while Malaysia Inc. privileged the conglomerates. Local parlance had it that one needed to pull "strong cables" to secure state contracts and projects and that one had to practice "money politics" in return. Allegations of impropriety, corruption and cronyism constantly attended privatization deals despite the trumpeting by those closest to such practices of the virtues of private sector initiative, public savings, efficiency, upgrading and so on, while overlooking the financial, social and moral costs to Malaysian society. But high economic growth created ample opportunities for even companies and individuals not coddled by the state or too small to engage in influence peddling; non-transparent privatization may have been regarded with envy or cynicism, but it was tolerated all the same.

Considerably different political reactions to these kinds of corporate and regime practices have been produced by July 1997 and especially September 1998. It is generally assumed that high-level corporate interests lurked behind the Anwar affair. There is a tacit understanding, in the eyes of the Islamic and non-Islamic opposition, that the conglomerates form an elitist camp of privilege and patronage. They provide refuge for cronies who are not only inefficient and incompetent but also arrogant and insecure. The 1997 crisis exposed their inefficiency and incompetence. After the crisis they showed their arrogance in considering it their birthright to profit from national resources when times were good, and, when times turn bad, to convert their private losses into public liabilities. They are insecure vis-à-vis the international market since they are unable to sustain a serious level of global competitiveness. Hence, they are constantly dependent upon state protection. Mahathirism was the ideology of this camp and it was particularly attractive when the camp reached its apogee before July 1997. The ideology drew its appeal and power from its inseparable association with Mahathir's person, because of Mahathir's political longevity and domineering conduct and the courage of his convictions. By the same token, shorn of success after the Asian crisis, and "beyond Mahathir," is it likely that such an ideology can continue to supply ruling ideas for another era?

Epilogue

We can now (June 2004) say that Abdullah Ahmad Badawi, who became prime minister in November 2003, chose to answer that question by assuming the responsibilities of premiership very differently than did Mahathir. Whereas Mahathir entered office with a slamming-of-doors and wasted little time imposing major policy re-orientations, Abdullah quietly slid into power. He did not rush to steer a post-Mahathir political course according to grand new visions, policies and directions. Instead, Abdullah chose to "de-Mahathirize" the political system, administrative framework and policy regime by interjecting ameliorative confidence-building measures. Not offering a political adrenalin rush, so to speak, Abdullah infused a sense of sobriety and gradualism, as if the society he led required a pause after the breathlessness of the Mahathir era.

In the first two months of his leadership, Abdullah emphasized selected issues of political economy, notably improvements in governance to check the inefficiencies and excesses of Malaysia Inc. and privatization. Most important were Abdullah's decisions to postpone a multi-billion ringgit double-track railway project[19]—controversially awarded to MMC-Gamuda shortly before Mahathir retired—and to delay the listing of the Federal Land Development Authority (Felda) on the Kuala Lumpur Stock Exchange, the listing being a recommendation of the last Budget presented by Mahathir in September 2003.

This was not the first time "reforms" introduced the "honeymoon" of a new administration. But Malaysia Inc. had to be reformed and Abdullah had compelling economic and political reasons to persist with governance issues. His moves partly reponded to the demands of foreign capital (both foreign direct investment and foreign portfolio investment) for "good governance" and "best practices."[20] These demands could hardly be ignored by an economy chronically dependent on foreign capital, or by a state already disadvantaged when it tried to tap global investment flows. Abdullah indicated, too, that it was time to balance the budget—since previous budget deficits[21] financed much of the post-1997 growth but were associated with "mega projects," bailouts and pump-priming—and show fiscal prudence to enforce adherence to other prudential standards.

At the popular level, the "good governance" drive indirectly responded to *reformasi* attacks on corruption and lent a patina of freshness to a leader whose regime was inherited and "old" but who had to call a general election. Some anti-corruption moves carried out at the "low-to-medium" political levels were popular even if they were inconclusive.[22] There were much publicized investigations into an alleged award of thousands of taxi permits to an individual applicant[23] and the suspected collusion of certain Customs officers in the import of luxury cars without the payment of duties,[24] the arrest of the head of a Malacca state government corporation for suspected bribery[25] and the removal of a bankrupt member from a Malacca district council.[26] Post-*reformasi* popular criticism held that only sustained governance reforms—stronger regulation, consistent oversight and stricter performance standards—could significantly diminish the rentierism and money politics that lie at the heart of many politico-corporate networks. Yet Eric Chia, former director of the ailing Perwaja steel mill, and Kasitah Gadam, a former minister from Sabah, were the most prominent people charged with acts of corruption; Chia and Kasitah were by then political "lightweights." The Anti-Corruption Agency did not charge anyone "higher," an indication that Abdullah was not ready to institute an uncompromising anti-corruption drive to cleanse high-level politico-corporate interests. Abdullah probably had neither the power nor the time to quickly dismantle or substantially restructure the many coalitions of interests without provoking instability, especially within UMNO.

Even so, anti-corruption moves, combined with other Abdullah initiatives, helped him secure his "own" national mandate via a general election. Abdullah's preparation for the March 2004 election disengaged from Mahathir's post-1999 Malay-bashing. Instead, Abdullah led UMNO to repair its damaged ties with the Malay grassroots and the Malay-dominated civil service—two often overlapping sources of dissident Malay voters during the last years of Mahathir's leadership. Reversing Mahathir's penchant for "mega projects,"[27] Abdullah "indefinitely postponed" the double-tracking project in favor of other "social priorities."[28] He delayed the politically risky move to list Felda on the KLSE,[29] and dismissed an unofficial proposal by the Employees Provident Fund to disallow its contributors from withdrawing part of their contributions prior to retirement.[30] In late December 2003, Abdullah introduced a RM 200 million "tuition" scheme to help 500,000 poor pupils "of all races, both in urban and rural areas," to cope with the change from Malay to English in the teaching of science and mathematics.[31] The same scheme was an indirect reward for schoolteachers, whose services and contributions had not been lauded in recent years.

Abdullah's measures signalled his strategy of re-orienting the government toward matters of rural development and social priorities—populist ones with NEP overtones at that, namely education, health care and housing. His "plebian" initiatives, consistent with the media's focus on Abdullah's "gentility," "religiosity" and "rusticity," bespoke his personal sensitivity toward rural Malay communities and the UMNO grassroots.

Thus was cultivated the "feel-good Abdullah factor" that influenced the outcome of the 2004 general election in circumstances that included reasonably good economic conditions, an absence of critical issues and the unravelling of the opposition following the historic unity of the Barisan Alternatif (BA) in 1999. PAS's decision to stake its political and electoral advance on its so-called "Islamic State" goal was a strategic mistake that alienated many potential allies and supporters. The Democratic Action Party (DAP) had no compelling grounds to recover from successive electoral defeats by its usual rivals—the Malaysian Chinese Association (MCA) and Gerakan Rakyat Malaysia (Gerakan). Parti Keadilan Nasional remained the heir to *reformasi* dissent, but the party had not yet acquired the qualities that had made for a formidable PAS challenge to UMNO in 1999, that is, a large and dedicated membership, an efficient electoral machinery and an ideological focus. Moreover, the Election Commission added new parliamentary seats throughout the country, with the exception of the PAS-governed states of Kelantan and Trengganu. The Election Commission's redelineation of constituencies in Kedah and Kelantan particularly disadvantaged PAS. The opposition had been virtually erased in Sabah after Parti Bersatu Sabah rejoined the BN, and in Sarawak there was no opposition presence to take advantage of intra-BN bickering.

Although PAS issued its Islamic State Document and Abdullah announced his Islam Hadhari in reply, the 2004 election was fought in the absence of Mahathir's controversial figure and beyond the Anwar Ibrahim affair. UMNO did not seek to out-Islamize PAS, but PAS itself could not out-politicize UMNO in other areas. Under these circumstances, UMNO was able to inflict heavy defeats upon PAS in the Malay heartland in general and, unexpectedly, in Trengganu and Kelantan. PAS lost control of the Trengganu state government and retained power in Kelantan by a very slim majority. The conduct of the election was sloppier than ever before and sparked many opposition complaints of irregularities and Election Commission bias in favor of the BN. Several election petitions, pending before the Election Tribunal, seek to challenge the results in parliamentary and state contests.[32] But the election outcome was truly surprising only in the lopsided BN win of 90 percent of parliamentary seats with less than 64 percent of the popular vote.

For Abdullah, in particular, the 2004 elections met two critical purposes. UMNO retrieved its lost legitimacy by defeating PAS in the Malay heartland and reasserted its dominance of the BN by regaining an outright majority within the coalition's representation in Parliament. It now remains for Abdullah to achieve a third purpose with his own mandate—to consolidate his leadership at the next UMNO party election and quell the tensions over succession that have so riven UMNO since the beginning of the Mahathir era.

Notes

1   This essay was first presented as a workshop paper in March 2002. As it was being revised for publication in June 2002, Mahathir unexpectedly

announced his plan to resign from political office on June 22, while making his closing speech at the UMNO General Assembly in Kuala Lumpur.

2   These accounts are instructive for emphasizing different dimensions of this crisis.

3   The term "bumiputera" refers to a person of indigenous background, but in Malaysian political economy it is practically consonant with "Malay."

4   The long and difficult disputes between the state and the Chinese education movement in Malaya are well documented in Tan Liok Ee 1997. The enrolment of non-Chinese (mainly Malay) children in Chinese-language schools is now estimated to be about 65,000.

5   For an analysis of the social and political implications of Mahathir's Bangsa Malaysia and Vision 2020, see Khoo 1995, 327–331.

6   Significantly, Anwar phrased the slogan in Mandarin rather than the official Malay language. Anwar's ideas on multiculturalism, elaborated within his discussion of an "Asian renaissance," are found in Anwar 1996.

7   The ringgit fell from a peak exchange rate of RM 2.493 to USD 1 in April 1997 to its lowest rate of RM 4.88 on 7 January 1998. KLSE's market capitalization declined from RM 806.77 billion in 1996 to RM 375.80 billion in 1997 and RM 182 billion in September 1998.

8   After the slogan, *kolusi, korupsi, nepotisme* ("collusion, corruption and nepotism"), coined by anti-Suharto forces in Indonesia.

9   Bank Negara instituted "exchange control mechanisms" that ended the free convertibility of the ringgit (*New Straits Times*, September 2, 1998). The ringgit, traded at RM 4.0960 to USD 1 on that day, was pegged at RM 3.800 the next day. Holders of offshore ringgit accounts were given one month to repatriate their funds to Malaysia: beginning October 1, the ringgit would not be traded overseas. For the money market, the most serious controls were those prohibiting non-resident correspondent banks and stockbroking firms from obtaining domestic credit facilities, and residents from obtaining ringgit credit facilities from non-resident individuals. Non-residents were required to deposit their ringgit securities with authorized depositories and to hold the proceeds from the sale of such securities in external accounts for at least one year before converting them to foreign currency (*New Straits Times*, September 2, 1998).

10   Ahmad Don, governor of Bank Negara, and his deputy, Fong Weng Phak, had resigned in late August 1998 in disagreement with Mahathir's move to impose capital controls.

11   The term "economic shield" was frequently used by the crisis managers and their spokespersons. See, for example, Mahani 2000, 184–199.

12 The Malaysian government's policies are set out in Malaysia 1998.

13 Jorgen Borhnoft, outgoing president of the Malaysian International Chamber of Commerce and Industry, expressed MICCI's "concern that there does not seem to be enough strong action against those people who were responsible for that massive spate of irresponsible borrowing, and just as irresponsible lending." He mentioned that MICCI supported the capital controls of September 1999 "on the basis that they are clearly seen to be short-term measures" and urged "serious structural adjustments" to some troubled companies (Dow Jones 1999).

14 Malaysia 1998, Box 1.

15 See "Capital controls erode" for a neo-liberal criticism of the capital controls.

16 On November 29, 2000, exactly one year after the 1999 general election, Barisan Alternatif (BA, or Alternative Front), through Parti Keadilan, led by Dr. Wan Azizah Wan Ismail (Anwar's wife), defeated BN in a by-election in Lunas, Kedah, a state assembly seat which the ruling coalition had held for forty-three years.

17 For accounts of Anwar's experience under detention, as recollected by a co-detainee, see Husin Ali 1996.

18 On July 10, 2002, the Federal Court, the highest court in Malaysia, dismissed Anwar's appeal against his conviction on charges of corruption and his six-year prison sentence arising out of his first trial, which ended in April 1998. The three judges who dismissed Anwar's appeal held unanimously that the trial hearings had shown "no errors in law" and "no travesty of justice." See Malaysiakini 2002.

19 Among other things, the award to the Malaysia Mining Corporation – Gamuda Berhad risked a severe deterioration in trade and diplomatic relations with India and China. Prior to the MMC–Gamuda award, the Indian Railway Construction Company and the China Railway Engineering Corporation had been issued "Letters of Intent" over the construction of different packages of the double-tracking project in a complex and broad government-to-government counter-trade deal. By local media standards, coverage of the risks of awarding the project to MMC–Gamuda was unusually open. See, for example, "Rail deal raises concerns over palm oil exports," *New Straits Times* (*Business Times*), November 12, 2003. With the election due in 2004, it was conceivable that any deterioration in relations with India and China could have an adverse impact on the attitudes of some ethnic Indian and Chinese voters whose support UMNO and Barisan Nasional critically need.

20 Summarizing a Citigroup risk assessment, the Malaysian news agency, Bernama, reported: "If as expected, the Government of Prime Minister

Datuk Seri Abdullah Ahmad Badawi secures a comfortable victory in the general election scheduled by end-2004, a greater push to liberalise the economy and promote regional economic integration as a means to attract foreign direct investments (FDI) can be expected" ("Greater push to liberalise if Dollah secures comfortable polls win," *New Straits Times*, December 11, 2003). It should be noted, however, that Abdullah expressed the need to shift from FDI to domestic direct investment since "foreign companies investing locally paid more attention to developing their own brands, technology as well as have limited involvement in the local production chains" ("Shift to domestic-led growth," *New Straits Times*, November 11, 2003). Actually Mahathir had earlier mooted the reduced emphasis on FDI because of increasing difficulties in attracting FDI in view of the changing directions of FDI flows within the East Asian region.

21 S. Jayasankaran, "Bated breath," *Far Eastern Economic Review*, May 15, 2003: 44, gives a summary of rising budget deficits, from 3.2 per cent of GDP in 1999 to an estimated 5.6 per cent of GDP in 2002.

22 Significantly, Abdullah made known his general views on the need to tackle corruption in both the public and private sectors in Parliament on November 3, 2003, when he tabled a motion of thanks to Dr Mahathir Mohamad. Abdullah's speech was reprinted as "Dr M a statesman ahead of his time," *New Straits Times*, November 4, 2003.

23 For summary coverage of a public quarrel between the Anti-Corruption Agency and the minister of Entrepeneur Development, Nazri Aziz, over the allegedly improper award of 6,000 taxi licences, see "Nazri summoned to meet ACA officials next week" (*New Straits Times*, December 5, 2003); "Probe: PM to meet ministers" (*New Straits Times*, December 8, 2003); and "Angry Nazri slams Nordin" (*New Straits Times*, December 9, 2003).

24 "Customs officers remanded," *New Straits Times*, November 18, 2003.

25 "State corporation head arrested," *New Straits Times*, November 28, 2003.

26 "PM orders Malacca Government to remove bankrupt from post," *New Straits Times*, November 20, 2003.

27 In what may be seen as a post-retirement statement in his own defence, Mahathir said, "Everything done to hasten the country's progress was labelled as a mega project and was opposed by the local NGOs and even sometimes by the local media" ("Dr M: Colonised mentality hindering Malaysia's progress," *New Straits Times*, December 5, 2003).

28 For an approving appraisal of this postponement on economic and political grounds, see Steven C. M. Wong, "Productiveness of our actions legitimises them" (*New Straits Times*, December 29, 2003).

29 "Welfare of settlers will be taken care of" (*New Straits Times*, November 6, 2003), reported Abdullah as saying, "What is important is that we do not want the settlers to assume that we have not given any consideration to their interests and welfare."

30 For a summary of the EPF's obviously unpopular "review" of its current practice of allowing contributors, when they reach the age of 50, to make a "pre-retirement" withdrawal of one-third of their savings, see "EPF withdrawal review" (*New Straits Times*, December 11, 2003).

31 This may be regarded as a politically imaginative solution to the uneasiness created by Mahathir's attempt to reintroduce the teaching of science and mathematics in English as a way to combat a general decline in the mastery of the English language, supposedly most keenly suffered by Malay pupils. See "Tuition for poor pupils" (*New Straits Times*, December 31, 2003).

32 For an unofficial summary of the election results, see *New Straits Times*, March 23, 2004. Philip Khoo, "A brave new world?" (*Aliran Monthly* 24, 3 [2004]: 2–7) analyzes some of the issues mentioned here.

References

Anonymous. N.d. Capital controls erode. *http://www.freemalaysia.com/economic/loss_of_control.htm*.

Anwar Ibrahim. 1996. *The Asian Renaissance*. Singapore: Times Books International.

Dow Jones. 1999. Foreign investors want more reform: MICCI. June 15. (*http://freemalaysia.com/reformasi_investors.htm*)

Gomez, Edmund Terence. 1990. *UMNO's Corporate Investments*. Kuala Lumpur: Forum.

Husin Ali, Syed. 1996. *Two Faces*. Kuala Lumpur: Insan.

Jomo K.S. 2001. *Malaysian Eclipse: Economic Crisis and Recovery*. London: Zed Books.

Kershaw, Roger. 1989. Within the family: The limits of doctrinal differentiation in the Malaysian ruling party election of 1987. *Review of Indonesian and Malaysian Affairs* 23: 125–93.

Khoo Boo Teik. 1995. *Paradoxes of Mahathirism: An Intellectual Biography of Mahathir Mohamad*. Kuala Lumpur: Oxford University Press.

Khoo Boo Teik. 2000. Economic nationalism and its discontents: Malaysian political economy after July 1997. In *Politics and Markets in the Wake of the Asian Crisis*, ed. Richard Robison et al., 212–237. London: Routledge.

Khoo Khay Jin. 1992. The grand vision: Mahathir and modernisation. In *Fragmented Vision: Culture And Politics In Contemporary Malaysia*, ed. Joel S. Kahn and Francis Loh Kok Wah, 44–76. Sydney: Allen and Unwin.

Mahani Zainal Abidin. 2000. Malaysia's alternative approach to crisis management. *Southeast Asian Affairs 2000*, ed. Daljit Singh, 184–199. Singapore: Institute of Southeast Asian Studies.

Mahathir Mohamad. 1991. Malaysia: The way forward. Working Paper presented at the Inaugural Meeting of the Malaysian Business Council. Kuala Lumpur, February 28, 1991. Reprinted in *New Straits Times*, March 2, 1991.

Malaysia. 1998. *Status of the Malaysian Economy* (*http://www.topspot.com/NEAC/*).

Malaysiakini. 2002. Anwar's guilty verdict upheld, unanimous decision. July 10. (*http://www.malaysiakini.com/*).

Searle, Peter. 1999. *The Riddle of Malaysian Capitalism: Rent-seekers or Real Capitalists?* St. Leonards, New South Wales: Allen and Unwin.

Shamsul A.B. 1988. The "battle royal": The UMNO elections of 1987. *Southeast Asian Affairs 1988*, 170–88. Singapore: Institute of Southeast Asian Studies.

Tan Liok Ee. 1997. *The Politics of Chinese Education in Malaya 1945–1961.* Kuala Lumpur: Oxford University Press.

Tan, Simon. 1990. The rise of state authoritarianism in Malaysia. *Bulletin of Concerned Asian Scholars* 22, no. 3 (July–September): 32–42.

9

Post-Crisis Economic Impasse and Political Recovery in Thailand: The Resurgence of Economic Nationalism[*]

Kasian Tejapira

The Root Cause of Economic Non-Recovery

Over three years following the severest financial crisis and economic recession in postwar Thai history, with the Democrat government of Prime Minister Chuan Leekpai and Finance Minister Tarrin Nimmanahaeminda having persistently pursued an IMF-prescribed, market-led, globalizing/ neo-liberalizing economic reform program since it came to power in November 1997, Professor Dr. Ammar Siamwalla, the finest and highly-respected senior mainstream economist in the country and one of the two Cassandras who had presciently and vocally warned of the impending devaluation of the baht and the resultant doom of the bubble economy prior to the crisis, published, after a long while, another of his influential articles in the local English press (Ammar 2000).[1] And again, despite his well-known sympathy for the general thrust of the Chuan-Tarrin government's economic reform policies, he had some bad economic news to tell.

Apparently, his article was a critique of a policy proposal, similarly put forward at that time by both the Thai Rak Thai Party—the foremost contender for governmental office in the general election on 6 January 2001[2]—and the former figurehead of the ruling Democrat Party's economic team,[3] to nationalize and take out the debilitating bad debts from the banking sector by setting up a national or "public" asset management company (AMC) to buy up its remaining intractable non-performing loans (NPLs), thereby allowing banks to capitalize faster and resume lending and thus reviving the country's so-far crippled and dysfunctional credit system as well as stalled economic recovery.[4] Macro-economically speaking, Ammar points out, this proposal rests on an assumed "virtuous circle" of a long chain of logic derived from the South Korean economic

179

recovery experience: expectations of high economic growth ⇒ higher borrowers' income prospects ⇒ increase in loan valuations ⇒ less bank capitalization ⇒ more bank lending ⇒ higher economic growth ⇒ higher borrowers' income ⇒ greater increase in loan valuations ⇒ etc., ad infinitum, hip, hip, hooray! (Iwasaki 2000). According to the national AMC advocates, this macro-economic miracle could be easily triggered off by the government's mere purchase of bad loans from the banks at a generous price.

However, the trouble is the whole magic scenario is based on a crucial but faulty presumption that, in Ammar's rendering: "bank lending is currently constrained only by their lack of capital, and that shortfall is due to the large amount of NPLs for which they have to find adequate reserves" (Ammar 2000). Actually, he argues, banks are now sitting on a huge pile of money.[5] That they are unwilling to lend has little to do with the question of insufficient money supply but everything to do with the lack of effective demand.

Thai entrepreneurs in the real sector of the economy do have a demand for loans but their demand is not effective because most of their companies do not have an adequate equity base to meet the banks' now much more rigorous globalized (read westernized or Americanized) standard, which has resulted from the IMF–Tarrin's reform of the financial sector. Thus, whereas formerly the average debt/equity ratio of Thai companies in the non-financial sector was conventionally between 2:1 to 3:1 and has presently become 2.8:1 as against that of less than 1:1 normally obtained in the Anglo- and Latin American West,[6] now the post-crisis Thai banks are trying to adapt to the latter ratio as the new requisite, globalized/neo-liberalized standard in considering corporate loan applications.[7] And yet, since many Thai non-financial companies (particularly the bigger ones) had borrowed extensively abroad during the good, old bubble days, especially through the BIBFs (Bangkok International Banking Facilities)' out-in financing channels set up in 1993 and consequently already had their equity wiped out by the 1997 sharp baht devaluation,[8] the resultant huge forex losses,[9] the stock market crash[10] and the three-year-long and still continuing deep economic recession,[11] how could they possibly maintain any presentable equity base to qualify for a new bank loan? Hence Ammar's hard-hitting diagnosis of the Thai economic disease as follows:

> The mistake of those believing that an AMC would help lies in the belief that only the banks are under-capitalised. Actually, the banks have gone some ways toward an adequate recapitalisation to meet a much more stringent standard than

previously. It is the non-financial corporate sector in Thailand as a whole that is under-capitalised. This is not just a post-crisis phenomenon, it has always been so...

It is this decapitalisation of the companies that is the root cause of the problem, far more so than the decapitalisation of the banks.

Thailand is an over-indebted country despite a saving rate that is quite high by international standards... We thus end up with a savings-rich, but equity-starved economy (Ammar 2000).

The Globalization or Death Impasse

From the above discussion, the following conclusions about the Thai economic malady may be inferred:[12]

1. The main problem of the current Thai economy is the contradiction between the globalized banking sector and the still "Thai-Thai" non-financial corporate sector.[13] It is precisely this contradiction or incompatibility between the two that has been paralyzing the credit system and preventing an economic recovery so far.[14] Evidently, a partial, halfway reform of the Thai corporate sector won't work and one needs either to complete or undo it, i.e., go further and also globalize or westernize the non-financial corporate sector, or revoke the too stringent new capital requirements and loan regulations officially imposed on the banks and revert more or less to the former culture of lending practice.[15]

2. If one chooses the former, it amounts to a daunting and strenuous attempt to transform the Thai capitalist economy from a hitherto localized or corrupted version of a bank-based, high-debt model a la German, Japan and East Asian system[16] to a market-based, prudential model a la Anglo- and Latin American system.[17] The choice, therefore, implies two further things, namely, the transformation of family or dynastic businesses into real public companies, and a need to push the latent rich savings of the middle and wealthy classes from the relatively secure safe-deposit boxes of the banks into the risky equities market through fiscal and financial policy adjustments and the building of many new and indispensable institutional mechanisms required for the proper functioning of an equities market-based economy.

However, given the fact that the Thai stock market consists mostly of small investors rather than institutional ones, that the latter are still limited in range and legally exclude potentially important big players such as pension funds and life insurance companies, that even if they are allowed to invest in the stock market, they will still need to build and/or develop the necessary mechanisms as well as to gain and accumulate the experience and skills in watching and checking the performance of the public companies whose shares they hold, that even when these outfits are all in place, the same information, the same rumors and the same information-processing apparatus (i.e., economic theory) that these institutional investors utilize will still lead them to display the same notorious herd instinct that accentuates the already high Thai stock market volatility, etc., given all the aforementioned, it is highly improbable or at least will take an awfully long time for Thailand even to approximate to the self-proclaimed and ideologically useful American "market-based" model.[18]

Hence the increasing pre-election public misgivings about and discontent with the Chuan–Tarrin government's globalizing/neo-liberalizing economic reform strategy, which basically consisted of keeping up the contradiction between the globalized banking sector and the "Thai-Thai" non-financial corporate sector, letting the ensuing suspended economic animation progressively undermine the capital base and will to survive of both the corporate debtors and bank creditors until either the living-dead entrepreneurs or the zombie bankers whose hands are at each other's throats become exhausted first, drop dead and then let go of their assets and equity as well as the ownership and management of their companies to foreign shareholders or buyers. If and when these "Thai-Thai" non-financial companies follow in the footsteps of those formerly Thai-owned banks and fall into foreign hands, then corporate good governance and transparency in the globalized American style will reign over Thai business community and the Thai economy will fully recover!?![19]

The bankers who were pressured by the Chuan–Tarrin government into strangling their delinquent debtors along the lines of the above-described "globalization or death" strategy have been hit hard by a boomerang effect of both new and re-entry NPLs in almost equal measure.[20] Thus, for instance, Mr. Banthun Lamsam, managing director of Thai Farmers Bank and the most outspoken and articulate among top Thai bankers, had become so disillusioned with the Chuan–Tarrin government's financial reform package, disheartened by the relapsing credit system and pessimistic about the prospects of a probably necessary new round of his bank's re-capitalization that he bitterly professed his inability to see other way out for his bank except "to sell itself out to foreign financial institutions...[or]...let the government take it over," a sentiment with which Kosit Panpiemras, executive chairman of Bangkok Bank, concurred.[21]

Not only the reformed but some of the reformers themselves also voiced growing unease and doubts about the effects and prospects of the reform plan. So admitted M.R. Chatumongol Sonakul, a self-proclaimed "laissez-faire capitalist economist," fiercely independent and sardonically blunt former permanent secretary at the Finance Ministry and then governor of the Bank of Thailand before being removed from office by the Thaksin government in mid-2001 for disagreement over financial policies, that: "The economy has yet to see light at the end of the tunnel...I used to think that I knew...but then when I found out that the foreign debt figures which had been supposed to be at a certain level were wrong, that they were actually 20 billion US$ higher than previously estimated, which are considered extremely high, I had to come back and attend to them again."[22]

And yet, when pressed for a way out, Chatumongol could only come up with the same "globalization or death" line, the only question being which institution would act as the local vanguard-cum-enforcer of economic globalization, the state or the central bank. Thus, he suggested if one wants to see good governance nationwide, it can be done in either way:

> 1) Someone takes care of the whole matter by passing a law that serves as the framework of good governance...The state or a strongman wades in to explain and draft a law to enforce it. What is against it is forbidden...
>
> 2) The Bank of Thailand (BOT) compels the financial institutions that constitute the dominant sector in the business community to observe good governance. When those non-financial business companies wish to borrow money from the financial institutions, they too would have to observe good governance otherwise the latter wouldn't lend.[23]

However, the crux of the matter is while the economic feasibility of all the Chuan–Tarrin, Chatumongol, Ammar or other variations on the same "globalization or death" line[24] had been and was still hotly debated and open to dispute, their common domestic political feasibility had progressively dwindled since the beginning of 2000 and fallen sharply in tandem with the waning popularity of the Democrat government, the approach of the January 2001 general election and the chronic economic recession-induced resurgence of populist-nationalist sentiment and movements. So much so that the surviving Thai NPL-capitalists, be they

Sino-Thai or royal, who still held on to their assets and equity, had dug themselves in in an all-out, last-ditch resistance to being globalized unto bankruptcy.[25]

The Debtors Strike Back

Thus, for example, Siam Cement, the largest and best-connected industrial conglomerate in the country with more than 100 subsidiaries and dealing in over 60,000 products, which was once a shining model of Thai corporate debt restructuring when it had worked out clear, neat plans to repay its then USD 5.4 billion debt after baht devaluation in mid-1997, had unexpectedly stalled its restructuring effort since the beginning of 2000. Hence, the sale of its non-core assets ground to a halt and the reduction in its remaining USD 4.6 billion debt was marginal with its debt/equity ratio worsening from 243 percent in the first quarter to 260 percent in the second quarter of 2000. The reason for not further selling its assets at fire-sale prices, as explained the company's president Chumpol Nalamlieng, was quite simple: "*Giving away something at a loss is really a disservice to shareholders,*" the most prestigious among whom, alas, was the royal family, which held 36 percent of its shares.[26]

Much more dramatically if rather desperately, Mr. Prachai Leophairatana, the once major shareholder and CEO of Thai Petrochemical Industry Plc. (TPI), the largest petrochemical conglomerate in Southeast Asia and the then biggest delinquent debtor in the country with a USD 3.7 billion debt or approximately 10 percent of the financial system's total NPLs, allegedly mobilized a 6,000-strong rowdy mob of his lay-off-fearing, non-unionized employees to lay siege to, riotously disrupt and successfully abort two attempts by TPI's 140 creditors to hold a court-prescribed meeting to vote on a rehabilitation plan. However, the creditors' third attempt to hold a meeting proved successful. Branded "*a slave indenture*" by Prachai, the plan stipulated a further reduction in TPI oil refinery's capacity utilization from 60–70 percent to 30 percent, the sale of TPI's non-core assets, and the swap of USD 700 million unpaid interest for its equity which made the creditor banks a major shareholder of TPI at 75 percent while reducing the Leophairatana family's holding in the company from 60 to 20 percent and costing Prachai his control over TPI's management.[27]

In the same vein, Mr. Wirun Techaphaibun, struggling NPL-entrepreneur and owner-cum-chief director of the multi-billion baht World Trade

Center (WTC) complex in downtown Bangkok, put the blame squarely on Finance Minister Tarrin's "14 August 1998" bank rehabilitation program for the inflexible stance typically taken by banks, especially government-majority-owned ones such as Bangkok Metropolitan Bank (BMB—actually his family's former flagship and convenient piggy bank),[28] in the debt restructuring negotiation process under the new and more stringent banking requirements and regulations. Hence BMB's rejection of his proposal for a 30 percent debt forgiveness out of WTC's total NPL of 1.2 billion baht, the breakdown in the negotiations and the consequent lawsuit brought against WTC by BMB. Wirun called on the next, hopefully non-Democrat government to change the existing financial policy and relax the banking regulations so as to reduce overall NPLs in the financial system, stimulate the flow of credit and bring about real economic recovery.

For the said purposes, he had turned into an activist-cum-politician, initiating and chairing a so-called Revivifying Businessmen Project, which aimed at piloting both the NPL-entrepreneurs and Thailand through economic troubled waters by dispensing business clinical advice.[29] Meanwhile, the then Senate committee on finance and fiscal affairs chaired by Senator Suchon Charli-krau had intervened in the TPI conflict on behalf of Prachai and company. by holding a hearing on the case as well as the controversial bankruptcy and eleven other related economic laws imposed by the IMF and passed under the Democrat government. Criticizing these laws for being unfairly negligent of small creditors', shareholders' and employees' interests as against those of major creditors, for lacking in mechanism for resolving hostile cases, and for providing no protection to new money injected by creditors in the debt restructuring process, Suchon planned other similar public events to push for their eventual review.[30]

And last but not least, Wirun also ran as a party-list MP candidate of the opposition New Aspiration Party (NAP) in the January 6, 2001, general election and slated to become a member of its economic team responsible for international trade.[31] Apart from Wirun, other prominent real-sector, NPL-entrepreneurs who had newly found their ways through economic nationalism to various parties' lists of MP candidates included, for example, Sawat Horrungruang (Chat Thai Party), the steel magnate and infamous author of the Thai NPL debtors' "Three Don'ts" battle-cry—don't pay interest, don't negotiate, don't run away—and Chirayuth Wasurat (NAP), businessman and former leading senator who had been a staunch critic of the Democrat government and IMF from the beginning. Among the political parties, the Chat Thai Party, the Seritham Party, the

Chat Phattana Party, NAP, TRT and the Thai Motherland Party were, to varying degrees and in ascending order of scope and seriousness, publicly committed to the revision of some or other elements of the IMF–Democrat government's economic reform package.[32]

On top of the fact that these anti-Democrat and IMF NPL-entrepreneurs were occupying strategic positions in many parties, pre-election public sentiment was also fed up with the Democrat leadership (especially Chuan and Tarrin)'s overconfidence and pigheadedness while TRT's openhanded, "populist" policies were also a major attraction for other parties' provincial MPs. And last but not least, in a highly unusual and politically-charged move, two of the remaining top Sino-Thai tycoons, chairman of Bangkok Bank Chatri Sophonpanich and head of the Charoen Pokphand Group Dhanin Chiraravanont, publicly endorsed TRT head Thaksin Shinawatra's bid for premiership, thus throwing the considerable weight of the Bangkok-based business and financial community behind him.[33] Therefore, chances were TRT was "three times" as likely to form and lead the next coalition government as the Democrat Party, in the stated opinion of an influential and experienced political activist-cum-public intellectual.[34]

All in all, as a foreign correspondent observed: "Most Thai companies have not shown the will to undertake the difficult managerial and operational overhauls that most analysts claim are necessary to return to profitability and stay competitive globally."[35] The key reason, as pointed out by Thanong Khanthong, a well-versed and well-informed Thai economic reporter-cum-columnist, is that Thai corporation owners refused to "reduce their debt load by *letting go of part of their assets and equity* in exchange for fresh capital and better management." This little-discussed refusal, in Thanong's opinion, "lies at the heart of the mother of all problems" (Thanong 2000a. Emphasis added.). Apparently, the financially cornered debtors had found another way out. They decided to strike back politically.

The Long March to Political Recovery

Cultural politically speaking, Thailand entered the age of "globalization" in the aftermath of the latest and second mass uprising that toppled the military-backed government of Prime Minister General Suchinda Kraprayoon in May 1992. Although the urban poor and slum dwellers made up a large part of the demonstrators along with the middle class and, in addition, bore the brunt of the violent suppression by the police and military, the political import and public meaning of the May 1992 uprising was almost exclusively hegemonized by the middle class and the incident itself often cited as evidence of, as well as becoming synonymous with, the political rise of the Thai middle class from under state authoritarian rule.[36]

Being fairly well-educated and affluent, earning their livings as small and medium entrepreneurs, investors and professionals in such modern economic sectors as print and electronic media, advertising and education, hotels and tourism, finance and securities, stock market and real estate development, retail trade and marketing, import and export, etc.,[37] the Thai middle class lead a typical globalized/westernized urban consumer lifestyle. The plurality being ethnic Chinese, they are, so to speak, the ungrateful offspring of past military dictators as well as the beneficiaries of three decades of state-promoted, continuous, unbalanced, unequal, inequitable and unsustainable socio-economic development under the latter, who had raised, nurtured and force-fed them economically while restricting them culturally and emasculating them politically on the Thai official nationalist pretext of keeping the un-Thai settlers at bay.

Hence two salient political cultural characteristics of the Thai middle class—their non-nationalist or anti-nationalist tendency and their liberal authoritarian as against democratic populist inclination. Having proven themselves time and again an opportunistic and unreliable ally of both dictatorship (in the 1973 and 1992 popular risings against military rule) and democracy (in the 1976 and 1991 military coups) alike, they yearn for a clean and kind, effective and efficient, accessible and liberal, enlightened and benevolent government that may not necessarily be a democracy, especially of the mass participatory type. Their respective attitudes towards different politically significant groups tell it all. They are nervous about military dictators, look down upon elected politicians from the provinces, distrust and don't really understand people's protest movements and NGOs, but trust high-ranking and seemingly respectable bureaucrats and look up to super-rich and successful professional managers or business CEOs (Kasian 1995).

The post-May 1992 spellbinding mantra of this culturally hegemonic and most loudly and blatantly globalized class in Thai society was of course "globalization." Its first Thai avatar, "Lokanuwat," which literally means "to turn with the globe," was coined by Professor Chai-anan Samudavanija, a maverick, colorful and versatile royalist political scientist-cum-public intellectual, and then widely and successfully propagated by the *Phoojadkan Raiwan* (Manager Daily), a leading and very popular business newspaper in the period from the May 1992 uprising until the July 1997 economic crisis, together with its various sister periodicals. So much so that "Lokanuwat" for a long while became the talk of the town and made its incessant, ubiquitous appearance, oftentimes uncalled-for or not obviously pertinent, in the press' headlines, columns and news reports, radio phone-ins, TV talk shows, TV advertisements for all sorts of products including a soybean sauce and even a birthday speech by King Bhumibol.

With its seemingly progressive, outward and forward-looking con-notations, the "Lokanuwat" discourse was adroitly used by Chai-anan, *Phoojadkan* and the globalizers among Thai public intellectuals to politically push the military back to their barracks and challenge the legitimacy of the rising elected politicians by branding their respective rule "counterclockwise," "against the trend of the globe" and "falling behind the trend of the globe." More ominously, it was also used to signify an aggressive and overconfident new national project of Thai capitalism with an expansionist implication for its neighbors. Symptomatic of this Thai bourgeois expansionist trend was the decision of the Royal Institute to adopt a new coinage as the official Thai equivalent of "globalization" in place of the pre-existing "Lokanuwat," namely "Lokaphiwat," which literally denotes "to turn the globe" (Kasian 1995).

One psycho-cultural impact of the 1997 economic debacle on the Thai middle class was to transform their collective imaginings of "globalization" from rosy to thorny one. Now they come to have a divided mind about it. On the one hand, they know they owed their hitherto rise and prosperity to a free market and an open economy but, on the other hand, they have also learned a costly and painful lesson that were the national economy and market to be thrown limitlessly open and fully free to outside competitors, they could be badly beaten and might not survive. It is precisely in the middle class' new-found hesitancy and ambivalence towards "globalization," now hanging over their heads like a two-edged sword, that a cultural opportunity structure has been opened up for a critical skepticism about "globalization" and a new turn towards economic nationalism.

Thus, in the aftermath of the 1997 crisis, Thai politics was mired in a triple impasse as follows.

First, the Thai electocratic political system by itself was incapable of coping with the financial crisis and salvaging Thai capitalist economy in the age of globalization but needed the help of IMF's credibility and directives in order to do so.[38] At the same time, the economically dominant Thai capitalist class and the middle class on their own were also incapable of mounting a protest movement strong and effective enough to push for political reform or a change of national leadership but needed the extraordinarily volatile and critical conditions of the economic crisis plus the informal support of such extra-parliamentary forces as the military, the IMF, people's organizations as well as the monarchy to achieve both.

Second, both the political system and the political leadership had a legitimacy deficit whereas the revival of Thai capitalist economy under the IMF program required a high degree of political legitimacy since its loan conditionality caused devastating socio-economic dislocation. Therefore, the IMF loan rescue-cum-economic restructuring program needed a technocratic consensus-based mass political passivity as a sine qua non for its success, i.e., people had to tamely believe that all economic problems were technical by nature, that these were best solely entrusted to technocrats to decide on their behalf, that their interests and well-being would be best served and taken care of by letting the technocrats lead them by the nose so as to follow in the IMF's footsteps.

Third, Thailand saw no alternative to the IMF line in solving its economic problems. Hence the utter meaninglessness and inconsequentiality of political reform, the new constitution or the new general election in terms of economic policy alternatives for they amounted to a mere selection of a group of people among many others to carry out a pre-determined plan devised by the IMF. That wasn't much different from having a bunch of kids compete with one another to do an exercise consisting of questions posed by Teacher IMF. Some kids might come up with better answers than others but basically that was all they could do. Nothing went far beyond the framework already laid down.

After languishing in the above-described impasse for three years, and despite the continuing economic non-recovery, Thai politics has staged a nascent recovery, i.e., mass protest movements have re-emerged in force all over the country, the Washington consensus-derived Thai technocratic consensus is being seriously challenged and rejected and alternative strategic visions other than the globalist/neo-liberal one are being actively and collectively constructed, publicly presented and widely publicized and debated. People who have been involved in this political recovery can be roughly divided into three groups as follows:

1. The so-called "Octobrists" (or *Khon deuan tula*): These are mostly well-known and established writers, thinkers, academics, public intellectuals and activists who used to take part in the historic radical student and popular movements of the 1970s and later joined the

communist-led armed struggle in the countryside or carried on their cultural political activities non-violently in the city.

2. The small but influential group of so-called "Senior Citizens" and "socially-outstanding good people": Members of this group are respectable and honest retired or active senior government officials. Ideologically a hybrid of royalism and communitarianism, they work mostly through development and grassroots NGOs to build up local community bases for socio-economic and political reform against the centralized state bureaucracy, corrupt elected politicians, capitalist economic globalization and consumerist culture.

3. Thai entrepreneurs in various trades and at all levels whose businesses are facing stiff competition from foreign business interests, or whose assets are being sold off and equity taken over by foreign creditors: Also included in this group are some outspoken and prominent independent nationalist academics, especially social scientists and economists.

The above-mentioned groups and their individual members have since mid-1997 mingled together and formed a variety of ad hoc loose nationalist groupings, e.g., the National Salvation Community (*Prachakhom kob ban koo meuang*), an early grouping of activists, academics and intellectuals who were concerned with the economic crisis; the Bangchak-lovers Club (*Chomrom khon rak bangchak*), which is opposed to the sale of the state-owned Bangchak oil refinery to foreign investors; the United Thai for National Liberation Club (*Chomrom ruam jai thai koo chat*), whose main aim is to prevent the sale of the nationalized Bangkok Metropolitan Bank and Siam City Bank to foreign banking interests; the Free Thai Movement (*Khabuankan seri thai*), a group of prominent academics and intellectuals whose namesake was the underground resistance movement against Japanese occupation during the Second World War; the *Withithas* Project, a publication project which has published a long series of radical leftist anti-globalization semi-academic pocketbooks since 1997; and the Thai Graduates' Group (*Klum bandit thai*), a staunchly anti-imperialist group of engineering lecturers at Chulalongkorn University whose leader, Dr. Sawai Danchaiwijit, was an Octobrist and ex-guerrilla.

There is the Patriotic People Club (*Chomrom prachachon phoo rak chat*), consisting of many thousand followers of a hugely popular and highly revered senior monk in northeastern Thailand, Luang Ta Maha Bua, who was resolutely opposed to the IMF-prescribed consolidation of accounts from the BOT's banking and issuing departments for fear that his followers' multi-million baht foreign currency and gold donations to the national reserves might be squandered by the government to compensate for the losses incurred in bailing out the bankrupt financial institutions; the Democracy for the People Group (*Klum prachathipatai pheua prachachon*), a group of ex-guerrillas and former radical student activists under the leadership of the charismatic ex-student leader and guerrilla fighter Dr. Seksan Prasertkul of Thammasat University, whose aim is to function as a nationwide coordinating, political umbrella organization for local people's groups all over the country; etc. Besides, there are pre-existing people's organizations, NGOs and academic groups which have also adopted a populist-nationalist stance against the IMF-Democrat government's economic policies such as the militant long-standing and well-organized Assembly of the Poor (AOP), the Friends of the People Group (ex-student activists and intellectuals who serve as the general staff and secretariat of AOP) and the Political Economy Center of Chulalongkorn University (established group of progressive, left-leaning economists).

Their intellectual activities and publicity campaign have been carried out through a continuing flow of books, periodicals, newspapers and radio programs with increasingly militant contents and rhetoric. The more important among them are: *Assembly of the Poor's Black-Covered Book: People's Handbook under IMF* (1998), the Withithas Project's pocketbook series edited by Thianchai Wongchaisuwan (aka "Yuk Sri-ariya," a Marxist intellectual) and Phitthaya Wongkul (a communitarian devotee), the re-published and renewed populist-nationalist *Journal of Political Economy* of Chulalongkorn University, the radical Buddhist *Pacharayasarn* magazine of the Sulak Sivaraksa group, the *Prachathas* newsletter of a coalition of NGOs, the *Bandit Thai* newsletter of the Thai Graduates' Group, the *Manager Daily*, the weekend Khleun Khwamkhid or Waves of Thought radio program on FM 101 MHz by Chatcharin Chaiyawat, etc.

They have separately and/or collectively engaged in many forms of public activism from academic seminars, panel discussions and collections for national economic crisis relief to demonstrations, signature campaigns, etc. The more prominent among them were the AOP's demonstration against IMF loan conditionality in 1997, the campaign against the sale of state-owned Bangchak oil refinery to foreign business interests in 1998–99, the campaign against the IMF-imposed eleven financial bills that gave greater advantage to foreign creditors in 1999, the anti-globalization/neo-liberalism demonstrations of NGOs and people's organizations during the UNCTAD 10th meeting in Bangkok and the annual ADB meeting in Chiang

Mai in 2000, the publicized opposition to the sale of nationalized banks with disadvantageous loss-sharing and yield-maintenance guarantees to foreign financial interests in 2000, Luang Ta Maha Bua's popular *Pha pa chuai chat* (donation to help the nation) project which turned unexpectedly into a massive signature campaign to oppose a major financial reform policy of the Democrat government as well as to impeach Finance Minister Tarrin in 2000, etc.[39]

Two factors played a key igniting, inspiring and boosting role in the foregoing process of political recovery through economic nationalism, namely, King Bhumibol's speech on "Setthakij pho-phiang" or "self-sufficient economy" given on December 4, 1997, which has been interpreted in such a way as to open public space for discourse on systemic alternatives to "trade economy" or capitalist globalization,[40] and the world-famous resurgent anti-globalization mass protest at Seattle in late 1999 that managed to shut down the millennium round of WTO meeting as well as the subsequent series of similar protests that has been staged in many places around the world.[41] Together, they constituted both an inspiration and a living example that pointed to new, emerging possibilities in resisting capitalist globalization in Thailand, the East Asian region and throughout the world.

From the said varied and diverse sources, an economic populist-nationalist trend that is anti-neo-liberal globalization has emerged from the political margins to reach the political center, from the masses to meet up with the elite, from the academia, the print and electronic media and Buddhist laymen's groups to coalesce into mass political movements, changing in the process from abstract theoretical discourse to concrete strategic and policy proposals and demands, an elaborate and path-breaking series of which has in late 2000 been successively presented to the public by such high-profile public figures as Dr. Virabhongse Ramangkura,[42] Associate Professor Rangsun Thanapornpun of the Faculty of Economics, Thammasat University,[43] Dr. Seksan Prasertkul,[44] Dr. Phijit Rattakul, head of Thai Motherland Party and former popularly-elected governor of Bangkok,[45] Princess Bajra Kittiyabha, the eldest daughter of the Crown Prince and a law graduate of Thammasat University,[46] a group of six prominent public intellectuals, a senator and a businessman,[47] and a self-proclaimed "neo-nationalist" group of Chulalongkorn academics and assorted businessmen and politicians.[48] These burgeoning political groups constitute a significant extra-parliamentary force under the new, more flexible and responsive, TRT-led government of Prime Minister Thaksin Shinawatra, checking and pressuring the latter as well as the electocratic parliamentary regime.

Conclusion: Whose Nation Is It? And Whither the Nation?

The domestic economic story of the latest and severest crisis of Thai capitalism is quite straightforward and familiar but which practical lesson and reform policy implication to draw from it are rather complicated and highly contentious. It is a story of "*mismatched investment on a grand scale*," in which the big Thai capitalists, taking advantage of cheaper foreign loans made easily accessible to them through the opening of the country's capital account and the liberalization of the financial market under the BIBFs since September 1993, overborrowed from abroad[49] and, under the name of business diversification, misinvested massively in non-traded and hence non-foreign currency-earning areas such as real estate, hospitals, construction materials, etc., due to their rather low-tech know-how and limited entrepreneurial skills.[50]

That massive misinvestment created inflated prices of non-traded goods that in turn caused cost-pushed inflation in the Thai economy in general and among Thai exports in particular.[51] Given the then fixed exchange rate regime, the overvalued baht made it impossible for overpriced Thai exports to compete with their cheaper counterparts from other countries in the global market, which led to a drastic fall in export growth, trade deficit and rising current account deficit in 1996/97.[52] The inevitable devaluation of the baht in July 1997 pricked the overinflated bubble. Thai capitalist economy then fell thundering down to earth and Thai companies lay in ruins.[53]

But, apart from the dithering and blundering Thai electocrats and the incapacitated Thai financial technocrats,[54] who were the main culprits to blame for this economic mess, the big Thai capitalists or their foreign creditors? Here mainstream opinions diverge along two main lines. The neo-liberal globalizers blame it squarely on the Thai "crony capitalists" and other domestic actors and factors, and call accordingly for further opening of the Thai economy to foreign investment in order to gain new infusions of capital that can increase competitiveness. On the contrary, the Thai NPL-entrepreneurs blame it emphatically on foreign loan sharks and international financial institutions, and call consequently for a nationalist fencing of their monopolistic economic turf from imperialist takeover. And yet, how could the big Thai capitalists make that gigantic 7-trillion baht worth mismatched investment in 1996 unless with the help of the USD 100 billion loans provided by the trusting and approving, soliciting and cheering crowd of foreign creditors? The two were thus more like Siamese twins, intimately and deeply complicit in and jointly responsible for the same bungled economic-bubble project.

Be that as it may, it was the big Thai capitalist class and not their
foreign creditors who have basically already gone bankrupt since the
July 1997 baht devaluation. Their wealth which had been accumulated for
many decades was all lost simply because they had borrowed many times
more than their companies' equity value. Thus, their national capitalist
project, which attempted to follow, overtake and then ride on the crest of
the economic globalization wave, was unexpectedly aborted and utterly
collapsed. They are not unlike some fisher folk on the Moon River who,
upon the completion of the Pak Moon dam at the mouth of the river, had
no choice but to change their job from fishing to garbage dump picking
in Bangkok, i.e., they have to switch from forming, accumulating and
expanding their capital base in a bank-based, high-debt economy to doing
the same things but in a completely new and different way in a supposedly
market-based, prudential one. They have to re-learn almost everything
anew and that is extremely difficult if not well nigh impossible.

A capitalist economic crisis of overproduction and overcapacity can be
solved only through the disposal of excess capacity or productive forces.
The more quickly the destruction is done, the more rapid the recovery will
be. This is precisely a necessary act of creative destruction capitalism occasionally demands of its practitioners. And part of the productive forces
that needs to be destroyed is the big Thai capitalist class themselves in
their role as losing owners and entrepreneurs of inefficient, uncompetitive
and unprofitable capitalist private enterprises. The delay in economic
recovery is actually caused by the slowness in their destruction. They
die too slowly and are still stubbornly hanging and clinging on to their
assets and company equity, struggling and resisting to survive. Until they
all drop dead, not as a rich individual consumer with still ample personal
savings but as a collectively impoverished and failed productive class, the
Thai economic paralysis will go on and on and the dawn of a new cycle
of productive activity won't arrive.

In that sense, the end result of neo-liberal globalization is a cosmopoli-
tan economic utopia devoid of any and all particular national characteristics and hence national capitalists.[55] Global capital is thus taking over
the material infrastructure of Thai capitalism with all its residual unfair,
monopolistic and exploitative character, as well as exerting greater and
greater influence over the pre-existing auto-colonial centralized state
structure that has since time immemorial been the main agent in transferring natural resources from the have-nots to the haves and commodifying
everything in the process. One has thus no future-proof reason to assume
that a further destruction of inefficient Thai capital and replacement by

new waves of foreign investment would in and of itself solve the deepest problems of the Thai economy.

The big Thai capitalist class are, alas, trying to defend themselves by invoking the Nation and putting the lives and well-being of poor common people at risk as its fences to ward off and dispel the unrelenting universal logic of capital.

Historically speaking, at its origin, the particular configuration of the Thai nation was officially imagined by the Thai absolutist and later military-bureaucratic state as an uncommunity, consisting of people of unequal status and incompatible plural ethnicities with the Chinese entrepreneurs, coolies and triads being the Other (Kasian 1997; Nidhi 1995). Other groups and classes of Thai people besides the royalty, the military and the state bureaucracy have found precious little of their own history, culture and community in this imagined uncommunity. Hence its rather hollowness and blurriness, irrelevance and worthlessness in the people's eyes as well as its repeated opportunistic abuses by the old royal or military-bureaucratic and new crony capitalist elites for their own particular group interests (Nidhi 2000). Mr. Prachai, Wirun, Sawat and their ilk are simply the latest comers in the long line of born-again nationalists who, out of a usual background of total disregard for the plight of their poor and pollution-suffering compatriots, suddenly feel and find an insatiable urge to make use of the imagined (un)community to indulge their urgent, unrequited desire for new re-capitalization.[56]

However, under the same nationalist banner, another different agenda that belongs to a separate political force is at work, i.e., the non-governmental and people's organizations which, through people's politics and direct participatory democracy, are pushing for a radical populist reformist agenda consisting of three major components as follows:

1. The economic sovereignty component: They want to restore the partially if increasingly-lost sovereignty over financial and fiscal macro-economic policies so that they can re-deploy them as an indispensable instrument to manage economic openness, mediate the risks and opportunities associated with economic globalization and mitigate the negative effects of economic liberalization on the people at large. More concretely, they want to push back trade and services liberalization to the pre-crisis level and keep it there in a standstill condition as of July 2, 1997. They also want to retreat from financial liberalization and reinstate control of the capital account. In short, in so far as economic liberalization is concerned, they want to turn the clock back to July 2, 1997, and stay there so as to restore,

reform and strengthen the domestic economy before opening it up again.

2. The resource manangement component: They want to decentralize power over natural resource management from the state to local communities, to stop any further commodification of naturally-endowed productive resources be it water, land and forests, as called for by some international and regional financial institutions-cum-creditors such as the ADB, and to radically redistribute these productive resources from the speculative capitalist class to the resourceless but potentially productive producers.

3. The state reform component: To achieve the foregoing objectives, it is essential that the Thai state be reformed from a centralized, bureaucratic, authoritarian, corrupted-to-the-core and actually auto-colonial structure into a popularly-controlled, socially responsive and responsible partner of civil society. Otherwise, the Thai state as it is and has been couldn't possibly serve as an instrument of the people's agenda. For that purpose, they insist that a nation-serving and protecting state needs not, nay, must not be a dictatorship.

As we can see, even though there are certain coincidences, overlap and similarities between the crony-capitalist agenda's call for the reversal of globalist/ neo-liberalist reform and the radical populist reformist agenda's call for restoration of economic sovereignty, the two agendas are basically different. They are imagining two different Thai nations and two disparate destinies for them.

It is thus incumbent upon the new advocates of economic national-ism to think hard—whose nation it is? And whither the nation? Thus, for example, to Finance Minister Tarrin's quip whether his critics wished to return to the past bubble years where growth came from asset price in-flation rather than genuine productivity gains,[57] an answer is provided by Seksan Prasertkul that he had no wish whatsoever to bring back pre-crisis social conditions which had been far from ideal and in which "*those who worked hard earned little income while those who earned a lot hardly worked...Truthful people were trampled on while deceitful people were rewarded*," and that his attempt at salvaging the Thai nation was "*by no means to pull up by a pulley the fallen heaven of the minority from the bottom of the ocean and leave the majority of people to go on languish-ing in poverty*" (Seksan 2000). And while the neo-nationalist Dr. Narong Petprasert insisted in an interview that Thai monopolistic or oligopolistic capitalists were indeed better than their Western counterparts,[58] Nidhi thought the exact opposite. Having redefined the Thai nation as consisting of "*the people, freedom and justice*," he concluded recently that:

The rejection of globalized capital doesn't mean the acceptance of crony capital. Be it which one of the two, both oppress and exploit the majority of people, deprive them of their freedom, and buy up justice for themselves alone alike. The difference between domestic capitalists and foreign ones in reference to the people's welfare, freedom and justice amounts to naught i.e. there is no difference (Nidhi 2000).

If we do not give meaning to these three factors (the people, freedom and justice), the nation is not worth preserving (quoted in Anjira 2000).

Postscript: One Year under Thaksin

What has happened so far during the past year under the new Thai Rak Thai government of PM Thaksin Shinawatra, which came to office on February 9, 2001? Rising to power on the crest of nationalist public sentiments and popular as well as oligarchic support, the Thaksin government understandably represents an unstable amalgam of the different and at times conflicting demands, interests and concerns of both political forces as refracted through the prism of the PM's own background and experience as a self-made Sino-Thai entrepreneur, a resourceful crony capitalist, a masterful bubble-economy speculator and a successful telecoms tycoon who has gone from rags to riches. Through him, the crony capitalists, especially the telecoms, media, auto-manufacturing and agribusiness oligarchic interests who are strongly represented in his cabinet and party, have won back their state. And through it, globalization and the financial ruins in its wake (that is economic liberalization, privatization of public enterprises, the remaining mountain of bad debts) have been re-managed in their favor at the expense of their domestic and foreign competitors, the Thai consumers and the public coffers. Under Thaksin, despite the continued stagnant economy doubly depressed by the new global recession and the impact of the 9/11 terrorist attacks on the US, the surviving remnants of Thai crony capitalism, now restructured and consolidated, with less local competitors and with him as their political CEO, are re-emerging relatively stronger and even more dominant than before.[59]

A holy if informal alliance of liberal intellectuals, mainstream economists, global corporate media and some of the local press arose and started to hit back monotonously and reverberatingly at the Thaksin government early on with a simplistic, economistic anti-populist discourse (Kasian 2001). Vulgarized at times as simply *"a platform that indulges the people's every whim or bribes them,"* their Specter of Populism has its origin in the World Bank's early 1990s neo-liberal critique of the economic redistribution policy of certain Latin American governments and can be reduced essentially to income redistribution without fiscal discipline (Castaneda 1993, 40–50). Being an economist-discursively engineered mutant from the classical pedigree populist as commonly understood by sociologists and political scientists, this nouveau populist has as its prototype not an anti-market Maoist revolutionary but a mere market-intervening and correcting Keynesian reformer (Suvinai 2001, 2–3). In this narrowly blinkered sense, most democratically elected governments could easily be pigeonholed as "populist" since they naturally need to market a platform that is attractive to voters for vote gains maximization in the next election (Rangsun 2001). Hence the neo-liberal critique of "populism" in effect reflects a discontent with democracy that implies a technocratic rejection of the people's will. Besides, in a polity long used to indulging the elite's every whim, bribing and receiving policy edicts from them while excluding and giving short shrift to the masses on the margins, Thaksin's "populism" is indeed a breath of fresh air (McBride 2002).

Although Thaksin's "populism" was actually begotten by a bunch of ex-communist guerrillas and former student activists among his close aides who put to good use the art and method of mass line from their Maoist past,[60] the other, non-economic radical populists, many of them also former comrades and ex-Maoists, aren't satisfied with mere income redistribution. If one defines "populism" in a broader political sociological sense as *"cross-class coalitional politics for redistribution,"* the radical populists would like to redistribute not just income but predominantly access to key productive natural resources and power over their management to local communities.[61] They therefore have found Thaksin's "populism" wanting and his government's nationalism mostly verbal and flip-flopping. In the name of "national interests," sovereignty has been invoked to protect his cronies rather than the people; on the other hand, public pressure has to be vigilantly and continually applied to prevent his government from yielding too readily to big powers' demands and interests. Land reform remains a mere proposal; a people-initiated Community Forest Bill is stalled in the Senate; the management of water resource is still state-centralized and geared to serve the non-agricultural sectors of the economy. While responsible government ministers have been too busy to meet with representatives of the people's organizations, the problems of poor people are frozen and left to rot in the bureaucratic labyrinth with government officials intransigently insisting on following standing bureaucratic rules and regulations rather than implement the relevant cabinet resolutions to help the poor. Meanwhile, several new mega-projects for infrastructure development are being pushed ahead around the country regardless of local people's concerns and opposition (Vanida 2001).

So, after having made peace with the Thaksin government in exchange for short-term concessions for a year, the NGOs and people's organizations are unlikely to continue their unconsummated honeymoon period with the government much longer. A showdown between the two populisms is looming.

Appendix

In Search of Alternatives to Neo-Liberal Globalization:
A Synopsis of Some Proposals to Salvage the Thai Economy[62]

1. Dr. Virabhongse Ramangkura, former deputy premier and finance minister[63]

Keywords:

"Let's beat a retreat to gather our strength first."

Regarding Globalization:

To go against the principles and trends of globalization, there needs to be regional co-operation and closer consultation among China, Japan and ASEAN.

There needs to be a leading country in the region to host a forum. Japan is ready to do that but South Korea and China have to co-operate and the US has to approve it.

We need to protect ourselves from disaster associated with capital movement and reduce the wild fluctuations of international currency flow by changing from a single currency-denominated payment system (USD) to a multi-currency one (yen and euro included), so as to lessen the weight of USD flow.

Regarding Domestic Affairs:

Asia including Thailand needs at least 10 more years of development to catch up with the West. (But how to achieve that, he has no idea.)

2. Assoc. Prof. Rangsun Thanapornpun, leading economist and columnist, Faculty of Economics, Thammasat University[64]

Keywords:

"Ask leave of WTO until 2007."

Regarding Globalization:

Review the development strategy so as to choose among: a) a globalization development strategy according to the neo-liberal economic line a la Washington consensus; b) a local community development strategy according to the self-sufficient economic line a la Bangkok consensus; or c) a combination of the two. In case of choice c), which is the optimal level of economic openness should we aim to achieve?

To heal our wounds from the malady of economic liberalism, we should halt our advance on its path and turn the clock back to July 1997.

Stand still on the path of free trade at the point where we reached on July 2, 1997. Liberalize our trade at that level and no more. Reject the Multi-lateral Agreement on Investment. Reject the introduction of social clauses into the new international economic arrangement. Ask for time off to review the WTO, AFTA and APEC obligations related to economic liberalization until 2007.

Beat a retreat on the path of financial liberalization. Strictly control and regulate the movement of short-term capital. We will review our advance on the path of financial liberalization only when we can efficiently deal with the footlooseness of international capital.

The tactics of asking leave of WTO is to unite with other Third World countries that also suffer hardships from economic liberalization so as to bargain with the advanced capitalist countries, beginning with the ASEAN and East Asian countries.

Build up relationships with the network of international People and Non-governmental Organizations so as to pressure the Great Power countries against pushing for economic liberalization too hastily while the Third World is not yet ready.

Regarding Domestic Affairs:

Reform the system of macro-economic management so as to delineate clearly the duty, responsibility and authority over the use of each policy instrument.

Co-ordinate harmoniously the making and implementation of fiscal, financial and public debt policies.

Reform the Bank of Thailand so that it has clear duty, responsibility and authority and is optimally independent. Enhance its academic potential and its capacity to regulate and inspect financial institutions, as well as to manage international capital flow.

Restructure the industrial sector so as to eliminate monopoly and promote competition. Stop open and hidden state subsidy for industry as well as tax benefits.

Reform the state bureaucracy to cut down on resource waste. Create accountability and transparency mechanisms to prevent and crack down on corruption and abuse of power.

Reform the legislative process. Pass legislation to promote efficient public administration and provide benefits for the poor and disadvantaged. Change the existing legislative convention to reduce the discretionary power of the Executive branch of government.

Reform education so as to promote among the young creative thinking, care and concerns for the lower classes and disadvantaged, historical and political awareness, as well as gratitude to the motherland.

Reform politics to achieve perfect competition in the political market and increase people's participation.

3. Dr. Seksan Prasertkul, head of the Democracy for the People Group, lecturer at the Faculty of Political Science, Thammasat University[65]

Keywords:

"Let's retreat for a while to review and correct the mistakes and remedy the weaknesses of our country."

"Let's beat a retreat to gather our strength and clean and repair our own house."

"Retreat from Neo-Liberalism."

"Withdraw from the obligations, rules and regulations set by big global capital."

"Ask leave of the rules and obligations of multi-national capital."

Regarding Globalization:

Retreat from or ask leave of globalization for a while but not permanently.

Open our country selectively. Accept socially constructive things. Make valuable and meaningful contribution to the world community to which we deem ourselves as belonging.

Oppose domination by multi-national corporations but hold no grudge against people in the West.

Oppose short-term profit seeking by foreign capital and the permanent takeover of entrepreneurial space by big global capital, but not long-term investment whose benefits are fairly shared between Thai people and outside investors. Reject monopoly under the guise of free competition, but not "free and fair" liberalization.

Retreat from WTO obligations.

Retreat from IMF obligations.

Abrogate the eleven laws that cost Thailand her economic independence.

Abrogate all unequal treaties with foreign countries.

Declare a moratorium on foreign debt payment for no less than 10 years.

Regarding Domestic Affairs:

We harbor no wish to bring back the pre-crisis social situation in which "those who worked hard earned little income while those who earned a lot hardly worked...Truthful people were trampled on while deceitful people were rewarded."

There is no ideal society. What we wish to see is Thai society as we know it minus a few evils and wrongs. Then we should be able to live together.

We must make the political power-holders change their minds, agree with the platform for economic independence and withdraw our country from disadvantageous obligations. We must pressure the political parties to accept the mandate of national salvation by clearly and concertedly voicing our demands everywhere.

We, the people, have to adapt ourselves and reconnect with one another into a new nation. It has to be composed of the concrete, tangible interests of people of all classes and provide everyone with a space for livelihood. Put an end to closed politics and government, restrictive economic development and elitist education. A powerful society needs to be just. Everyone has a right to its membership with honor and dignity. People must be equal in their humanity. Deal with one another with mutual respect and fairness. Everyone has to adapt especially those who used to be the advantaged groups.

We need to reconstruct the rural economy in tandem with salvaging the urban economy, strengthen it so that it will become the foundation of our use value and exchange value-production, trade and urban processing industry that grow on our own knowledge base. A national economic salvation platform must serve Thai people in both the rural and urban areas.

A state that serves the nation needs not be a dictatorship.

Rectify, purify and increase the efficiency of the governance system. It is the state's duty to protect Thai society from the domination of outside influences.

Allow the people every opportunity to check and take part in the exercise of power on a continual and systematic basis.

Expand the democratic system to accommodate civic politics in its decision-making and policy-making processes.

Liberalize the domestic economy so that every side has an equal opportunity. Reduce state power over society. Enhance people's power so that they can take care of themselves. However, state enterprises must not be replaced with the monopoly of big capital. The Thai state should not be bound by any rules or regulations to passively allow or even facilitate the domination of Thai economy and society by multi-national corporations.

Transform the educational system both in and out of school into a genuine and continual learning process. Use education as an instrument to lessen inequality of learning and opportunity among the majority population rather than a system to divide people in the nation. Thai people should gain occupational skills, work ethic, national consciousness and humanity from the educational system.

Oppose extreme consumer culture. Uphold a well-balanced material life, intellectual and spiritual happiness, harmony with nature, socially-constructive co-operation and a diverse but well-connected culture.

Call on the "Octobrists" in particular to gather their courage, bear again the burden of this historic task, form an intellectual vanguard, use their maturity and lessons from past struggle, unite with the people and lead the country out of darkness.

Call on the Thai people all over the country to turn towards one another, give each other mutual honor and justice so that we may proceed to ask for the same from the outside world.

4. Dr. Phijit Rattakul, head of Thai Motherland Party and former popularly elected governor of Bangkok[66]

Keywords:

"Liberate the motherland."

"Economic independence [from]"

"No recovery after 3 years of believing the white foreigners. Stop borrowing foreign debt...rely on ourselves."

"Salvage the nation back to freedom."

Regarding Globalization:

Aim at economic independence. Issue government bonds. Rely on domestic savings. No consolidation of accounts (from the BOT's banking and issuing departments). No sale of national assets to foreigners. Decentralize economic power to local communities.

Review and revise various rules and regulations including the eleven economic bills. Relax NPL-related regulations that prevent banks from lending to Thai businesses. Build economic independence through Thai wisdom and Thai-ism.

Negotiate a debt moratorium with IMF so that over 100 billion baht in tax revenue can be made available to national development.

Find liquidity through issuing 200 billion baht bonds for small investors at 5 percent interest rate. Use state banks to solve bad debts and revive Thai people's economy.

Control in- and outflow of foreign currencies to stabilize baht value and prevent forex speculation.

Promote the establishment of local banks by amending existing laws. Elevate the status of co-operatives. Support and develop community business and local industry.

No sale of state banks to foreigners on disadvantageous conditions. Keep good state enterprises rather than sell them dirt cheap to foreigners.

Regarding Domestic Affairs:

Carry through political reform. Strengthen local communities.

Create space and open channels for the people sector to take part in political decision-making and influence political movement. Lead the nation in the direction that the people can survive rather than perish.

5. Princess Bajra Kittiyabha, eldest daughter of the Crown Prince and a law graduate of Thammasat University[67]

Keywords:

"Slow down so as to seek opportunity...Stop to reconsider and review ourselves."

Regarding Globalization:

Find an opportunity to consider external context.

Avoid certain trends that emphasize the negative effects.

Learn to adapt oneself better.

Seriously reconsider and review ourselves to find out weaknesses that need to be redressed and strengths that may be a way out...through internal economic, social and political reform. Use internal strength as a pillar to create flexibility so as to transform international relations both at the regional and global levels.

Regarding Domestic Affairs:

Thailand is too dependent on the outside world.

The extended fixation on growth throughout the age of accelerated development may last just fifteen seconds in the scale of the long history of the Thai community.

Learn to use wisdom and caution in considering consumerism, which is the source of profligacy and brings out clearly the negative tendency of globalization.

People at all economic levels should follow the philosophy of sufficiency economy in their living and practice.

Accept and accord local wisdom that was once regarded as marginal a dignified standing in society.

Villagers are no aliens or Others that should be reconditioned and turned into people who admire and conform to the Center so as to diminish diversity.

Strengthen communities to accord with political reform through decentralization of power. Start from community power to achieve good governance. Make national politics an extension of local politics at the community level.

Notes

* This article was originally prepared for the Fifth Shizuoka Asia-Pacific Forum on "Governing in Post-Crisis Asia and the Prospects of a 'New Asia,'" organized by the Shizuoka Prefectural Government at the Hotel Century Shizuoka, Shizuoka City, Japan, December 1–3, 2000. Since then, some revisions and additions have been made to the text apropos later developments and as suggested by various friends and colleagues, especially Pasuk Phongpaichit, Chris Baker and the two anonymous *Critical Asian Studies* reviewers, to whom I would like to express my sincere gratitude. I would like also to thank the Core University Program and the Center for Southeast Asian Studies for supporting my research visit to Kyoto in March 2002 during which the revision of this article was completed.

1 The other Thai Cassandra was Dr. Virabhongse Ramangkura, a veteran academic-turned-technocrat who had formerly served as finance minister in the General Prem Tinsulanonda government in the mid-1980s. After the onset of the crisis in July 1997, he was again drafted by some well-acquainted top military figures into the then General Chavalit Yongchaiyudh government as deputy premier for economic affairs and finance minister.

2 Mitton 2000. The Thai Rak Thai (literally meaning "Thais love Thais") Party is a newly set-up political machine primarily devoted to the prime ministerial ambition of its founder and head, i.e. the billionaire telecoms tycoon, Dr. Thaksin Shinawatra (see his brief profile in Barnes 2000). At the time of the house dissolution on 9 November 2000, the party's war chest was reportedly stuffed with 179 million baht (or about USD 4 million, the current exchange rate being around 44 baht per USD), the biggest chunk of which (75 million baht) was donated by Thaksin's own wife, Khunying Pojamarn, making it, even by official count, the best-financed among Thai political parties ("Bunnak pojamarn khwak 75 lan borijak to.ro.to." [Loaded Pojamarn donates 75 millions to TRT], *Thai Post*, November 8, 2000). Unofficially speaking, though, TRT allegedly bid the most outrageous price for any defecting MP from other parties at 50 million baht each, to be paid in six rising-scale installments of 2-3-5-15-15 + 10 based upon steps taken by the sell-out MP from defection to re-election. This made TRT the prime target for resentment and envy of other outbid and outraged parties which altogether had lost hundreds of MPs to it and hence branded it as "Phak Dood" or "the suckering party" (Suthichai 2000). The total sum of money said to be spent legally or otherwise by all parties on the campaign trail in the January 2001 general election was estimated at more than 20 billion baht.

3 Nominally headed by the deputy prime minister for Economic Affairs, minister of Commerce and the designated director-general-to-be of the WTO, Dr. Supachai Panitchpakdi, the so-called economic "real team" of the Chuan government (so named against the nightmarishly blundering economic "dream team" of the former General Chavalit government) was actually a one-man band run by Finance Minister Tarrin, whose typically

methodical but pigheaded and solo working style is legendary. Answering directly only to the prime minister, he often clashed with and prevailed over dissenting "real team" members and advisers such as Dr. Supachai, Minister for the Prime Minister's Office Mr. Abhisit Vejjajiva, and the prime minister's economic adviser Mr. Boonchu Rojanastien. Prime Minister Chuan's absolute trust in, complete reliance on and full and consistent support for Tarrin on all matters concerning economic policy against the caution, dissension, objections and opposition raised by these dissidents had incurred rising political cost which weighed heavily on the Democrat Party's prospects in the general election of January 2001. So much so that Dr. Supachai had refused to run again and yet the party leadership dared not give pride of place to the increasingly unpopular Tarrin as head of the economic team, leaving the election campaign in disarray. See "Chuan Eyes New Finance Minister," *Far Eastern Economic Review*, 16 November 2000; Gearing 2000.

4 "Interview: Thaksin Shinawatra—How to Save Thailand," *Far Eastern Economic Review*, November 16, 2000. Kitii Limsakul, an economics professor at Chulalongkorn University and founding member-cum-economic adviser of TRT, called the national AMC proposal "our most important policy in that it will make the most difference," (Wichit 2000b). Dr. Supachai's slightly different "public" AMC proposal sought to transform and widen the function of the already existing but rather under-utilized state-owned Asset Management Corporation by injecting 300 billion baht of the government money that remained from Finance Minister Tarrin's rather unsuccessful "August 14, 1998" bank rehabilitation program into it. He cautioned against the government holding a majority stake in the public AMC as too much of a financial burden and advised it to wait and see the performance of the recently-launched AMC unit of the government's Krung Thai Bank before taking any decision. See Holland 2000; and "Tho.po.tho. fai khieu kho.po.no. luanglook amc" [Bank of Thailand gives the green light to the Corporate Debt Restructuring Advisory Committee to oversee AMCs], *Thai Rath*, November 21, 2000: 8. Having peaked at 2.7 trillion baht or 47.7 percent of total outstanding debts in May 1999, the banking system's NPLs have since declined partly through the government-mediated debt restructuring program and mainly through the fire sale or transfer of some bad debts by certain banks to their own asset management units and, according to the latest available figures, stood at around 800 billion baht or 17.6 percent of total credit as of mid-2001 ("Khlang tho.po.tho. tham jeng 2.7 lan lan nayobai dokbia-kae bank" [Finance Ministry &

BOT lost 2.7 trillion through interest and bank restructuring policies], *Phoojadkan Raiwan*, November 8, 2000; and Nareerat 2000; the figures therein have been updated). The seemingly substantial overall reduction in NPLs notwithstanding, Federation of Thai Industries' vice chairman Mr. Praphad Bhodhivorakhun pointed out that NPLs in the industrial sector remained high. Small and medium enterprises in particular made up as much as 60–70 percent of total NPLs as the government had focused on solving big companies' problem loans. In the same vein, Kosit Panpiemras, executive chairman of Bangkok Bank, warned that the reduced NPL figures didn't signify a successful solution to the NPL problem since most of them resulted from the mere transfer of NPLs to the banks' own AMCs whereas the problem loans themselves remained unsolved ("World trade yua srinakhorn ud mattrakan 14 so.kho. lom lew" [World Trade Center fumes at Bangkok Metropolitan Bank, attacks the 14 August Measure as a failure], *Thai Post*, November 8, 2000; "Bad loans still plague Thai banks," *The Straits Times*, October 20, 2000). If the written-off debts and the private AMCs-held NPLs were also taken into account, then the figure of problem loans would stand at 1.5 trillion baht.

5 As pointed out by an SCB Research Institute report, the abundant baht liquidity was reflected in the fact that, despite six US inter-bank overnight loan interest-rate hikes from June 1999 to May 2000, Thailand's domestic interest rates had indeed declined ("A second crisis is not likely, says institute," *The Nation*, November 25, 2000: B8).

6 Wade and Veneroso 1998; and Supat 1999.

7 According to a well-informed economist colleague-cum-business researcher of mine, the said adaptation process among Thai banks is uneven, still in its early stage and has yet a very long way to go. It has proceeded farther in those banks majority-owned by foreign capital (Pichit Likitkijsomboon, Personal e-mail correspondence, October 20, 2000).

8 At its worst, the value of the baht plummeted precipitously from 25 to over 50 baht per USD in late 1997 to early 1998 ("Thai Danu Bank paints scenario for Bt48 slide," *The Nation*, November 23, 2000: B12). Currently, it hovers around 44 baht per USD.

9 The total foreign debt of Thai non-financial private sector stood at USD 85 billion at year-end 1997 ("Tua lek ni nok mai phung ik 2 meun lan dol" [New foreign debt figures up 20 billion US$], *Matichon Daily*, 1 July 2000: 8) and is estimated to be about USD 33.6 billion in the year 2000 and USD 29.4 billion at year-end 2001 (Bank of Thailand, "Key Economic Indicators: Table 9 External Debt," at *http://www.bot.or.th/bothomepage/*

databank/EconData/KeyEcon/tab09e.asp). One can simply multiply these figures by 15 up to 25 baht depending on the fluctuating exchange rate to form a rough estimate of the forex losses incurred. However, there have been some important improvements in Thailand's external debt structure over the period from 1997 to 2001, i.e., the ratio of short-term debt to long-term debt, which was 42:58, has changed to 13:54, and the ratio of private debt to public debt, which was 85:15, has become 39:28 ("A second crisis is not likely," *The Nation*, November 25, 2000: B8; and Bank of Thailand, "Key Economic Indicators: Table 9 External Debt," at *http://www.bot.or.th/bothomepage/databank/EconData/KeyEcon/ tab09e.asp*). This has made public debt a matter of growing concern while the restructuring of big private companies' operations seems to have slid down their Thai owners' list of priorities, as will be discussed later.

10   The benchmark Stock Exchange of Thailand composite index has plummeted from the pre-crisis height of 1,700 to around 300 in 2001 (The Stock Exchange of Thailand, "Statistical Highlights of the Stock Exchange of Thailand," at *http://www.set.or.th/static/market/market_u13.html*). In the year 2000 alone, it was down more than 40 percent ("Shadow of bank NPLs continue to darken," *The Nation*, November 22, 2000: B14).

11   The Bank of Thailand records the country's annual GDP change of –1.4 percent in 1997, -10.8 percent in 1998, 4.2 percent in 1999, and 4.4 percent in 2000 (Bank of Thailand, "Thailand's Macro Economic Indicators," at *http://www.bot.or.th/bothomepage/databank/EconData/Thai_Key/Thai_ KeyE.asp*). The World Bank predicts Thailand's GDP to grow annually at 3.7 percent in the 2000–04 period (World Bank, "Thailand at a glance," at *http://lnweb18.worldbank.org/eap/eap.nsf/7a4109e5442319dc85256 7c9007162e0/ dfc257dce375d674 852567c900719142?OpenDocument*). Meanwhile, the Federation of Thai Industries reported the average capacity utilization of the industrial sector as of November 2000 to be as low as 50 to 60 percent (Nareerat 2000). Actually, industrial capacity utilization has stalled at that level since 1997 while the rate of unemployment has shot up to over 4 percent as one million more workers lost their jobs during the same period (The Economic Team 2000; and "To.ro.to. yeoi dreamteam po.cho.po., nae chuan um tarrin to" [TRT insults the Democrat Party's Dream Team, advising Chuan to go on supporting Tarrin], *Matichon Daily*, November 12, 2000: 2).

12   This inference is entirely my own doing and by no means implies Ammar's prior concurrence.

13   By "Thai-Thai" here I mean the normal credit practice of pre-1997 bank-based Thai "crony capitalism," which Ammar, in his personal correspondence to me, succinctly elucidates as follows: "What took

place in the good old days went something like this. The banker's cronies would have an investment project, which required financing. The normal debt/equity ratio in Thailand would be 3:1. Now in normal low growth economy, setting such a high ratio would imply that the bank is taking a quasi-equity in the venture, even though officially it is lending a fixed amount of money for a fixed interest. Other devices were used to bolster the idea that this is a bank loan, e.g. extensive use of collateral. The banks in the days before the capital market liberalization in about 1990 were willing to lend for what is essentially a long-term risky investment at the (cheap) price of a fixed interest loan because the bankers (not the banks) were able to get various 'fringe benefits,' in the form of shares in various companies, or a share in the money that was siphoned off the companies. Hence the power of the banking families. All this began to be seriously threatened by the liberalization of the 1990s. But as usual the high growth rates saved the day, and everyone coasted merrily along. You cannot imagine the power of an 8 percent growth rate in hiding all kinds of sloppiness. It is not completely flippant to say that the old system has some of the character of a Mae Chamoy system [i.e., a disreputable pyramid share-selling scheme in the mid-1980s—author], and is addicted to a high growth rate to keep the system going" (Ammar Siamwalla, personal e-mail correspondence, October 4, 2000).

14 Bank loans had contracted by about 10 percent since the onset of the financial crisis in mid-1997 until year-end 2000 (The Economic Team 2000; and "To.ro.to. yeoi dreamteam po.cho.po.," *Matichon Daily*, November 12, 2000: 2).

15 These post-crisis globalized requirements and regulations of the banking industry decreed by the Bank of Thailand under the Chuan–Tarrin government include, among others, debt reclassification which shortens the period of default of interest payments before problem debts turn into NPLs from 12 to 3 months, full provisions against possible loan loss by year-end 2000 and the maintenance of capital-to-risk-asset ratio of 8.5 percent.

16 Wade and Veneroso 1998, I owe my conceptualization of this issue to Dr. Ammar (Ammar, personal e-mail correspondence, October 4, 2000). In contrast with the original German or Japanese system, the Thai legal system had been much looser and provided far weaker protection for the creditors. In the pre-1997 financial crisis past, it had been precisely the high growth rates that had helped shield the economy from the adverse consequences of such a system and thereby partly concealed its weakness. (For further details, see Ammar 1999.) The Thai credit-

related legal system was indeed successfully changed in favor of the creditors by the Chuan–Tarrin government through an American and Singaporean-derived, IMF-imposed legislative program of 11 bills in 1999. These controversial 11 financial laws have since become a major bone of contention that sticks in the throat of the noisily-protesting big Thai NPL-capitalists ("Kathao pleuak setthakij thai, thammai mai feun ?" [Cracking open the Thai economy: Why no recovery so far?], *Matichon Daily*, October 1, 2000: 2). For a concise account of the contentious passage of the eleven bills, see Pasuk and Baker 2000, 167–68.

17 For an extensive review of recent literature that gives a general idea and critical perspective of how the stock market-based American system is supposed to work, see Madrick 2000.

18 I owe the information and prognosis in this passage to Ammar, personal e-mail correspondence, October 4, 2000. I use the term "self-proclaimed and ideologically useful" advisedly as testified by the ongoing energy corporate giant Enron scandal that belies any facile claims of transparency, good corporate governance or free market-driven efficiency of the American model. Enron's use of magic accounting tricks and complicated financial products to mislead investors about its value, its use of money to buy elections and political connections so as to shape US energy policy and avoid regulations, the complete absence of transparency and good corporate governance in its management and organizational culture, etc., are stark evidence and irrefutable proof of bad, old crony capitalism, American style. Suffice it to point out that Enron contributed USD 623,000 to the political campaigns of George Bush Jr., handed over a further USD 200,000 just to give a little pizzazz to his inauguration as president and has made contributions to 71 current members of the Senate and 189 members of the House of Representatives of both main parties since 1989, including, notably, John Ashcroft, the current US attorney general. Far from being an exception, much of what Enron did was not illegal. Its auditors claim that its central practices were within the law; that thousands of American firms do the same! See Stiglitz 2002; Stephen 2002; Solman 2002.

19 In more conventional and low-key economic parlance, the Chuan–Tarrin government's economic reform approach can alternately be described in contrast with the South Korean one as follows: "Korea implemented a quick-fix solution, throwing money at the problem, bailing out the financial and corporate sectors and pushing through the restructuring of the chaebols. Thailand had a more market-based approach with some banks setting up their own private asset-management companies (AMCs). Corporations were forced to restructure their debt profile on a case-

by-case basis while the government focused on creating a legislative structure consistent with a more appropriate relationship between the corporate and financial sectors" ("South Korea's quick fix now stalling," *The Nation*, November 25, 2000: B8).

20 "Shadow of bank NPLs continue to darken," *The Nation*, November 22, 2000: B14; Anoma 2000b. All in all, about one third of restructured debts (13 billion out of 40 billion baht) had turned sour again whereas new-entry NPLs amounted to 18.8 billion baht under the Chuan government ("Industry calls for national AMC," *The Nation*, November 3, 2000: B1, B4).

21 *Nation Weekender* 9, no. 434 (September 25–October 1, 2000): 11–3.

22 "Lai huang khong mom tao, so.ko. thai praobang sangkhom rai tha-mmaphibal" [M.R. Tao's many worries, Thai economy remains fragile, society without good governance], *Matichon Daily*, September 9, 2000: 2; and *The Nation*, 22 December 1999: B1. The hitherto unreported USD 20 billion foreign debts were uncovered only after a newly improved and expanded survey had been conducted and new data gathered from 6,000 additional private companies. See "Tua lek ni nok mai," *Matichon Daily*, July 1, 2000: 8.

23 "Lai huang khong mom tao," *Matichon Daily*, September 9, 2000: 2.

24 While cautiously reticent about how to break the current economic impasse in his anti-AMC article, more recently Ammar, in a seminar on "Transparent and Corruption-less Society," did suggest a course of further reform action similar to Chatumongol's second BOT-led approach, to which he added two more elements i.e. enhancing the power of creditors to foreclose on a loan, especially of those that were juristic persons, and making it possible for financial institutions to hold equities in companies (*Matichon Daily*, November 19, 2000: 23).

25 An insider of Thai tycoon circles estimated shortly after the baht devaluation in July 1997 that 65 percent of them had been wiped out by the resulting financial crisis and he himself had become "a yesterday's tycoon." See an interview with Chatri Sophonpanich, chairman of Bangkok Bank, in *Matichon Weekender* 17, no. 892 (September 23, 1997), 24.

26 That Chumpol could afford to stall his company's debt restructuring process might be partly owing to the fact that much of its remaining debt had already been converted to baht currency and from short-term to long-term. See Crispin 2000.

27 *Matichon Daily*, November 13, 2000: 9; November 15, 2000: 9; November 16, 2000: 8; November 17, 2000: 16; November 18, 2000: 18; and

Somluck Srimalee, "Ten thousand TPI workers set to rally," *The Sunday Nation*, A1–A2. TPI's major creditors include the World Bank-affiliated International Financial Corporation, US Exim Bank, Citibank, Bank of America and Bangkok Bank.

28 The Techaphaibuns are a long-established and well-known Sino-Thai tycoon family whose Bangkok Metropolitan Bank (BMB) became insolvent and was taken over by the Democrat government during the financial crisis in 1998. In the process, the family's multi-billion baht holdings in the bank were written down to almost naught. The latest round of negotiations to sell BMB to Hongkong and Shanghai Banking Corporation in late 2000 met with widely-publicized, aggressive protests from a group of nationalist businessmen and economists before eventually falling through. See Kasian 1999, 32–7; "Tarrin lan mai yokloek khai srinakhorn" [Tarrin declares the sale of BMB won't be scrapped], *Matichon Daily*, November 21, 2000: 9.

29 "World trade yua srinakhorn," *Thai Post*, November 8, 2000; and "Kathao pleuak setthakij thai," *Matichon Daily*, October 1, 2000: 2. One of the more vociferously nationalist panelists in the project's launching public discussion at the World Trade Center complex in late September 2000 was none other than the embattled Prachai Leophairatana of TPI.

30 Pichaya Changsorn and Somluck Srimalee, "TPI protests set bad precedent—Staporn," *The Nation*, November 24, 2000: B1, B4; "So.wo. dan kae ko.mo. setthakij tai imf" [Senators push for revision of economic laws passed under IMF], *Matichon Daily*, September 1, 2000: 27.

31 "Wad keun team setthakij 5 phak yai" [Gauging the competence of the 5 big parties' economic teams], *Phoojadkan Raiwan*, November 16, 2000.

32 "Poed phoi khunphol setthakij" [Baring the economic commanders], *Thai Rath*, November 16, 2000; Wichit 2000a; Wichit 2000b. A quick glance at their policy statements in the election campaign yields the following result: the Chat Thai Party was open to the idea of a foreign debt moratorium and the suspension of some obligations imposed by WTO agreements; the Seritham Party called for a four-year collective IMF- and World Bank-debt moratorium by debtor countries; the Chat Phattana Party wanted a review of existing financial laws and agreements with foreign countries, a quick solution to the NPLs problem and adjustment of regulations and requirements governing financial institutions in accordance with current economic conditions; NAP advocated a stop to the sale of state enterprises to foreigners and protectionist measures for Thai companies in all kinds of business and at all levels; TRT planned to reverse all key economic policies formulated by the Democrat government through setting up a

national AMC to buy up NPLs, relaxation of banking regulations, a three-year suspension on debt repayments for indebted farmers, provision of facilities to incubate micro-savings at the village level, large-scale support for small- and medium-sized enterprises and a possible imposition of the Tobin tax, etc.; the Thai Motherland Party's proudly and emphatically nationalist-populist economic platform included most of the main policy ingredients enumerated above and more.

33 Jiwamol 2000. An accompanying news analysis commented that while Finance Minister Tarrin appeared to have lost the support of the big Thai bankers, Thaksin still had to earn foreign investors' confidence (Thanong 2000b.)

34 So said Thirayuth Bunmi, a suave and sharp former student leader-turned-revolutionary-turned-academic at Thammasat University, in another of his timely personal press conferences on the January 6, 2001, general election. See Thirayuth 2000.

35 Crispin 2000. According to Yodchai Choosri, senior director of the BOT's debt-restructuring department, of all the 951 debt-ridden companies that had sought the aid of the Corporate Debt Restructuring Advisory Committee (CDRAC) in mediating debt-restructuring agreements with their creditors since mid-1998, only 51 percent did sign a debtor-credit agreement. Of these, only 57 percent managed to complete debt restructuring while another 20 percent were still in the process. The remaining 23 percent had failed. See Anoma 2000a.

36 For arguments in detail, see Kasian 1997.

37 The economic formation of the Thai middle class during the economic-bubble boom is most succinctly and concisely captured in Suvinai 1994, 147.

38 By "electocracy" I mean a systematically corrupted representative form of government. The term originated in Thai as "rabob leuaktangthipatai" during the heyday of substantially unchecked and unbalanced parliamentary democracy in the mid-1990s after the military had returned to their barracks in the aftermath of the May 1992 popular uprising against the military-backed government of PM General Suchinda Kraprayoon. Mr. Khamnoon Sitthisaman, a top-notch journalist and the then political editor of *Phoojadkan Raiwan*, a leading business daily of that period, coined it. A comprehensive historical and analytical account of Thai electocracy appears in Kasian 1999b.

39 A more detailed general account of these various campaigns and activities is given in Chapter 7, "Selling the Nation, Saving the Elephant," Pasuk and Baker 2000.

40 Bhumibol's entire speech in his own English translation appears in a
    CD-Rom entitled "Cycles of Life, Cycles of Development: A Collection
    of HM King Bhumibol Adulyadej's Speeches Given on the Occasions
    of His Birthday Anniversaries from 1993–1999" (Bangkok: Princess
    Maha Chakri Sirindhorn Foundation, 1999). Pasuk and Chris Baker, in
    their latest book, have differently translated and extensively quoted and
    discussed those parts in this particular speech related to his concept of
    "self-sufficient economy" in the context of similar ideas that had been
    laboriously if less noticeably worked on and advanced over the years
    by other communitarian commoner-public intellectuals (see Chapter 8,
    "Walking Backwards into a Khlong: Thinking Social Alternatives," Pasuk
    and Baker 2000). Interestingly enough, the authors' rendering reads both
    more fluently and literally than Bhumibol's own. Since the late 1980s,
    Bhumibol's annual birthday anniversary speech has become a highly
    significant and at times defining cultural political event of the year, a
    fact that testifies to his role as a top-ranking Thai public intellectual
    par excellence. Bhumibol again discoursed on "setthakij pho-phiang" in
    his 1998 birthday anniversary speech not only to confirm and elaborate
    on its meaning and practical implications but also to rein in and tame
    some of its more overzealously dogmatic or extremist as well as radical
    interpretations. In the later speech, he also subtly but notably changed
    its English translation from "self-sufficient economy" to "sufficiency
    economy."

41 For a detailed, eye-witness account of the Seattle protest, see St. Clair
    1999. Some AOP leaders such as Bamrung Kayotha who had traveled
    to Seattle and personally taken part in the protest there talked later in
    glowing terms about it and admitted he was tremendously inspired by
    it.

42 "Tong thoi pheua ruk ik khrang : ro.so. do.ro. virabhongse ramangkura"
    [We must retreat so as to go on the offensive again: Assoc. Prof. Dr.
    Virabhongse Ramangkura], *Nation Weekender* 9, no. 434 (25 September–1
    October 2000): 14.

43 Rangsun 2000.

44 Seksan 2000.

45 "Roojak nayobai thin thai, phak nong mai style phijit rattakul" [Intro-
    ducing Thai Motherland Party's platform, a new party in Phijit Rattakul's
    style], *Matichon Daily*, October 7, 2000: 24.

46 Phrachao lan thoe phraong chao bajra kittiyabha, "Prathet thai nai krasae
    lokaphiwat" [Thailand in the globalization stream], *Matichon Daily*,
    October 25, 2000: 2. The unusually radical contents of the supposedly

"academic" public address plus the status of the deliverer herself carried profound significance.

47 They were Dr. Prawase Wasi (retired physician, widely-respected and influential royalist-communitarian social critic and political reformer), Prof. Chai-anan Samudavanija (royalist political scientist and a former judge of the Constitutional Court), Prof. Nidhi Aeusrivongse (foremost historian and academic columnist), Rangsun Thanapornpun (a leading economist-cum-columnist), Seksan Prasertkul, Dr. Bowornsak Uwanno (a French-trained royalist expert in public law), Senator Sophon Suphaphong (former reform-minded royalist head of Bangchak oil refinery-turned-senator) and Mr. Narong Chokewatthana (a politically outspoken nationalist manufacturer). See Prawase et al. 2000.

48 The group's spokesman is Dr. Narong Petprasert of the Political Economy Center, Faculty of Economics, Chulalongkorn University. Two interviews with Dr. Narong were published in Nantiya 2000 and Sineeporn 2000.

49 Thailand's private borrowing from overseas rose from 16 billion US$ in 1989 to 100 billion US$ by 1996. In the year 1995 alone, more money flowed into the country than over the whole decade of the 1980s!

50 Although the country's national investment skyrocketed from 2 billion baht in 1980 to 7 trillion baht in 1996, its returns had become shockingly diminished. Of the 300 listed companies on the Stock Exchange of Thailand in 1996, 187 or almost 62 percent of them did not even earn enough before tax to pay the interest on their loans.

51 Ammar was quoted as estimating that domestic inflation in Thailand had grown higher than its foreign counterpart at an annual rate of around 1–3 percent from 1987/88 to 1996, hence the equivalent loss of its export competitiveness over the same period. See "Dokbia ja lod mai dai tha mai mi kan lod khangoen" [Interest rate can't be reduced without devaluation], *Corporate Thailand* 1, no. 9 (January 1997): 65–66.

52 Ammar estimated that the baht currency was overvalued at around 10–15 percent before devaluation ("Dokbia ja lod mai dai," op cit.). After many successive years of dynamic growth, Thailand's export slowed down and stalled in 1996 and grew only 3.7 percent in 1997. In 1997, the country also recorded a trade deficit of –4.6 percent and a current account deficit of –3.1 percent compared to the previous year. See Bank Of Thailand, "Thailand's Macro Economic Indicators," at *http://www.bot.or.th/ bothomepage/ databank/EconData/Thai_Key/Thai_ KeyE.asp.*

53 Unless otherwise indicated, data used in this passage and the accompanying notes are from Pana Janviroj, "Business caught in time warp," and "Policies 'off the track'," *The Nation*, 3 September 2001: 2A. However, I don't share the conclusion of Pana's analysis for I think he casts his

critical net too narrowly and catches only Thai big fishes while letting the foreign sharks off lightly.

54 For details, see Kasian, "The Political Lesson of the Thai Economic Crisis," op cit.

55 See Wolfgang Sachs, "Chapter 8 Globalization and Sustainability," *Planet Dialectics: Explorations in Environment and Development* (London: Zed Books, 1999), 129–55; and Aijaz Ahmad's series of hard-hitting essays on 20th century world history entitled "A Reflection of Our Times" in the *Frontline* fortnightly magazine of India, especially "Colonialism, Fascism and 'Uncle Shylock': A Reflection of Our Times—IV," *Frontline* 17, no. 17 (19 August–1 September 2000); "Globalisation: A society of aliens? A Reflection on Our Times – V," *Frontline* 17, no. 20 (30 September–13 October 2000).

56 Some skeptical reaction to this born-again NPL-nationalism in the Thai English-language press can be found in Chang Noi (Pasuk Phongpaichit and Chris Baker), "Nationalism in the noodle shop," *The Nation*, 24 October 1997: A5; "Nationalism and the White Peril," *The Nation*, 13 November 2000: A5; and Thanong Khanthong, "Nationalism is the last refuge of bankrupts," *The Nation*, 24 March 2000: A4.

57 Post Reporters, "History will judge fairly," *Bangkok Post*, 13 November 2000: business section, 1.

58 Nantiya, "Using nationalism," *The Sunday Nation*, 5 November 2000: A3. To Nantiya's question whether Thai capitalists were any better than their Western counterparts, Dr. Narong answered: "Yes. In a broader sense, Thai companies may be a monopoly or oligopoly, but the wealth still stays in the country. If we have a good government and legal mechanisms, the wealth can be better distributed..."

59 I owe this perceptive interpretation of Thaksin's political role to Pasuk and Baker 2001 and Chang Noi 2002.

60 Suvinai 2001, 16.

61 I owe this definition of "populism" to Jomo 2001.

62 Originally prepared for a seminar of the Core University Program, "Round Table on Contemporary Thai Economy and Politics," organized by the Center for Southeast Asian Studies, Kyoto University, at the said premises on March 21, 2001.

63 "Tong thoi pheua ruk ik khrang : ro.so. do.ro. virabhongse ramangkura" [We must retreat so as to go on the offensive again: Assoc. Prof. Dr. Virabhongse Ramangkura], *Nation Weekender* 9, no. 434 (September 25–October 1, 2000): 14.

64 Rangsun 2000.

65 Seksan 2000.

66 "Roojak nayobai thin thai, phak nong mai style phijit rattakul" [Intro-
    ducing Thai Motherland Party's platform, a new party in Phijit Rattakul's
    style], *Matichon Daily*, 7 October 2000: 24.
67 Phrachao lan thoe phraong chao bajra kittiyabha, "Prathet thai nai krasae
    lokaphiwat" [Thailand in the globalization stream], *Matichon Daily*,
    October 25, 2000: 2.

References

Ammar Siamwalla. 2000. AMC: An idea whose time has gone. *The Nation*,
    October 3: A5, A8.
Ammar Siamwalla. 1999. Nak setthasat farang mong wikrit asia: bot samruaj
    khwamroo [Western economists' views of the Asian crisis: A survey
    of literature]. Unpublished paper presented in a panel discussion on
    Western Economists' Views of the Asian Crisis: A Survey of Literature
    organized by the Economic Association of Thailand, Imperial Queen's
    Park Hotel, May 26; available at *www.info.tdri.or.th*.
Anjira Assavanonda. 2000. Academics propose a way out of morass: Eight
    strategies to end economic crisis. *Bangkok Post*, November 13: 2.
Anoma Srisukkasem. 2000a. Debt plans to help recovery—BOT. *The Nation*,
    November 21.
Anoma Srisukkasem. 2000b. Several banks see a rise in NPLs. *The Nation*,
    November 24.
Barnes, William. 2000. Wealth comes to the party for ambitious tycoon. *South
    China Morning Post*, September 25.
Castaneda, Jorge G. 1993. *Utopia Unarmed: The Latin American Left after
    the Cold War*. New York: Alfred A. Knopf.
Chang Noi [Pasuk Phongpaichit and Chris Baker]. 2002. PM Thaksin's pluto-
    populism. *The Nation*, February 18: 5A.
Crispin, Shawn W. 2000. Losing momentum. *Far Eastern Economic Review*,
    October 19.
Gearing, Julian. 2000. Taking the heart. *Asiaweek* 26, no. 46 (24 November).
Holland, Tom. 2000. Debt debate. *Far Eastern Economic Review*, September
    28.
Iwasaki, Yoshihiro. 2000. The 5th column: Asia's recovery on track. *Far
    Eastern Economic Review*, December 14: 38.
Jiwamol Kanoksilp. 2000. BBL chief supports Thaksin. *The Nation*,
    November 28: B1.
Jomo K.S. 2001. The political economy of populism: Global experiences

and Southeast Asian perspectives. Talk at the Economics Department, Thammasat University, Bangkok, October 12.

Kasian Tejapira. 1995. *Wiwatha lokanuwat* [Debate on globalization]. Bangkok: Phoojadkan Press.

Kasian Tejapira. 1997. Imagined uncommunity: The Lookjin middle class and Thai official nationalism. In *Essential Outsiders: Chinese and Jews in the Modern Transformation of Southeast Asia and Central Europe*, ed. Daniel Chirot and Anthony Reid, 75–98. Seattle and London: University of Washington Press.

Kasian Tejapira. 1999. Ruang lai mangkorn [Fallen dragon motif]. In *Thin ka khao: setthakij kanmeuang thai tai ngao imf* [The land of the white crows: Thai political economy under IMF's shadow]. Bangkok: Komol Keemthong Foundation Press.

Kasian Tejapira. 1999b. The political lesson of the Thai economic crisis: A critical dissection of electocracy. Unpublished paper presented at the workshop, What Lessons We Learn from the Crisis?, organized by Professor Takashi Shiraishi at the International House of Japan, Tokyo, 14 June 1999.

Kasian Tejapira. 2001. Pisaj populist [The specter of populism]. *Matichon Daily*, January 20: 6.

Madrick, Jeff. 2000. All too human. *The New York Review of Books*, August 10.

McBride, Edward. 2002. Pleasing the voters. *The Economist*, March 1.

Mitton, Roger. 2000. Down, and likely out. *Asiaweek* 26, no. 37 (22 September).

Nantiya Tangwisutijit. 2000. Using nationalism to defend the economy. *The Sunday Nation*, November 5: A3.

Nareerat Wiriyapong. 2000. Industry calls for national AMC. *The Nation*, November 3: B1, B4.

Nidhi Aeusrivongse. 1995. Phasa thai mattrathan kab kanmeuang [Standard Thai language and politics]. In *Khone, carabao, namnao lae nang thai: waduai phleng, phasa lae nana mahorasop* [Khone, carabao, stinking water and Thai movies: On songs, language and various theatrical performances], 136–71. Bangkok: Matichon Press.

Nidhi Aeusrivongse. 2000. Chat [Nation]. *Matichon Daily*, November 24: 6.

Pasuk Phongpaichit and Chris Baker. 2000. *Thailand's Crisis*. Chiang Mai: Silkworm Books.

Pasuk Phongpaichit and Chris Baker. 2001. Thailand's Thaksin: New populism or old cronyism? Paper written for Johns Hopkins University-SAIS, Washington DC, 27 November.

Prawase et al. 2000. *Kho sanoe yutthasat kae wikrit chat* [Strategic proposal to solve the national crisis]. Bangkok: Local Community Development Institute.

Rangsun Thanapornpun. 2000. Kho wen wak...wto" [Ask leave of...WTO]. *Phoojankan Raiwan*, October 19: 6.

Rangsun Thanapornpun. 2001. Ammar Siamwalla vs Thaksin Shinawatra. *Phoojadkan Raiwan*, November 21.

Seksan Prasertkul. 2000. *Amnaj kanmeuang, wikrit setthakij lae thang ok khong prachachon* [Political power, economic crisis and the people's way out]. Bangkok: The Democracy for the People Group.

Sineeporn Mareukphithak. 2000. Thang rod thi leuak mai dai: sangkhom-niyom + chatniyom = chatniyom mai [The inevitable way out: socialism + nationalism = neo-nationalism]. *Nation Weekender* 9, no. 439 (October 30–November 5): 18–9.

Solman, Paul. 2002. Accounting alchemy. Public Broadcasting Service Television news program, January 22.

St. Clair, Jeffrey. 1999. Seattle diary: It's a gas, gas, gas. *New Left Review* 238 (November/December): 81–96.

Stephen, Andrew. 2002. Just making a dishonest buck or two. *New Statesman*, January 21.

Stiglitz, Joseph. 2002. Crony capitalism is nothing new in US. *The Nation*, February 14: 5A.

Supat Tansathitikorn. 1999. Defining economic self-sufficiency. *The Nation*, November 26: B3.

Suthichai Yoon. 2000. Anyone for 2-3-5-15-15 plus 10? Bingo! *The Nation*, July 19.

Suvinai Paranavalai. 1994. *Tunniyom fong saboo* [Bubble capitalism]. Bangkok: Duang Kamol Miti Mai Publisher.

Suvinai Paranavalai. 2001. *Vision 2002 parithas* [Review of vision 2002]. Bangkok: Jedi Publishing House.

Thanong Khanthong. 2000a. How to staunch the bleeding of capital? *The Nation*, October 13: A4.

Thanong Khanthong. 2000b. Tycoon makes inroads on Democrat turf. *The Nation*, November 28: B1, B4.

The Economic Team. 2000. Sam pi bon samoraphoom leuad, wad pholngan setthakij tua to tua ratthabal chuan 2, doen na klab soo wikrit ik rob, thing raboed fak wai doo tang na [Three years on the bloody battlefield, measuring the second Chuan government's economic performance, heading back towards another crisis, leaving behind a remembrance bomb]. *Thai Rath*, November 6: 8.

Thirayuth Bunmi. 2000. Thirayuth kang khamphi-chi leuaktang, pid chak yuk chuan, thaksin mai chai thang leuak mai [Thirayuth professorially predicts the elections will end the Chuan era but Thaksin is not really a new alternative]. *Matichon Daily*, November 27: 2.

Vanida Tantiwitthayaphithak. 2001. Siang khon jon [Voice of the poor]. *Matichon Daily*, November 30: 6.

Wade, Robert, and Frank Veneroso. 1998. The Asian crisis: The high debt model versus the Wall Street – Treasury – IMF complex. *New Left Review* 228 (March/April 1998): 3–23.

Wichit Chaitrong. 2000a. Thai Rak Thai wants greater credit flow; Proposal to relax bank laws. *The Nation*, 15 June: B1, B4.

Wichit Chaitrong. 2000b. Thai Rak Thai to reverse fiscal policy. *The Nation*, August 15: B1.

10

Recent Social Movements in Thailand in Global Perspective

Pasuk Phongpaichit

Since around 1990, Thailand has seen an outburst of demonstrations, protest marches and new organizations by people of various walks of life. In 1978 there were forty-two demonstrations and protest marches, rising to 170 in 1990 and 988 in 1994 (Praphat 1998, 34, 35, 39). These protests have not been one-shot events. In most cases, participants have organized into a movement to demand their rights or fight to protect the environment and their livelihood on a long-term basis.

This paper is based on research into social movements in Thailand, funded under the Thailand Research Fund's Senior Researcher (*medhi wijai awuso*) program and carried out between 1999 and 2001.[1] The project covered eight movements by eight research teams. The sample of movements was not "representative" in any scientific sense, but it includes many of the most prominent movements and indicates something of the variety. This upsurge of political activity cannot be assigned to one group, one grievance or one cause. The movements are both varied and complex. Collectively they mark a significant change in Thai society and politics. The aim of this paper is to understand something of that change. Let me first summarize the eight studies.

Kritiya Atchwanitkul and Kanokwan Tharawan studied the movement among women to gain full control over their bodies and sexuality, using four specific cases: the struggle for women's right to abortion; the campaign for the right to choose a woman as a lover; the women's movement on AIDS; and the fight to eliminate violence against women. Voravidh Charoenlert's study dealt with women workers' struggle for health and safety in the work place, while Nalinee Tanthuvanit and Sulaiporn Chonvilai looked into the roles of poor rural men and women in the fight against dam projects that destroyed natural forests and fish breeding grounds, thus taking away means of livelihood and dispersing communities. Sayamon Kaiyunwong, Atchara Rakyutitham and Krisada Bunchai examined the northern hill farmers' movement to win the right to manage local natural resources and to maintain their cultural identities and Praphat Pintoptaeng and Anuson Unno covered the movement by small-scale fishermen in southern Thailand to protect the coastal environment. Maneerat Mitprasat investigated the slum dwellers' movement for housing rights and participation in urban development, while Nualnoi Treerat and Chaiyos Jirapruekpinyo traced the rural doctors' movement against bureaucratic and political corruption in the public health ministry. Finally, Narumol Tapchumpon and Charan Ditthapichai focused on the movement for the new constitution of 1997 and its aftermath.[2]

These studies ranged from the northern hills to the southern coasts, from hill minorities to educated civil servants, from local issues about natural resources to national concerns over constitutional principles. The nature of the peoples' struggles, their novelty and variety, motivated the research. For the social movements are not only the expression of today's discontent; they also represent the collective wishes of large numbers of people. "Society itself is shaped by the plurality of these struggles and vision of those involved" (Escobar and Alvarez 1992, 5).

Social movements are controversial. Some political analysts have argued that modern social movements are a dangerous delusion because they emphasize civil society rather than class, networks rather political parties and local action rather than the capture of the state. As such, they result in a futile populist strategy with no hope of success against the entrenched power of the internationalized capitalist state (Brass 1994). Defenders have responded that such criticism simply ignores contemporary realities. Class has become much more complex in the globalized, post-industrial world (Veltmeyer 1997), and states with impressive resources and broad foundations of tacit support are unlikely to be overthrown by old-style movement parties. Social movements have arisen precisely because of these characteristics of the modern world, and we need to reconcile to these facts rather than cling to an idealized past (Omvedt 1993; Byres 1995).

Several thinkers have rediscovered the Gramscian discussion of hegemony as a way to reconcile social movements with leftist thinking. Whereas old-style political movements sometimes succeeded in capturing the state, they often failed to disturb deeper hegemonic ideas such as the domination of one group over another, the exclusion of minorities, the necessity of hierarchy or the privileges of an elite. Social movements, by contrast, mount direct attacks on such hegemonies from the base of civil society.

Social movements and NGOs have also been criticized for retarding the development of a political party system which would truly represent society, particularly the urban and rural mass. By deflecting people's interest away from the establishment of political parties, these critics suggest, social movements and NGOs cede this realm to old elites and business gangs who directly represent only a minute portion of the population. Social movement activists respond that party politics are not the only type of politics, nor necessarily the most effective for the mass of the people, given current structural conditions and money politics (see below).

The flow of the paper is as follows. First it will present a brief summary of the worldwide theoretical debate on social movements that has developed since the 1960s. Secondly, it will analyze some of the lessons from past debates on social movements, followed by a discussion of the main features of recent popular movements in Thailand. The paper ends with a conclusion and dedication.

International Debates on Social Movements since the 1960s

Social movements are simply collective actions—many people acting together. The phrase "social movement" has taken on new meanings since the 1960s, when it was first used to describe anti-war, anti-nuclear, student rights, feminist, gay and environmentalist movements. Some writers dubbed these campaigns "new social movements" because participation cut across class lines and included a large number from the educated white-collar middle class. The "new" tag distinguished them from class-based movements, such as trade unions, communist parties and socialist movements. The "social" tag was used because the movements were not directly political. They had no aim to capture or overthrow the state and tacitly accepted the political framework of liberal democracy. Some wanted to establish different cultural identities or make society accept different ways of life (gay or lesbian). Many were about quality of life and asserted the rights of the individual or community.

The US Debate
Political scientists argued that these movements demanded new theoretical approaches, different from both the Marxian paradigm of class and mainstream theories about interest groups and political recruitment. The first attempts at theorizing in the 1960s and 1970s occurred in the United States; these focused not on why the movements took place (this was seen as self-evident), but on how they were organized and why some were more successful than others. *Resource mobilization theory,* for ex-

ample, purported to show that the success of a movement depended on the resources available (people, money, allies), and the ability to mobilize these resources (by persuasion, organization, networking). This theory was wholly about the *strategy* of demanding change in government policies or legislation. It focused on political action and paid no attention to civil society. A variant of this approach became known as *political process* or *political opportunity theory* and analyzed the success or failure of movements in terms of the "opportunities" available. If the government is strong and committed to repression, then the *political* opportunity is small and the movement likely to fail. And vice versa. Analysts in this school paid less attention to the "resources" available, but concentrated on the interaction between the movement, on the one hand, and the state or other forms of established power, on the other.

Western European Debate

Debates in western Europe began in the 1970s and, from the start, differed from those in the US. This reflected a big difference in the two continents' political history and traditions of political theory. At issue in the western European debate was essentially the same phenomenon—new movements about the environment, women and sexual identities. But instead of focusing on strategies and requirements for success or failure, the European debate focused on *why these non-class-based movements arose.*

The early theorists came mostly from the tradition of Marxist political economy. They were concerned that Marxist analysis of social movements, which stressed the importance of consciousness, ideology, social struggle and solidarity, seemed inadequate to characterize and explain these new movements. They argued that theories which stressed the primacy of structural contradictions, economic classes and crisis in determining collective identities were inappropriate to understand movements which did not appear to have a class base or to be related to any crisis or structural contradiction. European theorists were also quite unimpressed by US theories of resource mobilization and political process. They asserted that present day collective action is not confined to negotiations and strategic calculations to gain political access. Rather, movements involve issues of social norms and identity, and the struggle takes place in the realm of civil society rather than in the realm of politics.

Prominent European theorists such as Alain Touraine and Jurgen Habermas linked the upsurge of new social movements to the failure of the democratic system in postmodern society to guarantee individual freedom, equality and fraternity. In the view of these theorists, the state has become more subject to the market and democratic processes are being crushed by the growing power of authoritarian technocracy. The power which people once enjoyed through their role in the production process has been eroded by technology and managerial technique. The main socioeconomic role of individuals is not as workers but as consumers, and in this role they are manipulated by the technologies of media and markets.

For Touraine, as the technologies of state control, mega-corporation economics and mass communications advance, the liberty of the individual diminishes (Touraine 1995). For Habermas, the expanding structures of state and market economy colonize the public and private sphere of individuals, which he calls the *lifeworld*. This lifeworld includes the domains in which meaning and value reside—such as family, education, art, religion. So private life becomes steadily more politicized by this double encroachment (Habermas 1973; Foweraker 1995, 6).

For Habermas, social movements are defensive reactions to protect the public and private sphere of individuals against the inroads of the state system and market economy. Similarly, Touraine sees participation in social movements as the only way the individual can recover liberty. For both Habermas and Touraine, the main role of social movements is the mobilization of "actors" or "subjects"—their terms for human beings in their full role as free and creative members of a pluralistic society, as opposed to victims of state and market domination.

Social movements in European theory involve a process of self-awareness to create human and social identities free of domination by the technocratic state and the market. But the creation of these identities is part of the process of a social movement, not its ultimate goal. The social movement is a collective form of action to contest abuses of political and economic power and to change political and market institutions in order to produce a better society. Social movements come into conflict with existing norms and values. As stated by Cohen and Arato (1992, 511), "collective actors strive to create group identities within a general identity whose interpretation they contest."

Both the United States and Europe are advanced industrial societies with established democratic systems, yet the analysis of social movements in the two continents has differed widely. Foweraker explained this difference by reference to the historical context. Western Europe has a history of social democracy, welfare states, institutionalized trade union movements and strong corporatist traditions linking trade unions with the state (Foweraker 1995). European theorists try to explain the appearance of a new type of social expression by reference to shifts in society and culture. They conclude that the new social movements are concerned with the construction of new social and political identities in opposition to the power of market and state. In the United States, by contrast, there has been no tradition of social democracy, no trade union corporatism and no powerful labor movement. Social movements are thus explained not as a consequence of social or structural change, but as part of the political maneuvering whereby groups mobilize resources to gain political representation and realize social change. American theorists are not interested in why social movements arise. They concentrate only on why some succeed and some fail.

Debates in Latin America

The debate on social movements in the developing world surfaced first in the late 1980s and early 1990s in Latin America as a result of close historical connections between Europe and that region, and because of heavy American involvement in the politics of the region. Latin American theorists found many of the insights from the western debate useful because many movements (women, gay, environmental) were either concerned with similar issues or linked to the US and Europe in increasingly international arenas of debate. However, the Latin Americanists also found that the local movements that arose in the region in the 1980s had many features which required extension or adjustment of the western theories.

First, the early Latin American movements were primarily urban-based, formed in response to problems of rapid urbanization due to industrial development, the capitalization of agriculture and resulting shifts from rural to urban areas. These urban social movements often revolved around the demand for public utilities or access to land and water. The movements gained momentum in part because of the crudeness of the government reaction. Thus the movements themselves were affected by the repressive policies of the state and the suppression of traditional forms of organization, such as trade unions and political parties.

Second, older forms of organization and agitation such as trade unions and agrarian movements did not disappear. But many new social actors came onto the scene, such as women, teachers, students, ethnic groups and environmentalists, to co-exist and even collaborate with these "traditional" forms of popular organizations. Third, the movements often involved a struggle to establish rights, including rights to livelihood, rights over the body, rights to land and "the right to have rights." Such movements were not so much expressions of civil society as something much more basic: attempts to *create* or *recover* civil society in the face of state power, dictatorial repression and exclusionary hegemonies. (Foweraker 1995, 6).

Fourth, these movements were not divorced from the political process, but often by necessity overflowed from civil society into the political realm. Movements were often locked in contest with authoritarian regimes. As part of their strategy, they demanded democratization, political participation and constitutional change. While some movements appeared to have the postmodern, non-class-based, networking form of the European model, others were much more obviously class-based and directly political.

Fifth, these movements were much more likely than European movements to be concerned about material issues such as access to and control over land, water and means of livelihood. Sixth, while European theory situated new social movements as an extension of the traditions of liberal individualism, many social movements in Latin America were based in communities, leveraged community solidarities and demanded community rights. Foweraker, for example, studied how the Chiapas movement drew on customary practices within the community as part of network building and evolved demands for the rights of Mexican Indians as a community (Foweraker 1992). Finally, the success rate in Latin America was not impressive. Repression by the state was tough and very effective in disrupting and preventing meaningful success.

Latin American theorists adopted some of the vocabulary and approaches of the western literature, but found that they confronted some important differences. At the close of the 1980s, these theorists advanced some tentative conclusions. First, they argued that the question of the class base of social movements was an empirical matter. In the advanced world, many movements were either middle class or cross-class. But in Latin America, most were attempts by the poor and disadvantaged to gain basic rights and improve their economic standing. Second, they proposed that the success or failure of movements was related not simply to the *local* strength of the state, but also to the neo-colonial framework and *international* backing for local state power. Touraine's observations about the domination of the state system, market economics and mass communications had to be modified to stress the extreme nature of this domination in a situation where the power base of state, market and communication media was remote from the local context and hence even more difficult to oppose.

In the early 1990s, two new developments in the Latin American movements prompted still further extension and adaptation of social movement theory. The first development was the much greater prominence of *rural* social movements, as land-grab movements spread and the Chiapas peasant resistance exploded. The second was the paradoxical development in the political economy that saw a revival of democratic forms of government running in parallel with a rapid widening of the gap between rich and poor, powerful and powerless. The explosion of rural movements emphasized the importance of competition over resources and drew the focus back to issues of identity, culture and community. Many Latin American movements were centered among minority groups who drew some of their movement's strength from the reassertion of identity. Even in cases where ethnicity was not an explicit issue, movements drew on a background of rural identity and culture raised in opposition to a dominant urban ideology of market and state. Similarly, movements drew on concepts of community that found little place in the theories worked out within the liberal-individualist traditions of the West.

The paradox of democracy and social division drew attention to the special conditions of subordinate societies within an increasingly globalized world. Latin American theorists argued that the region's urban centers and urban elites were being annexed (politically, economically and culturally) to a globalized world system dominated by the United States. In this process, the power of the national state was diminished. Hence, although dictatorships were being replaced by democratic politics, there was no space for meaningful negotiation of social and economic demands. The strength of internationally backed repression meant that local political defiance was increasingly ineffective. The decline of trade unions and welfare provisions was evidence of this trend. Hence, social movements acquired a new importance as a basis for defiance (Escobar and Alvarez 1992; Escobar 1995; Alvarez, Dagnino, and Escobar 1998).

Debates in India

In the 1980s, the debate spread more widely in the developing world. In India, there was a long tradition of socialist and communist movements, and this had an impact on the social movements that developed in the 1980s. On the one hand, Indian social movements emerged at a time when many old causes had declined in importance. The trade union movement, for example, had previously campaigned heavily for nationalization of industries or for increasing the state's role in managing privately-owned industrial enterprises. Over the 1980s, this issue disappeared. Similarly, the movement for land reform—in the sense of reallocating land from big landlords to the landless—diminished in importance. On the other hand, movements related to community, minorities, religion, women's rights, natural resources and the environment began to grow in importance. Untouchables demanded that the government increase their quota of civil service posts, while environmental movements protested big dam projects and demanded alternative development strategies. Local communities asserted their right to manage local resources, and small farmers petitioned for specific forms of government support. None of these new movements adhered to the old socialist ideology and none seemed to have a definite idea of an "ideal society."

According to Omvedt (1993), Indian social movements in the 1980s differed significantly from those occurring previously. The participants showed no interest in class analysis, but insisted on the specific nature of the exploitation they suffered. They were unimpressed by socialist ideology as a way to explain their position. They rejected alignment with leftist political organization as a strategy for redress.

Omvedt concluded that these new movements in India required researchers and analysts to reimagine the whole of Indian society. The varied movements expressed a new cultural dynamism. Although scattered and diverse, together the new movements amounted to a rejection of old ideologies and values, namely dominant high-caste Brahmanism, the state system constructed since independence and the integration of Indian society into post-cold war global capitalism. The aim of the movements was to find new ways to affect change (Omvedt 1993, 313, 318).

Orthodox Marxists reacted strongly against Omvedt's analysis. Utsa Patnaik argued that their emphasis on culture and identity were signs of backwardness and anti-modernism. Brass (1994) argued that the new movements were suffused with various forms of false consciousness (postmodernism, communitarianism) and were a threat to the traditions of socialist political organization. But Omvedt countered that leftists had to accept the new movements for what they were, rather than arguing for what they *should* be. She urged theorists to analyze new social movements in order to adapt old ideas of class analysis and political mobilization to fit the new reality. In her view, there must be a reinterpretation of revolution (Omvedt 1993, 312, 319).[3]

Learning from Past Debates

From the above discussion, we can pinpoint two important comparative elements to help us understand the history of the Thai social movements. First, the movements that emerged in Thailand in the 1990s have many similarities to the Latin American and Indian cases. Second, theorists in Latin America and India found many useful elements in studies of social movements in the West, but also found many differences in their local situations. Before turning to the Thai experience, let us therefore summarize four key areas where the Latin American/Indian debates have modified or rejected western models.

Double Domination

Touraine (and other European theorists) argue that new social movements are specific to a postmodern society—by which he means a society in which the major part of the workforce is educated, skilled, white-collar and likely in service industries. However, the technocratic state, market forces and mass communications that Touraine identifies as the forces oppressing humanity and making social movements necessary are clearly present in societies which cannot yet be called postmodern. Indeed, this domination is a global process. Hence the diminution of liberty, which this dominance entails, is also present in non-western societies and also needs to be opposed. Indeed, many of the new movements in the non-western world have been focused precisely against the power of the state, the expansion of big business at the expense of small and the monopolies over modern communications.

But the problems have become more complicated in non-western countries by the extra dimension of subordination to or dependency upon a western-dominated world. The dominating forces which Touraine identifies are globalized. The big businesses are multinational. The mass communication systems are US-owned and global in scope. National state systems are being weakened and coopted. Touraine talks about social movements contesting directly against corporate and state power. In non-western countries, the contest is more complex because these powerful forces are more remote and the balance of power even more unequal. Social movements in developing countries must be seen in the context of a double repression: at the local level by the power structure of the society and the market forces in question; and at the global level by the forces of world capitalism and multinational corporations.

Social or Political?

Theories constructed for the West are concerned with movements that focus on quality of life, rather than the material aspects of life. The movements' actors are often middle class. In non-western countries, where the material aspects are still a problem, many social movements are about bread-and-butter issues, particularly access to resources. The actors involved in many cases are the underprivileged, the marginalized, workers and poor farmers.

In a sense, Latin America and similar parts of the world are experiencing *at the same time* two different types of movement which in the West took place in *historically separate phases.* Moreover, these two types cannot be easily separated. Because they exist in the same place and time, they are inevitably interrelated—through people, organizations, networks and shared context.

Two important features of the recent movements in the developing world have been struggles for livelihood and demands for basic rights. In most cases, these struggles are by definition political, because they have to challenge the political control of resources and political arrangements for the allocation of rights. Hence, it is questionable how far these movements deserve to be labeled "social" in the sense that this label suggests they are not "political." It is also questionable how far they deserve to be labeled "new" when much of their content is very traditional. Because of this, the use of the term "new social movement" has declined in use and been replaced by "popular movement."

From Democracy to People Politics

Many of the movements arising in developing countries since the 1980s aimed to establish or strengthen democratic systems and structures in the belief that this was an important precondition for removing oppression, allowing participation and overcoming many of the inequalities and injustices in the society and economy. But recent experience suggests that this democratizing goal is important but insufficient. States have retained their authoritarian character even while taking on many of the outward forms of democracy. They have access to the modern technology and communications of social control. Their authoritarianism is sometimes reinforced by global forces. Theoretical equality under a democratic system is ineffective when large differences in income lead to "money politics." In these circumstances, democratization is ineffective in challenging economic inequality or embedded social hierarchy. Hence there has been a shift away from democratization to "people politics," which implies more direct participation of people in the decision-making process on matters affecting their livelihoods and ways of life.

Individual and Community

Touraine and other western thinkers write firmly in the historical tradition of western liberalism with its emphasis on the individual. Touraine is explicit in wanting to revive the French Revolution ideals of liberty, equality, fraternity—especially liberty. In the non-western world, however, which has different historical traditions and a much shallower experience of advanced capitalism, such an emphasis on individual liberty is either absent or much weaker. Often it is an importation with uncertain local roots. Local traditions of philosophy and political practice place more emphasis on the role of communities and groups. Touraine has to go through some complex argument to explain why a *social* movement (which involves collective action) is a way for an *individual* to reclaim liberty. In the non-western context, this stage of theorizing can be (and often is) conveniently by-passed. Communities are resurrected, reinvented or reimagined as the basis of new movements of defiance against the power of state and markets, as well as the guide for alternative development of a desirable future society.

Many social movements in the developing world since the 1970s have been based in poor, peripheral or minority communities. The Chiapas movement in Mexico is a classic case in point. In Thailand, movements among small farmers, small fishermen and hill peoples all have a base in the community or are community movements, not movements of individuals. Chairat (1995) has analyzed the discourse on community culture in Thailand as a social movement based in the village community. These movements have pressed for alternative development strategies or imagined ideal future societies different from those of the ruling mainstream. Sometimes they have sought to protect community rights against the inroads of market individualism. Sometimes they have actively revived community solidarity and community cultures as a political strategy. Sometimes they have demanded that the broader society accept and respect the culture and values of a minority or repressed community.

In sum, while European theory describes middle-class movements which operate in civil society, reject old forms of political organization, challenge postmodern forces of state and market and seek to defend traditions of liberal individualism, those that have appeared in the non-western world seem very different. They are often movements of the poor and oppressed. They cannot avoid confronting the political structure. They are increasingly involved in combating forces of globalization. They are often based in the community and draw on its strengths.

Recent Popular Movements in Thailand

The upsurge of popular movements in Thailand over the past decade obviously shares many similarities with the experience of Latin America and India—the broad base of participation, rejection of old forms of organization, emphasis on the environment and role of community discourse. But there are certain ways in which the details or emphasis of the movements in Thailand have been importantly different.

Historical Shift

A large number of movements of great variety have arisen within a very short time. In a broad sense, this is a result of changes in the global and local context. The end of the Cold War has led to the decline of dictatorship, and the opening up of democratic politics has created more space for social agitation and political expression. The global discourse on topics such as rights, identity and environmental protection has stimulated reactions within Thailand. At the same time, the rise of the modern state, market-oriented economy and new forms of global power (hegemonic states and dominant multinationals) has caused conflict over resources, the dislocation of communities and the erosion of ways of life. In sum, the combined impact of democratization, economic growth and globalization creates contradictory results. These forces encroach on people's lives and livelihood, and at the same time they open up political opportunities and give legitimacy to social movements.

The new movements in Thailand include a wide variety of social groups. But most significant is the great participation by the "little people" who have traditionally been excluded from having a political voice, including hill peoples, small fishermen, marginal peasants, slum dwellers and working women. They have become more assertive than before about their rights and roles in society, their stronger voice partly the result of the passing of the Cold War and the era of dictatorial rule. But there has also been an important synergy between these various different movements. The space created by one movement is available to another and their various experiences feed off one another and become cumulative. The sum of several movements is thus greater than their individual contributions suggest.

This upsurge is significant because it represents a break from the past. Thai society has had little or no experience of mass political mobilization. Nationalism was historically orchestrated by the elite, and in the absence of a colonial power, there was no anti-colonialist mass movement. After World War II, socialism was crushed within the context of the Cold War. Hence the social movements of the 1990s represent some of the first sustained examples of mass social action. With an ever faster pace of globalization, social movements are definitely here to stay in Thailand.

Democratic Limits

In different ways, the various movements express frustration over the poor operation of Thailand's parliamentary democracy. The rapid rise of "money politics" has stimulated middle-class support for constitutional reform and campaigns against corruption, such as that in the public health ministry. The failure of representative democracy to provide meaningful representation for poor and marginal groups has also stimulated many agitational campaigns. Despite wide differences in social background, these various movements share a feeling that politicians and bureaucrats imagine themselves as a ruling caste rather than as public servants.

This shared perspective can become a basis for common action. The Assembly of the Poor supported the constitutional movement, although the constitution was peripheral to its major concerns.[4] Many of the activists in the constitutional and anti-corruption campaigns have lent moral and organizational support to little people's campaigns for rights and resources. Of course, such cooperation has strict limits. But in the short term it helps to create a "snowball" effect of benefit to many contemporary movements.

Environment

About half the movements covered in this research on social movements in Thailand are concerned in some way with the environment and competition over natural resources.[5] Over the past half century, natural resources have been captured and destroyed for private gain, the process often justified by discourses about development and national interest. Those most sensitive to the loss of such resources are the little people who depend most heavily on nature for their livelihoods and culture. Attempts to halt this process and protect both resources and livelihoods has become a current that transcends any particular local campaign and acts as a common base for alliance between groups of various backgrounds.

The past pattern of development assumed that lots of little people could be sacrificed in the business of creating modern industrial society on the western model. But recent movements make it more difficult to maintain that belief. The government will have to think more seriously about pursuing old policies and strategies without regard to the effects on people.

Women

One striking feature of the recent upsurge of popular movements has been the role of women. This includes involvement in issues specifically affecting women—abortion, AIDS, violence against women—but also the assumption of leading roles in other campaigns.[6] Women have been a major force in the labor movement, in slum campaigns, in rural protests and in the constitutional campaign. This is significant because it offers a strong contrast to the extreme male bias in Thailand's formal public life. The female share among parliamentarians, senior bureaucrats and local politicians is very small. Traditionally, women had a strong role in Thai society. In the realms of the family and local community, there have never been traditions of suppressing the female contribution. The male bias in formal politics developed within the modern bureaucracy and political system based on western models. The strong and often leading roles taken by women in modern popular movements represents a reassertion of traditional female power.

Culture, Identity, Alliance

As in other developing countries, Thai social movements mobilize concepts of culture and identity to build solidarity and inspire action. This is similar to earlier western movements, but also importantly different. The cultures and identities mobilized are very often those of the poor, the peripheral and the excluded. This focus gives the movements some of the moral power (against injustice) of old-style class-based action. But at the same time, the fact that these movements are *not* founded explicitly on class concepts and motivated by class antagonism makes it easier for them to mobilize support from a broader public. Appeals to universally acceptable concepts—protection of the environment, health for all, eliminatin of corruption—make it possible for movements of the underprivileged to build support from the educated middle class through links forged by non-governmental organizations (NGOs).

NGOs

Around the world, the role of NGOs has become controversial. To what extent do they actually *create* the movements which they claim only to facilitate? What is the moral or political justification for their role? Are they a force *for* democracy, or are they helping destroy democracy by diverting attention from parties, parliaments and other official democratic institutions? Are they part of the globalizing forces which are undermining sovereignty and national government? Our project did not set out to be an in-depth study of the role of NGOs. But these questions are so much part of current debate that it is worth offering some tentative conclusions which arise from the research.

In terms of its resource base, the Thai NGO movement remains rather weak. The number of people directly involved on a full-time basis is small, and funding is very limited. Foreign funds and assistance are available and important, but they are not large.

At the same time, NGOs have played an important role in all of the movements studied in the project. This role has arisen because of the upsurge of popular movements, on the one hand, and the authorities' attempt to combat these movements by a mixture of constructive neglect and the exercise of traditional power, on the other. It is probably fair to say that without the NGO contribution, these movements would be significantly weaker and less effective. What explains the fact that the NGO movement is weak in resources but able to have such an impact? In part it is due simply to the levels of effort and commitment on the part of a small number of people. But there are also structural and strategic aspects.

The roles played by NGO workers are very specific. They accumulate practical political experience which makes them effective advisors on strategy and tactics. They transmit information between groups and across movements, which allows local groups to shorten the learning curve. They have contact networks which can bring in expertise from international sources, academics and researchers and can disseminate information to the press and other media. They are educated, having important skills for compiling documents, conducting negotiations, framing publicity and so on. In none of these roles do the NGOs have the ability to *create* movements, although they certainly can contribute to making them stronger. NGO workers themselves argue that whatever role they have is dependent on the strength of the popular movement which they assist.

Finally, the NGOs are often described as a "middle class" element. As a recent study has shown, many of the older (1970s) generation of Thai NGOs did have middle class backgrounds and were motivated by political commitment. However, those of the new generation (1990s) are more likely to come from a rural or urban lower-class family, to have climbed the ladder of educational achievement and to have made a decision to remain true to their roots.[7]

Strategies

Among those in Thailand committed to social and political change, three general strategies for action are being debated. The first is to work within the existing system and press for changes in law, law enforcement, institutions and mindsets through various forms of social action and political lobbying. The second alternative is to form a political party to provide a more direct channel for change. The third alternative is the so-called New Anarchism, calling for people to simply ignore the state, pursue their preferred way of life and seek strength within the community and through networking between communities.[8]

Most popular movements in Thailand adopt the first option. The anarchist solution is problematic because of the intrusive power of the state (particularly in control over natural resources) and because of the difficulty of evading various forms of hegemony handed down from history. The option of establishing a new political party has been actively debated in recent years, but most activists to date fear the result would be infighting, disunity and distraction from the goals of direct social action and counter-hegemonic political activism.

Conclusion and Dedication

The project on social movements upon which this paper is based was an academic research project, but it was also conceived as a contribution to the movements being studied. All of the principal researchers and their assistants working on the eight case studies were chosen because they are committed activists. I hoped they would profit in some way by being asked to research these movements and reflect on the forces behind them, the strategies adopted, the successes and the failures. That much was intentional. Beyond that, the subjects of the research got involved in the project in ways I had not expected. In an early work-in-progress seminar, one activist was orchestrating the fishermen's blockade of Phangnga Bay over his mobile phone from the back of the room. At the final seminar in October 2000, several of the dam protesters attended and cheered on the researcher. Leaders of the doctors' movement came to the presentation on the public health scandal, contributed advice and information and insisted on presenting a garland to the research team. And one man from the Hmong hill community attended the seminar to get tips on helping his home village, which had been ransacked a few days earlier by vigilantes covertly encouraged by the Forest Department. An important aspect of modern popular movements is that they are not confined within any one formal framework.

This research is dedicated to all those who believe that Thai society can and should be moved ahead by collective action of various kinds.

Notes

1 The author would also like to thank the Center for Southeast Asian Studies Core University Program at Kyoto University for the invitation to spend time at the Center, where parts of this paper were written.

2 All the studies are published in Pasuk et al. 2002.

3 For criticism by other Marxist writers, see Brass 1994; and Veltmeyer 1997. Garner and Tenato 1997 reviewed the literature on social movements from 1945 to 1995, including analysis of the Marxist standpoint.

4 On the Assembly of the Poor, see, for example, Suthy 1997; Missingham 2000; and Praphat 1998.

5 See chapters 3, 4, 5 and 6 in Pasuk et al. 2002.

6 See chapters 2 and 3 in Pasuk et al. 2002.

7 For an excellent analysis of NGOs and social movements, see Missingham 2000. See also Prudhisan and Maneerat 1997; Narong 1999; and Somchai 2001 (on the northeast).

8 Somchai (2001, chapter 3) gives a good discussion of the debate within NGOs working in the northeast of Thailand on the community culture approach and the political economy approach.

References

Alvarez, Sonia E., Evelina Dagnino, and Arturo Escobar, eds. 1998. *Cultures of Politics, Politics of Cultures.* Boulder, Oxford: Westview Press.

Brass, Tom. 1994. Postscript: Populism, peasants and intellectuals, or what's left of the future? *Journal of Peasant Studies* 21, no. 3 and 4 (April–July).

Byres, T. J. 1995. Preface. In *New Farmers' Movements in India,* ed. Tom Brass. London: Frank Cass.

Chairat Charoensinolarn. 1995. Kanmuang baep mai khabuan kan khluen wai thang sangkhom baep mai lae watthakam kan phatthana chut mai [New politics, new social movements and the new discourse on development]. *Thammasat Journal* 1 (January–April).

Cohen, Jean. L., and Andrew Arato. 1992. *Civil Society and Political Theory.* Cambridge: MIT Press.

Escobar, A 1995. *Encountering Development: The Making and Unmaking of the Third World.* Princeton: Princeton University Press.

Escobar, A., and Sonia E. Alvarez. 1992. *The Making of Social Movements in Latin America.* Boulder: Westview Press.

Foweraker, J. 1992. *Popular Mobilization in Mexico: The Teachers' Movement 1977–87.* Cambridge: Cambridge University Press.

———. 1995. *Theorising Social Movements.* London, Boulder Colorado: Pluto Press.

Garner, Roberta, and John Tenato. 1997. *Social Movement Theory and*

Research: An Annotated Bibliographical Guide. McGill Bibliographies, Lanham Md. and London: Scarecrow Press.

Habermas, J. 1973. *Legitimation Crisis.* London: Heinemann.

Missingham, Bruce D. 2000. The Assembly of the Poor in Thailand: From local struggles to national protest movement. PhD diss., Australian National University.

Narong Petchprasert, ed. 1999. *Setthasart kanmuang en ji o* [Political economy of NGOs]. Bangkok: Political Economy Centre, Chulalongkorn University.

Omvedt, Gail. 1993. *Reinventing Revolution: New Social Movements in South Asia.* London, New York: Routledge.

Pasuk Phongpaichit et al. 2002. *Withi chiwit withi su: khabuankan prachachon ruam samai* [Ways of life, means of struggle: Contemporary people's movements]. Chiang Mai: Silkworm Books.

Praphat Pintoptaeng. 1998. *Kanmuang bon thong thanon: 99 wan prawatisat kan doen khabuan chumnum prathuang nai sangkhom thai* [Politics on the street: 99 days of the Assembly of the Poor]. Bangkok: Centre for Research and Production of Textbooks, Krik University.

Prudhisan Jumbala and Maneerat Mitprasat. 1997. Non-governmental development organization: Empowerment and environment. In *Political Change in Thailand,* ed. Kevin Hewison. London and New York: Routledge.

Somchai Phatharathananunth. 2001. Civil society in northeast Thailand: The struggle of the Small Scale Farmers' Assembly of Isan. PhD diss., University of Leeds.

Suthy Prasartset. 1997. Paet banyat waduai samatcha khon jon [Eight propositions about the Assembly of the Poor]. *Warasan setthasat kanmuang pu chumchon chabap thi nung* [The political economy journal, edition for the community, no. 1]. Bangkok: Chulalongkorn University.

Touraine, A. 1995. *The Critique of Modernity.* Massachusetts: Blackwell.

Veltmeyer, Henry. 1997. New social movements in Latin America: The dynamics of class and identity. *Journal of Peasant Studies* 25, no. 1 (October).

Index